# New Applications of Data Bases

*Academic Press Rapid Manuscript Reproduction*

Based on proceedings of a workshop held at
Churchill College, Cambridge, England
on 2 and 3 September 1983

# New Applications of Data Bases

*Edited by*

## G. GARDARIN

*University of Paris VI and
INRIA, Le Chesnay, France*

## E. GELENBE

*ISEM, University of Paris-
Sud, Orsay, France*

1984

## ACADEMIC PRESS

(Harcourt Brace Jovanovich, Publishers)

London   Orlando   San Diego   New York

Toronto   Montreal   Sydney   Tokyo

ACADEMIC PRESS, INC. (LONDON) LTD.
24-28 Oval Road,
London NW1 7DX

*United States Edition published by*
ACADEMIC PRESS, INC.
Orlando, Florida 32887

**British Library Cataloguing in Publication Data**

New applications of data bases.
1. Data base management   2. File
organization (Computer science)
I. Gardarin, Georges   II. Gelenbe, Erol
    001.64'42   QA76.9.D3

    ISBN 0-12-275550-2
    LCCCN 84-70478

PRINTED IN THE UNITED STATES OF AMERICA

85 86 87 88      9 8 7 6 5 4 3 2

# CONTENTS

# PREFACE

Over the last ten years, research on data base systems has concentrated on producing elegant and effective methods for designing information systems for storing and retrieving alphanumeric data.

In parallel with this research effort, and as a consequence of the much wider usage of computers as general purpose tools for handling natural or synthetic images, natural or synthetic sounds, communications, elaborate texts, and so on, the variety of information which has to be stored and retrieved has considerably evolved.

Applications for these relatively new computer media have moved into general purpose information processing and are becoming quite widely used. The much greater accessibility of graphic workstations at a far lower cost has been a major factor in this trend.

Text processing, general office applications, and of course CAD/CAM (computer aided design and manufacturing) have had a major impact on opening up the usage of computer systems offering a much richer man-machine interface and thus posing complex problems of data storage and representation.

The purpose of the ICOD-2 workshop on New Applications of Data Bases was to call upon researchers who are actively investigating the representation of such complex data oriented towards human interfacing. The emphasis was placed on groups who were considering these issues in practical terms, since it is our belief that in this area we are still at a stage where experimentation should precede theory. Papers were thus sought in order to bring together contributors who are pioneering a data base approach to the treatment of data which is not formated in traditional alphanumeric mode.

Much of the most interesting work in this area is being done close to the application areas and away from traditional academic or research environments. Therefore it is often difficult to reach via the usual conference mechanism such work which may be deeply imbedded in industrial or applied development projects.

Thus we do not claim to have brought together in these Proceedings all of the best or most representative work in the area. We do hope, however, to have been able to focus greater attention on these new and important topics, and to encourage further investigation.

Contributions for this workshop were selected, by a call for papers, on the basis of extended abstracts. Complete papers were then presented at the workshop for possible inclusion in these Proceedings. The papers were judged on the basis of the oral presentation by the authors and their written contents. Recommendations concerning their inclusion in the published proceedings after some possible revision were then made.   The papers published here have all gone through this process, except for two articles which have been included on the basis of their relevance and interest.

The papers contained in this volume cover five main areas:
   - Image and pictorial data bases
   - Text oriented systems
   - High-level (user oriented) interfaces
   - Expert systems and data bases
   - Engineering (CAD/CAM) oriented systems.

In the first area, the papers by McKeown and by Brouaye *et al.* address the important issue of image representation, in natural or artificial pictures, while M. Créhange *et al.* present an "assistant" for information retrieval from a picture data base. The papers in the second area are similar in that they are concerned with modelling textual data bases, though their approaches are dissimilar; the paper by Bancilhon and Richard was not presented at the workshop. The papers in the third area are quite dissimilar: Barbic *et al.* assume a static user interface (forms) for office information systems, while Boguraev and Jones consider a general purpose natural language interface.

The fourth theme (expert systems and data bases) is of broad interest. Marque-Pucheu *et al.* examine the general problem of interpreting a PROLOG-like language in terms of the relational calculus, a central issue to the "fifth generation" concept. This concept is described in the introduction by Gardarin, which indicates how the different areas covered in the workshop contribute to the development of fifth generation systems. The paper by Jarke and Vassiliou discusses representation common to both data bases and expert systems, while Bouzeghoub and Gardarin show how one can use an expert system for data design. The papers by Gray and Katz both discuss specific issues of data base management for CAD/CAM applications.

I would like to express my sincere thanks to the organizers

of the ICOD-2 Conference, in particular to Dr. Deen who en-
thusiastically supported my initiative concerning this workshop, and to Dr. Hammersley who made the arrangements which
allowed it to take place. The workshop committee (G. Gardarin,
W. Litwin, F.B. Manola and R. Williams) sought out papers and
Professor Gardarin and Dr. Litwin contributed significantly
to the paper selection process. Professor Gardarin put in
considerable effort towards the preparation of these
proceedings, including a special introductory paper. Mrs
M-Th. Bouvier generously contributed her time and effort to the
preparation and distribution of the call for papers. Special
thanks are due to the ISEM laboratory at Orsay (Université
Paris-Sud) for providing the administrative support. The set-
ting of Churchill College, Cambridge University, was most
appreciated by all participants. Finally - and most
important - my special gratitude goes to the contributors
and to the workshop participants.

Erol Gelenbe
Workshop Chairman

# CONTRIBUTORS

A. AIT HADDOU   CRIN, BP 239, 54506 Vandoeuvre Cédex, France

F. BANCILHON   INRIA, BP 105, 78153 Le Chesnay Cédex, France and LRI, Bât 490, Université Paris-Sud, 91405 Orsay, France

F. BARBIC   Dipartimento di Elettronica, Politecnico di Milano, Piazza Leonardo da Vinci 32, 20133 Milano, Italy

B.K. BOGURAEV   Computer Laboratory, University of Cambridge, Corn Exchange Street, Cambridge CB2 3QG, England

M. BOUKAKIOU   CRIN, BP 239, 54506 Vandoeuvre Cédex, France

M. BOUZEGHOUB   INRA/SABRE, BP 105, 78153 Le Chesnay Cédex, France

G. BRACCHI   Dipartimento di Elettronica, Politecnico di Milano, Piazza Leonardo da Vinci 32, 20133 Milano, Italy

P. BROUAYE   Laboratoire de Formation, Centre Mondial Informatique et Ressource Humaine, Paris, France

M. CARLI   Dipartimento di Elettronica, Politecnico di Milano, Piazza Leonardo da Vinci 32, 20133 Milano, Italy

M. CRENHANGE   CRIN, BP 239, 54506 Vandoeuvre Cédex, France

J.M. DAVID   CRIN, BP 239, 54506 Vandoeuvre Cédex, France

O. FOUCAUT   CRIN, BP 239, 54506 Vandoeuvre Cédex, France

G. GARDARIN   INRIA and Université Paris VI, BP 105, 78153 Le Chesnay Cédex, France

M. GRAY   IBM UK Science Centre, St Clement's Street, Winchester, England

M. JARKE   Graduate School of Business Administration, New York University, New York, USA

G. JOMIER    ISEM, Bât 508, Université Paris-Sud, Orsay, France

R.H. KATZ    Computer Science Division, Electrical Engineering
and Computer Sciences Department, University of California,
Berkeley, California 94720, USA

M.R. LAGANA    Dipartimento di Informatica, Università di Pisa,
Pisa, Italy

E. LOCURATOLO    Istituto di Elaborazione dell'Informazione
del CNR, Pisa, Italy

D.M. McKEOWN JR    Department of Computer Science, Carnegie-
Mellon University, Pittsburgh, Pennsylvania 15213, USA

J. MAROLDT    CRIN, BP 239, 54506 Vandoeuvre Cédex, France

G. MARQUE-PUCHEU    Ecole Normale Supérieure, 45 rue d' Ulm,
75005 Paris, France

J. MARTIN-GALLAUSIAUX    ISEM, Bât 508, Université Paris-Sud,
Orsay, France

T.H. MERRETT    School of Computer Science, McGill University,
Montreal, Quebec H3A 2K6, Canada

B. PERNICI    Dipartimento di Elettronica, Politecnico di Milano,
Piazza Leonardo da Vinci 32, 20133 Milano, Italy

T. PUDET    Laboratoire de Formation, Centre Mondial Informatique
et Ressource Humaine, Paris, France

P.RICHARD    INRIA, BP 105, 78153 Le Chesnay Cédex, France

K. SPARCK JONES    Computer Laboratory, University of Cambridge,
Corn Exchange Street, Cambridge CB2 3QG, England

R. SPRUGNOLI    Istituto di Elaborazione dell'Informazione del
CNR, Pisa, Italy

Y. VASSILIOU    Graduate School of Business Administration, New
York University, New York, USA

J. VICARD    Laboratoire de Formation, Centre Mondial
Informatique et Ressource Humaine, Paris, France

# Introduction

# TOWARDS THE FIFTH GENERATION
## OF DATA MANAGEMENT SYSTEMS

### G. Gardarin

*INRIA and University of Paris VI*
*BP 105, 78153 Le Chesnay-Cédex, France*

## 1. INTRODUCTION

In 1981, Japan initiated a vast program in research and development to design and elaborate a new
generation of computers. Quickly, Japan was followed by
the United-States and Europe. In the view of most
scientists, this new generation should derive from
three fundamental disciplines [SPECTRUM83] :

. microelectronics, which will produce the needed highly parallel hardware widely based on VLSI
. artificial intelligence, which will supply the concepts and algorithms for handling data, knowledge and
  inferences
. computer systems and architecture, which will provide
  the methodologies and technics to integrate all the
  ingredients.

What will be the place of data base management in
this future generation ? Most experts agree that the
Data Base Management System (DBMS) should be a central
component of the fifth generation computer.

Data management systems have evolved from file systems to relational DBMS. Like computer systems
[DEITEL82], they have undergone a series of stages of
development that we refered to as generations. Todays
fourth generation of DBMS is composed of relational
systems which are now available as software products.
Therefore, from a research point of view, we are at the
end of the fourth generation. Thus, research has to grow

to design and experiment the new DBMSs of the fifth generation which should encompass new types of applications.

In this paper, we would like to summarize first the
characteristics of the four generations of data management systems which already existed. Then we focus on
the coming fifth generation of DBMSs and try to define
what it could look like. In the final section, we present the various papers of this book and show that all
of them tackle important issues of the fifth generation
DBMSs.

## 2. PAST GENERATIONS OF DATA MANAGEMENT SYSTEMS

### 2.1. The first generation (1950's) :

The first generation of data management systems was
strongly based on sequential files. Data were grouped
in records sequentially written on tapes, or on what
was the logical view of a tape, that is a sequential
file. This first generation was oriented towards batch
processing.

### 2.2. The second generation (1960's) :

With the advent of time-sharing systems, sequential
processing of files was no longer satisfactory. To support an interactive and conversational mode, direct
access files were developed. Therefore, the second generation was strongly characterized by the appearance
of file systems supporting multiple access methods, such as indexing and hashing.

### 2.3. The third generation (mid-1960's to mid-1970's) :

The third generation of data management systems began with the advent of IDS.1, the first integrated data
base management system. This generation was mainly based on access models, that is data models allowing the
data base administrator to describe the physical structure of the data base. The data base programmer was
seen as a navigator through the various access paths of
the data base [BACHMAN73]. The CODASYL 1971 recommendations [CODASYL71] are probably the keystone of the
third generation whose leader was C.W. BACHMAN.

2.4. The fourth generation (Mid-1970's to present) :

Fourth generation DBMS are the current systems coming in the industry. They  are strongly based on the
relational approach [CODD70]. The end-user only sees a
logical view of a part of the data base ; this view is
composed of a set of tables. The data manipulation language is assertional in the sense that the user has to
specify the what and not the how : in other words, the
user defines the set of data he wishes to get with a
first order logic formula, and the system determines
how to get this set of data. Probably, the ANSI report
[ANSI83] on a normalized SQL language for describing
and manipulating relational databases is the keystone
of the fourth generation whose leader was E.F. CODD.

3. THE FORTHCOMING FIFTH GENERATION DBMS

The fifth generation DBMS is not yet here. However,
researchers seem to agree that a fifth generation database should include the following ingredients :

(1) facts represented as relational tuples ;
(2) complex objects as texts, graphical images, pixel
    structured images ;
(3) general documents composed of an ordered set of
    complex objects and facts.

In addition, the DBMS should supply deductive func-
tionalities to support the definition of inference rules and the derivation of objects. These rules would
allow the user to deduce, from the stored objects, derived objects having the semantic and the shape that
the user wishes. Such rules could include certain
transformations of objects from one form to another
e.g. texts to relations, relations to texts, graphical
images to relations...

Several interfaces should be offered by a fifth generation DBMS. Such interfaces could include logic based languages, natural languages, access through forms,
navigation through images, speech recognition
devices...

Although there does not yet exist a commonly agreed
architecture for the future fifth generation DBMS, a
typical architecture could be based on the three following layers :

(1) <u>A multi-media associative memory</u> would supply the
    storage capabilities for the various types of ob-
    jects and the associative access methods to retrie-
    ve objects. This layer would manage magnetic and
    optical secondary memories in a highly parallel
    fashion. The external interface of this layer would
    probably look like an extended relational algebra,
    including operations on complex objects.

(2) <u>An object transformer</u> would supply an object trans-
    <u>formation calculus to</u> the external layer. This
    layer would perform the basic combinations and
    transformations of objects, useful for all types of
    applications. The external interface of this layer
    could probably be richer than Prolog questions
    [CLOCKSIN81], including basic transformation func-
    tions of complex objects from one form to another.
    Its role would then be to decompose complex re-
    quests received by the layer in sequences of exten-
    ded relational algebra operations executed by the
    previous layer. For reasons of performances, some
    inferences should be carried out at this layer but
    most deductions could be performed at the next
    one, as a specific type of application oriented
    functions. Also, the layer could provides facili-
    ties to control the structurations and manipula-
    tions of objects, such as application independent
    integrity control devices, generalized transaction
    concepts, authorization verifications...

(3) <u>An application oriented layer</u> would supply for each
    <u>type of application the specific</u> functionalities
    and for the end-user very high level interfaces. This
    layer could be strongly based on the notion of da-
    ta base view : the concept of view can be usefully
    extended to include several types of complex trans-
    formations of the underlying database [WONG83].
    We can envision in particular the following types
    of modules at the application oriented layer :
        . image retrieval and presentation
        . text processing and edition
        . form management and utilization
        . document entry and composition (i.e. mixed
          objects entry, retrieval and presentation)
        . computer aided design/manufacture applications
        . expert system interfaces

. deductive databases
. natural language interfaces
. speech recognition and synthesis

Finally, the architecture of a fifth generation DBMS
is tentatively portrayed figure 1.

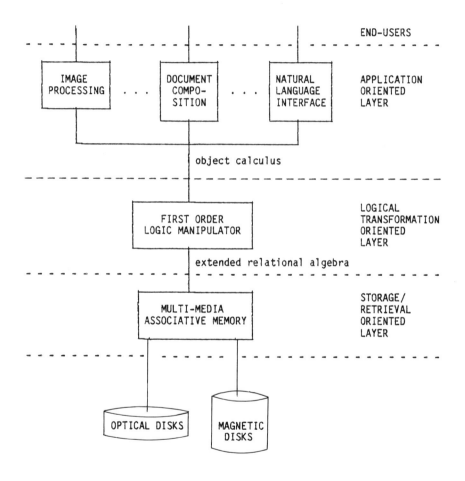

Figure 1. : Tentative architecture
for the fifth generation DBMS

Many problems remain to be solved and breakthroughs
are urgently required to be able to develop such a
fifth generation DBMS. The workshop papers suggest a
set of problems which must be studied. A tentative
classification of these problems according to the three
layers we distinguished above is given below.

Layer 1 : Multi-media associative memory

1.1. How to physically memorize facts and texts ?
1.2. How to physically memorize images ?
1.3. How to physically retrieve sets of (possibly
     mixed) objects ?
1.4. What are the physical controls performed ?
1.5. What is the parallel sub-system architecture ?
1.6. What are the mass storage devices ?
1.7. What access paths to data are managed ?

Layer 2 : Logical transformation functions

2.1. How are knowledge rules represented ?
2.2. What are the possible transformations of data ?
2.3. What type of inference is possible ?
2.4. How inference is performed ?
2.5. How rules are enforced ?
2.6. What is a transaction ?
2.7. What optimisation is performed ?

Layer 3 :

3.1. How can we enter rules ?
3.2. How can we enter facts, texts, images ?
3.3. What image retrieval and presentation functions
     are supplied ?
3.4. How can we retrieve and compose documents ?
3.5. What generalized query language is offered ?
3.6. How is natural language understood ?
3.7. How can we convert knowledge from one form to
     another ?

Probably, many other problems have to be solved. The
papers in this book address most of the questions in
our list, and many others.

## 4. PRESENTATION OF THE PAPERS

The papers have been grouped in five sections. Each section describes a type of advanced application. In the following, we give a short summary of each paper and we try to characterize what specific topics is tackled by cross-referencing addressed questions (see list above). We hope that this will help the reader select certain of his main interests. The abstracts are composed by the editors and thus express their viewpoint rather than that of the author.

### 4.1. Pictorial databases :

#### DIGITAL CARTOGRAPHY AND PHOTO INTERPRETATION FROM A DATABASE VIEWPOINT

Addressed questions : 1.2, 2.2, 3.3, 3.7

In this paper, D.M. McKEOWN addresses the problem of cartographic databases. First, he classifies such spatial databases in three categories :
(1) Image databases are composed of a set of images related to descriptive attributes, including the location of the image.
(2) Map databases contains a set of maps, possibly at different scale, generated by digitizing paper maps.
(3) Image/Map databases include both images and maps and relate them at different levels.

Then, it is shown that the image/map database approach is a very powerful model allowing the system to perform a great variety of tasks, such as image selection, spatial computation, semantic computation, image synthesis. Finally, D. McKEOWN describes the MAPS system which uses an image/map integrated model to manage a large set of aerial photographs, digitized maps and database descriptions of features in the Washington D.C. area.

#### EXPRIM : AN EXPERT SYSTEM TO AID IN PROGRESSIVE RETRIEVAL FROM A PICTORIAL AND DESCRIPTIVE DATABASE

Addressed questions : 3.2, 3.3, 3.6

M. CREHANGE et al. address certain problems which arise when manipulating an image base. The paper focus on a user interface problem : how to choose some pictures among a large collection. This problem is not simple when the user has a very fuzzy idea of pictures he wishes to select ; that is the case, for example, when a journalist asks a press agency for images to illustrate a paper. The solution M. CREHANGE et al. propose is based on an expert system which infers the selected images from a dialogue with the end-user, using rules defined by experts in images.

## MANAGING THE SEMANTIC CONTENT OF GRAPHICAL DATA

### Addressed questions : 1.2, 1,3, 2.1, 2.2, 3.7

P. BROUAYE, T. PUDET and J. VICARD propose to store the semantic of graphical pictures as expressions of geometric primitives. These primitives reference objects which are defined in environment dependent contexts. The expression of geometric primitives, called an abstract image, is a syntax-tree. Leaves are terminal objects and internal nodes represent functions combining these objects. The drawing of an abstract image is performed by a postfix traversal of the syntax-tree materializing each node as specified in the context. The authors also propose a hierarchical organization of abstract images in order to provide tools to build complex images with low-level images considered as context objects. Finally, the paper shows that representing graphical images as expressions allow the system to tackle the semantic of the images. That facilitates the development of several applications including image transformation, searching and animation. Good examples are discussed, such as queuing network and electrical network drawing.

### 4.2. Textual databases :

### MANAGING TEXTS AND FACTS IN A MIXED DATA BASE ENVIRONMENT

### Addressed questions : 1.1, 3.4, 3.5, 3.7

F. BANCILHON and P. RICHARD address the problem of mixing textual and factual data in the same system. While others have suggested the design of a new model for handling facts and complex objects as text or to extend the relational model, F. BANCILHON & P. RICHARD explore a multi-base approach to that problem. They propose

that the user sees two distinct databases, a textual
one and a relational one, with possibilities of exchange of objects between the two, namely text interpretation and text generation. They also propose a rela-
tional-oriented text manipulation language called TQL.

## FIRST STEP TO ALGEBRAIC PROCESSING OF TEXT

Addressed questions : 1.1, 3.5, 3.7

T.H. MERRETT takes in a certain sense an opposite
approach to that of BANCILHON and RICHARD : he suggests
that a textual database could be represented as a set
of relations. The main problem with that is to represent
sequences as relations : a simple solution is proposed
based on a sequence number attribute. Then, MERRETT
considers a word as a sequence of tuples, each being a
letter, and a sentence as a sequence of tuples, each
being a word. Suprisingly, this approach allows the
user to express complex transformations of texts, such
as concordance building, dictionary searching, cryptography, statistical analysis, as very simple relational
algebra expressions.

## A MODEL FOR WORD PROCESSING SYSTEMS

Addressed questions : 1.1, 2.5, 3.2, 3.4

M.R. LAGANA et al. present a model for a word processing system. The model consists mainly of three
components, texts, a screen and a dictionary. Each
element of the model is detailed, and a notion of consistent state is introduced. Then, operations on modelled objects are introduced, such as formatting,
inserting, deleting... Finally, a system implementation of the model is suggested. Such an implementation
would probably be supported by a relational database,
as suggested in the previous paper.

## 4.3. High level interfaces :

## A TOOL FOR FORM DEFINITION IN OFFICE INFORMATION SYSTEMS SPECIFICATION

Addressed questions : 3.1, 3.2

F. BARBIC et al. propose a form definition system for an office environment. A form is seen as a set of attributes. Each attribute is described by a name, a set of properties of its content, and a graphical representation on a particular displaying device. The main contribution of the paper is a language to describe forms ; in particular this language allows the user to define the type, format, modality, constraint and automatic filling-in procedures (if any) for each attribute. Many more features are available with this language, such as the possibility of defining views of forms.

## A NATURAL LANGUAGE FRONT-END TO DATABASES WITH EVALUATIVE FEEDBACK

Addressed questions : 3.5, 3.6, 3.7

In their paper, B.K. BOGURAEV and K.S. JONES describe a natural language pre-processor for a relational DBMS. The system, which is transportable, is composed of an application independent analyser which generates a logical representation of the English query. This logical representation is then translated into a general query representation and also reformulated in English for validation by the end-user. Finally, a system specific convertor derives the target query. Each component of the system is carefully described in the paper, with good examples. This system is really operational at Cambridge.

### 4.4. Expert systems and databases :

## DATABASE AND EXPERT SYSTEMS : OPPORTUNITIES AND ARCHITECTURES

Addressed questions : 2.3, 2.4, 2.5, 2.7

An expert system can be seen as an application oriented system inferring query answers from a base of facts, using a base of rules. In their paper, M. JARKE and Y. VASSILIOU study the possible benefits of the two technology combinations. It is suggested that the expert system approach can be used to enhance existing database systems in at least three areas : view mapping, query optimization and integrity checking ; these three functions could include deduction-based transformation strategy. Converseley, it is shown that expert systems

need use of database systems to increase the number of
facts they are able to handle. Finally, the authors
conclude by examining the various possible architectures of the coupling : an intelligent DBMS with integrated deduction, an expert system coupled to an independent DBMS, or an expert system with a DBMS integrated
in it.

## DESIGN OF AN EXPERT SYSTEM FOR DATABASE DESIGN

Addressed questions : 2.1, 2.2, 2.3, 3.7

The authors propose an expert system to design the
relational schema of a data base application. The expert system encompasses a dialogue module, an interpretor, a base of rules, a base of facts and an
inference engine. Using the dialogue module, a database
expert defines the base of rules which includes general schema design rules such as normalization
algorithms, but also system oriented rules such as optimization criteria. Then, users (i.e. database
administrators) describe the application using a subset
of the natural language. The interpretor generates from
this description a semantic network with specialized
arcs representing generalizations, aggregations and
instantiations. The inference engine reduces the semantic network by successive application of the rules,
with the help of the database administrator. Such an
approach seems to be very promising to get out of the
database design mess.

## INTERFACING PROLOG AND RELATIONAL DATA BASE
## MANAGEMENT SYSTEMS

Addressed questions : 2.3, 2.4, 3.5

G. MARQUE-PUCHEU et al. tackle the problem of interfacing Prolog and relational data bases. Prolog is a
computer programming language able to infere answers to
questions about a set of facts and a set of rules. A
possible way for interfacing Prolog and relational DBMS
is to assume that the set of facts seen by a Prolog
program is a relational database. With such an
approach, we get a very powerful tool allowing the user
to deduce any possible fact from a relational database.
Unfortunately, the system becomes very inefficient with
the Prolog strategy which instanciates all variables

appearing in a rule. To solve this problem, the authors propose a high level interface between Prolog and the DBMS, where queries are not given individually, but rather as a tree of recursively defined queries. The interface primitives, which generalize the transitive closure, can then be optimized globally by the DBMS.

## 4.5. Engineering data bases :

### DATABASES FOR COMPUTER-AIDED DESIGN

Addressed questions : 2.1, 2.5, 2.6, 3.4

In his paper, Mike GRAY analyzes the requirements of CAD systems in terms of database management functions. He examines the many problems which arise, among them :
- data may be added very frequently ; consequently, the schema must be able to evolve rapidly ;
- the problem of updating through views needs to be solved ;
- the data model has to support complex structures, with several layers of attributes interlinked in many ways ;
- consistency and transactions are hard to define ;
- constraints are very complex and defined at several levels.

### TRANSACTION MANAGEMENT IN THE DESIGN ENVIRONMENT

Addressed questions : 2.5, 2.6, 3.2

R. KATZ addresses the problem of defining the transaction concept to support VLSI design activities. In such an environment, designers extract a large portion of the design from the data base into their private workspaces. Then, they access and modify their private data during a long period of time. Finally, they try to commit their transaction updates. At commit time, the modified data must pass a series of consistency tests before being integrated in the data base. The previous version of the design must be kept. Also, if a consistency test fails, the transaction is not aborted but the design, which should be improved, is possibly partially integrated in the data base. Therefore, transactions are not all or nothing. Starting from these observations, R. KATZ suggests several new approaches to manage transactions in the design environment, among them :

- a design transaction is any sequence of database operations that maps a consistent version into a new
consistent version ; thus design transactions are
continuous activities ;
- locking could be performed as book reservation in a
library ;
- at certain consistency points, new versions should be
made visible to other users ;
- recovery should not undo the whole user activity, but
rather consider that transactions are continuous,
i.e. roll-back the transaction to the last consistency
point.

## 5. REFERENCES

[ANSI83] ANSC X3H2 : "SQL database language", X3H2-26-15,
         ANSI Report, Sept. 1982.

[BACHMAN73] BACHMAN C.W. : "The programmer as naviga-
         tor", Comm. of the ACM, V.16, N.11, Nov. 1973.

[CLOCKSIN81] CLOCKSIN W.F., MELLISH C.S. : "Programming
         in Prolog", Book, Springer-Verlag Ed., 1981.

[CODASYL71] CODASYL DATA BASE TASK GROUP : "Report of
         the DBTG", ACM New York Ed., April 1971.

[CODD70] CODD E.F. : "A relational model of data for
         large shared data banks", Comm. of the ACM,
         V.13, N.6, June 1970.

[DEITEL82] DEITEL H.M. : "An introduction to operating
         systems", Book, Addison-Wesley Ed., 1983.

[SPECTRUM83] IEEE SPECTRUM : "Next generation", IEEE
         Ed., V.20, N.11, Nov. 1983.

[WONG83] WONG E. : "Semantic enhancement through exten-
         ded relational views", ICOD-2 Conf., Wiley-
         Heyden Ltd Ed., Cambridge, 1983.

# Pictorial Data Bases

DIGITAL CARTOGRAPHY AND PHOTO INTERPRETATION
FROM A DATABASE VIEWPOINT

D.M. McKeown, Jr

*Department of Computer Science,*
*Carnegie-Mellon University, Pittsburgh,*
*Pennsylvania 15213, USA*

## Abstract

This paper gives an overview of database issues in digital cartography and aerial photo interpretation. A classification of database systems based on the method of data acquisition and underlying spatial representation is described. We also present a brief overview of MAPS, the Map Assisted Photo interpretation System. MAPS is a large integrated database system containing high resolution aerial photographs, digitized maps and other cartographic products, combined with detailed 3D descriptions of man-made and natural features in the Washington D. C. area.[*]

## 1. Introduction

This paper gives an overview of database aspects of the cartographic process. Although database systems have been developed to manage imagery and some collateral information, for the most part the use of sophisticated intelligent spatial databases is unknown in the map production community. Spatial database research requires the integration of ideas and techniques from many areas within computer science such as computer graphics, image processing, artificial intelligence, and database methodology as well as from the traditional area of photogrammetry. The problem is complex along many dimensions. First, digital cartography requires a massive amount of raw data: image, map, textual, and collateral data. Recently various estimates of the amount of data associated with cartographic production[1] have been brought forth by the three major users of remote sensing and aerial imagery in the United States: the U.S Geological Survey (USGS) $10^{12}$ to $10^{14}$ bits, the National Aeronautics and Space Administration (NASA) $10^{16}$ bits, and the

---

[*] This research was sponsored by the Defense Advanced Research Projects Agency (DOD), ARPA Order No. 3597, monitored by the Air Force Avionics Laboratory Under Contract F33615-81-K-1539. The views and conclusions contained in this document are those of the author and should not be interpreted as representing the official policies, either expressed or implied, of the Defense Advanced Research Projects Agency or the US Government.

Defense Mapping Agency (DMA) $10^{19}$ bits. Further, DMA estimates that by 1995 they will require support for 1000 on-line users, each having a local database context of $10^{14}$ bits. Second, the number and variety of spatial entities, their description, attributes, and the rich set of spatial relationships between entities will not be handled by precomputed tables of relationships. Finally, the extraction of man-made and natural features from source imagery using automated image analysis tools will require a map database as a source of knowledge to guide the extraction and interpret the processing results. This is a chicken-and-egg problem of grand proportions.

In Section 2 we discuss models for classification of spatial database systems based on what is represented in the database, how it is represented, and how information is acquired. Section 3 presents a description of tasks and criteria for evaluation of spatial database designs. some models for spatial databases. Section 4 gives an overview of the MAPS system developed at Carnegie-Mellon University. The application of the MAPS database to 3D scene generation, image segmentation, and rule-based systems for image interpretation is discussed in Section 5.

## 2. Classification of Spatial Databases

Image acquisition and map production has begun to move from a film based medium (hardcopy) to digital imagery (softcopy) due to the advent of remote sensing satellites such as LANDSAT series and the Thematic Mapper. As a result, there has been a need for the organization and structuring of digital image and map data for cartographic applications. Systems reported in the literature could loosely be categorized as paper studies and proposals, research vehicles, or production-oriented systems for particular well-defined subtasks of the general cartographic problem.[2, 3, 4, 5, 6] It has been difficult to evaluate the capabilities and limitations of various approaches since there were few common denominators by which systems could be compared. Research vehicles generally had a high degree of organizational complexity tested on very small scale databases. Systems used in production environments tended toward simple models running very large-scale databases. Further, while the tasks being performed involved the analysis of aerial or satellite data, it is often unclear whether the image data was an integral part of the resulting database, or simply used for manual data acquisition.

This section describes a classification of spatial database systems for cartographic applications. We assume that the following minimal capabilities hold: (1) on-line display of digital imagery and map data, and (2) ability to query interactively about attributes of the imagery and map using high-resolution color raster displays as a medium for interaction. Query systems with purely textual interfaces, which cannot relate queries to the display of imagery or map data, do not provide an interactive user with the proper tools for photo interpretation or cartographic analysis. Additional important capabilities include (3) maintenance of photogrammetric relationships between imagery and map data, and (4) representation of complex spatial relationships between map database entities. We will see, however, that criteria (3) and (4) are usually missing or deficient in most cartographic database implementations.

The following classification of the capabilities of three models that can be used to compare various existing systems or approaches. These models are the Image Database (ID) model, the Map Picture Database (MPD) model and the Image/Map Database (IMD) model.

## 2.1. Image Databases

The Image Database model (ID) is the simplest and most common database model. It is organized to relate attributes about the sensed image such as sensor-type, acquisition, cloud cover, or geodetic coverage.[**] These databases generally do not represent the content of the scene, but rather attributes of the scene. When the semantics of the scene are present, the location of cartographic features are represented in the image (pixel) coordinate system. This poses obvious limitations to the application of relevant knowledge from other images or from external sources, since there is no general mechanism to relate map feature position between images that overlap in coverage or to an external map. Although the features represented may appear to be map-oriented, it is difficult to compute general geometric properties using the image raster as the coordinate system.

Although relational database techniques have been applied to the ID model, we feel these techniques are not appropriate to spatial database organizations for several reasons. First, using the basic ⟨attribute, value⟩ tuple to represent vector lists of map coordinate data requires that all of the primary key attributes be duplicated in each relation, since there is no mechanism for allowing multiple valued (sets, lists, order pairs) as a primitive attribute in a relation. Further, the relational database operations such as union, intersection, join, project, are not good primitives for implementation of inherently geometric operations such as containment, adjacency, intersection and closest point. Operations such as feature intersection are reduced to searching for line segments that share the same pixel position. Finally, in any large system, a logical partitioning of the database must be performed in order to avoid extensive and often unnecessary search when performing spatial operations. Partitioning is difficult to achieve in relational systems since the relational model restricts itself to homogeneous (only one record type) sequential sets. Previous work advocating such organizations did not address the issues of system scale, and focused more on issues of query languages using relational models for geographic databases than the actual construction of complex systems.[7, 8, 9] When measured by the number of images, image-based features, and by the complexity of the relationships represented, these systems were quite simplistic.

---

[**] using flight annotation such as the center point and corner points not using general image-to-map correspondence

## 2.2. Map Picture Databases

The Map Picture Database model (MPD) describes databases that are generated by digitizing cartographic products, such as pre-existing maps and charts. These databases are attractive in environments where paper maps have played a large role in planning and analysis. There are, however, some major limitations to spatial systems based on digitized cartographic products. First, in the original map production, spatial ambiguity has been rectified by the cartographer in a manner that is not often reversible. The cartographic process involves simplification (generalization), classification (abstraction), and symbolization of real-world ambiguity. Constraints imposed by the scale of the map often determine which world features can be depicted despite the desirability of portraying a complete spatial representation. Therefore, map icon and symbol placement may not be as accurate as the original source material. Since the deduction of the actual spatial arrangement of objects from an iconic representation is an open problem, MPD's represent chaos masquerading as rationalized order. The key issue is that MPD's are pictures of a map (however detailed) rather than the underlying map structure and spatial organization. Although the graphics display of MPD appears to convey a great deal of semantic information, that impression is a result of the human observer, not a reflection of an underlying map representation.

When a map is digitized into a map picture, another subtle simplification occurs. The digitization process results in a map image on a rectangular grid whose size is generally limited either by custom or as an artifact of the digitization process. Common limitations are scanner resolution, maximum size of image raster, and the physical size of source map. One popular representation is to subdivide regions of the map picture into a regular decomposition such as quad-tree,[10, 11] or k-d tree.[12] The implementation of this representation is greatly simplified in MPD models since one no longer has to contend with positional ambiguity of map features because of the cartographic process outlined above, and the discrete nature of the digitization process.

One common use for the MPD model is in geographic information systems for land use and urban planning. In these systems, aggregate values such as population of an area and crop yield of an area are computed. The scale of the original map becomes the limiting factor for accuracy in information computation. However, the grain of computation is usually large enough that these inaccuracies are not a practical problem. Incremental update of the database due to new residential and industrial areas and the concomitant loss of rural areas is a difficult problem since database update requires careful map editing tools not usually associated with these MPD systems.

A recent trend has been to take existing MPD databases and add a map feature database component, usually relational, to describe attributes of various features. We believe that augmenting traditional MPD databases with semantic information has merit in those environments where analysis is being performed by humans, since information synthesis is not a requirement of the database system. However, once such a system is in place, there is a tendency to attempt to automate analysis functions requiring spatial interpretation, and the generation method of the MPD model has several drawbacks for use in photo-interpretation and cartography. The chief problems are the method of generation as outlined above, the lack of semantic information about map features, and the requirement that a map exist at the appropriate level of detail for the area under consideration. The IMD model discussed in the following section addresses these issues.

## 2.3. Image/Map Databases

The Image/Map Database model (IMD) relates map features to image database through camera models. It therefore has the capability to describe relationships between features acquired from different images through the map database. This capability is in contrast to the image database model where the feature descriptions can only be related if the descriptions come from the same image.

Since the map database is built directly from aerial imagery in the IMD model, the resolution / accuracy issue is a function of the ground resolution of the imagery, the intrinsic position measurement error due to camera model, ground control, etc. rather than an artifact of the map depiction scale as in the MPD model. A greater variety of feature descriptions is possible since they are not restricted to those that can be portrayed in a cartographic product. Further, the complexity of a particular feature description is independent of any particular task requirement and can represent a rich set of attributes, semantic interpretations, and knowledge from diverse sources. This flexibility is a key element for map data representation as we look toward spatial database systems with applications in cartographic production and expert photo-interpretation.

However, just as the cartographer must resolve ambiguity, so the spatial database must be able to represent inconsistency in a consistent manner. For example, errors in correspondence between images and the geodetic model cause the same point on the earth to be given a different geodetic position, ie., when viewed from different images the same geodetic point produces a different world position. If this point is on a common boundary between two features, say a political boundary, there should be ambiguity as to which region the point belongs. By the same token, if two large residential areas are found to intersect because of positional uncertainty, and the result of the intersection is several small polygonal areas, the IMD model should be able to rectify this ambiguity. This rectification might take the form of a symbolic relationship that indicates that the residential area share a common boundary, while maintaining the ability to represent the original errorful signal data. Since the original data is maintained in the database, the symbolic relationships do not have to be static. For example, these relationships can be dependent on attributes similiar to those used by cartographers when they perform simplification and generalization. The link from the symbolic interpretation back to the original source data is not possible in MPD systems.

## 2.4. Spatial Knowledge

We believe that spatial databases for digital cartography and photo interpretation should be designed using the IMD model because it gives us the tools to construct our map database from "first principles" and tie together partial spatial knowledge at different levels of detail. This is possible because individual map features may be specified directly from source imagery. This capability is precluded by the derivative nature of the MPD model. That is, it is difficult to assimilate new and possibly errorful knowledge because of the mismatch between the new errorful data and the cartographic rectification of ambiguous data.

The representation of a multiple levels of detail paradigm is often invoked as a part of a coarse-fine or hierarchical matching strategy in image processing and interpretation. Given the scale and digitized ground resolution of an image, the IMD model can generate a map description that will suppress any features that would be too small to be recognized, with remaining descriptions at the appropriate level of detail. This technique is more than camera scaling and transformation, since the criterion for "too small" can be an attribute of the map feature itself. Consider the map feature description of a university campus. At some level of detail corresponding to pixel ground resolution distance (GRD), features such as playing fields, dormitories, instructional buildings and offices, access roads, and campus greenery are all individually distinguished. Using spectral properties of the features and spatial relationships between these features, we can determine those feature boundaries that are likely to be muddled, and those with sufficient detail to be recognized. For example, roads preserve linear properties until the GRD approximately equals the width of the road. The multiple level of detail paradigm need not be applied in a homogeneous manner. A large scale spatial organization containing urban, residential, and rural areas will require flexibility to represent the high feature density and complexity in the urban area as well as significantly lower density in rural areas.

Flexible knowledge acquisition is necessary because in photo-interpretation and cartography, world knowledge is inherently fragmented. There are diverse sources of knowledge that are used to acquire map feature information. Some of the most common are direct measurement from imagery, old maps and charts, sketches, and collateral data. Further, there is a certain amount of specialization in cartography. Analysts may specialize in a particular area of the world, be knowledgeable in hydrology, geology, local construction customs, or political matters. In the production of large scale maps it is rare to find map generalists, although this may not be true for low level feature extraction activities. This specialization tends to fragment knowledge, and is often given as a justification for building database systems that provide access to a wide range of map knowledge and may have general capabilities for knowledge synthesis.

The IMD model methodology provides a mechanism for feature unification in a cohesive framework. It provides a framework to relate symbolic descriptions to their original data sources. It is not tied to a particular cartographic representation nor to limitations of cartographic production.

# 3. Tasks for Image/Map Database

In this section we give a classification of tasks that are common to applications in photo-interpretation and digital cartography systems. The four tasks are *selection* of image, terrain, or map data based on attributes of the data, *spatial computation* of map feature relationships, *semantic computation* of map features, and *synthesis* of imagery, terrain and map data.

## 3.1. Task Classification

### 3.1.1. Selection

The selection task requires that the spatial database system be able to select from a potentially large set of database entities based on attributes of image, terrain, and map database features.    The selection task does not require image-to-map correspondence, and is the task normally performed by ID model systems.   For example:

- select imagery with particular intrinsic characteristics: sensor, scale, date, cloud cover, processing history
- select map features based on symbolic description, partially specified description, similarities in image acquisition

### 3.1.2. Spatial Computation

Spatial computation is ubiquitous in cartographic and photo-interpretation tasks. A spatial database system must provide tools to compute common spatial relationships such as containment, closest point, adjacency, and intersection.   One issue is how to structure the environment in order to constrain search and thereby avoid unnecessary computation. Consider four views of the same problem:

- given a geodetic area, which images cover, or partially cover this area
- which roads can be found within the image
- which images contain this building
- given an image, find all images which overlap it

### 3.1.3. Semantic Computation

There are a number of tasks that require more than basic spatial computation, or where the appropriate spatial operation depends on the meaning of the map objects. Are there intrinsic high-level properties of map features that we can extract from basic spatial geometry that give a meaning to the feature? Semantic computation needs to be investigated as we develop more complex spatial databases.   For example, what is the semantics of 'intersection' for the following pairs of map objects?

- intersection of two roads
- intersection of bridge and river description[***]
- intersection of a building and a road

---

[***] We will discuss an example of this semantic computation in Section 4.6.

### 3.1.4. Synthesis

One goal of any database system should be to bring together diverse sources of knowledge into a common framework.  Synthesis is the generation of new information using a new method of presentation, computation, or analysis.  For example:

- cartographic superposition of map data on newly acquired image
- 3D display of terrain and cultural features from map database including man-made structures, political boundaries, neighborhoods, arbitrary collections of physically realized features
- to predict spatial (location) and structural (appearance) constraints; where to look and what to look for based of task knowledge, previous experience, or expectations
- a spatial framework within which to embed task-specific knowledge

### 3.2. Some Criteria for Spatial Databases

In this section we list some criteria that can be uses to evaluate database systems in four general areas.  These areas are image-to-map correspondence, map feature representation, spatial computation, and database synthesis.

### 3.2.1. Image-to-Map Correspondence

- can the it relate image-based features to a map coordinate system
- can these features be projected onto new imagery using the correspondence mechanism
- what capabilities exist for incrementally updating feature descriptions based on updates to the camera model, or to intrinsic changes to the feature itself.

### 3.2.2. Representation

- what are the capabilities for feature representation; what complex spatial relationships can represent; how is inconsistency recognized and handled
- can the user describe features and associated attributes in a flexible manner; what is the variety of attributes.
- can the representation accommodate map-based information coming from a variety non-imagery sources
- what is the relationship between the representation of signal and symbolic data
- what synthesis tasks does the representation support

### 3.2.3. Spatial Computation

- does the system support dynamic spatial queries
- what spatial relationships does the system compute directly from the underlying data, which relationships are specified by the user, how do they interact, how does one maintain consistency
- what mechanisms are available to partition the search space when computing spatial relationships

### 3.2.4. Database Synthesis

- imagery, terrain and map data are components, each with an appropriate representation, operation semantics, and utility; in what ways does the database support synthesis of these components
- what concrete tasks requiring synthesis are performed

## 4. MAPS Overview

In the previous sections we have attempted to raise issues of Image/Map Database organization, tasks, and capabilities. In this section we discuss MAPS, the **Map Assisted Photo interpretation System.** MAPS is a large integrated database system containing high resolution aerial photographs, digitized maps and other cartographic products, combined with detailed 3D descriptions of man-made and natural features in the Washington D. C. area. We will only briefly describe some of the system aspects; a more complete treatment is found in McKeown.[13] For a more detailed description of the image segmentation program (Section 4.1.1) and the image-to-map correspondence program (Section 4.3) see McKeown.cite[MCKEO81] For a detailed description of the CONCEPTMAP database see McKeown.[14]

### 4.1. BROWSE: Interactive Image/Map Display

BROWSE[15] is an interactive window-based image display system. It provides a common interface to all of the MAPS system components to display results of queries, graphical prompts for interactive image-to-map correspondence, superimposition of map data on imagery, and other similar functions. While often viewed as an application issue, a flexible, functional user interface is critical for building more complex tools. BROWSE provides the user with a window-oriented interface, which greatly increases the effective spatial resolution of the frame-buffer, and provides multiple processing contexts which allow users to manipulate dynamically the size, level of detail, and visibility of imagery. Photograph 4 shows a multiple window display of several images over the Foggy Bottom area of Northwest Washington.

### 4.1.1. Interactive Image Segmentation

SEGMENT is an interactive image segmentation program which uses the BROWSE window facility to provide an interface to our frame buffer. Users can extract image-based descriptions of map features, edit existing features, and assign symbolic names to the features. SEGMENT produces a standard format [SEG] file that is used throughout the MAPS database to represent image-based descriptions of point, line, and polygon geometric data. Database routines discussed in Section 4.5 are available to convert the [SEG] description to a map-based description [D3].

### 4.2. Image Database

The MAPS system currently contains approximately 100 digitized images, most of which are low altitude aerial mapping photographs. Typical ground resolution distances (GRD) are 120cm$^2$, 360cm$^2$, and 600cm$^2$ per pixel. The imagery is mainly comprised of three data sets taken in 1974, 1976 and 1982. In addition to aerial mapping photographs, we have several digitized maps including a USGS topographic map, and tour guide maps. Figure 1 gives the current status of the MAPS Washington D.C. image database. Although we have several LANDSAT,

Skylab and high altitude aerial photographs taken over the Washington D.C. area, we have focused our work on those images that provide the greatest ground detail.

```
                           IMAGE  DATABASE
    CLASS    NUMBER    SCALE      RASTER        COMMENTS
    ---------------------------------------------------------------
    ASC'74     25     1:36000    2048x2048x8    Aerial mapping BW
    WGL'76     37     1:12000    2200x2200x8    Aerial mapping BW
    AER'79      2     1:124000   2288x2288x8    Color infrared
    ASC'82     29     1:60000    2300x2300x8    Aerial mapping BW
    MAP'71      1     1:24000    4096x4096x8    USGS topo map
    MAP'74      1     1:160000*  4096x3880x8    D.C. region map
    MAP'79      1     1:16000*   4096x4096x8    Tourist guide map

    * not cartographically accurate.
```

**Figure 1:** MAPS: Image Database Component

### 4.2.1. Generic Image to File Mapping

The MAPS system uses a generic naming convention to refer to images in the database. The generic name is a unique identifier assigned to the image when it is integrated into the database. For example, DC38617, DC1420 are representative generic names that correspond to flight line annotation on the photographic film. All types of image access that require the filesystem name of the image, or require associated image database files, use the generic name mechanism to construct the appropriate physical file name. It is possible to change the logical and/or physical location of imagery by updating the generic name file or to add another image to the database. As we move to larger image/map systems this naming isolation allows us to construct a database that can be distributed over multiple processors based around a centralized or distributed file organization. The decoupling of name with physical or logical location fits well with name server organizations usually employed with such distributed systems.

The following table lists the database files associated with each active image in the MAPS database. Each is accessible using the generic image name.

- [GENERIC]  **image-to-file system mapping**
  - contains the file system location of the database image
  - identifies which reduced resolution images are computed and available for hierarchical display
- [SDF]  **scene description file**
  - contains image specific information: source, date, time of day, raster size, digitization, image scale, geodetic corner points, camera information
- [COE]  **image-to-map coefficients file**
  - contains camera model coefficients, error model, polynomial orders solved, best correspondence (default polynomial order)

- independent coefficients for <latitude>, <longitude>, <image row>
- [COR] **correspondence pairs file**
  - mapping of ground control points to image point specification
  - lists of landmark names and their geodetic position combined with image pixel position of landmark specified by user
- [HYP] **hypothesized landmark file**
  - lists of landmark names which are within the image geodetic coverage, but were not used to perform image-map correspondence

### 4.2.2. Image-Based Segmentations

MAPS maintains several types of image segmentations and map overlay descriptions associated with each image in the database. These segmentations either are feature descriptions generated using the image as the base coordinate system, or the projection of map features onto the image using map-to-image correspondence, or segmentations from other images registered to the image. In the latter case, image-to-map correspondence is used to register the two images. Users can point to segmentation overlay features using the display interface in BROWSE and CONCEPTMAP, identify the segmentation feature name and retrieve its image and geodetic coordinates. For the [DLMSSEG] and [CONCEPTSEG] segmentation descriptions, the name of the segmentation feature is used to retrieve the associated DFAD (see Section 4.4) or CONCEPTMAP description. The following table is a list of image segmentations associated with each image in the database. Segmentations that require map correspondence for their generation can be automatically recreated when image camera model is updated.

- [HANDSEG] **hand (human) segmentation**
  - collection of all hand segmentations performed on this image
- [HCOMPSEG] **composite hand segmentation**
  - collection of all features in the [HANDSEG] database that are spatially contained in this image
- [MACHSEG] **machine segmentation**
  - collection of all machine segmentations performed using the image
- [MCOMPSEG] **composite machine segmentation**
  - collection of all features in the [MACHSEG] database that are spatially contained in the image
- [DLMSSEG] DLMS **map overlay**
  - all features from the DLMS digital feature analysis database that are spatially contained in the image
- [CONCEPTSEG] CONCEPTMAP **map overlay**
  - all features from the CONCEPTMAP database that are spatially contained in the image
- [COVERSEG] **image coverage overlay**
  - all images whose area of coverage is overlapped or wholly contained within the image

## 4.3. Image-to-Map Correspondence

The MAPS system uses an interactive image-to-map correspondence procedure to place new imagery into correspondence with the map database. It has three major components: a landmark database, a landmark creation and editing program, and an interactive correspondence program. The process of landmark selection, description, and interactive correspondence has been described in detail in McKeown.[16]

### 4.3.1. Landmark Database

MAPS maintains a database of approximately 200 geodetic ground control points in the Washington D.C. area. Landmarks are acquired using USGS topographic maps, but in principle can be integrated from any source that provides accurate geodetic position ⟨latitude/longitude/elevation⟩. Users can query the database to find landmarks by name, within a geodetic area, or the closest landmark to a geodetic point. Landmark features are also integrated into the CONCEPTMAP database and can be found using the ⟨role-derivation⟩ attribute (see Section 4.5.2) of a concept role schema.

### 4.3.2. LANDMARK

LANDMARK is an interactive tool used to generate new landmarks, their text descriptions, and associated image fragments. The following information is maintained by LANDMARK to support landmark database access.

- [LDM] **landmark name directory**
  - associates the list of landmark names with their geodetic position
  - sorted for spatial proximity
  - partial name matching also provided
- [ETY] **landmark text description**
  - contains a detailed text description of the location of the landmark and general factual properties of the landmark
  - stores the location and name of the associated image fragment file [LIMG], and replicates the geodetic position from ldm file
- [LIMG] **landmark image fragment**
  - contains a high-resolution image fragment which clearly shows the ground control point and scene context around the point

### 4.3.3. CORRES

CORRES is an interactive image-to-map correspondence program. It uses the BROWSE window interface, the LANDMARK database, and image database routines to interactively build an image-to-map correspondence. Once an initial guess of the corner points is performed and the [COR] and [COE] files have been created in the image database, CORRES automatically suggests new possible landmark points using the image database [HYP] files. The LANDMARK database [LIMG] files are used to display the ground control point when the user selects it from the list of hypothesized points.

## 4.4. DLMS: An External Database

The ability to rendezvous with externally generated map databases is a key capability in order to integrate information from a variety of sources. One example of the flexibility of the MAPS database is illustrated by our experiences with the Defense Mapping Agency's (DMA) Digital Landmass Simulation System (DLMS)[17]. DLMS is composed of a digital feature analysis database (DFAD) which describes man-made cultural features and a digital terrain elevation database (DTED) which is organized as a raster elevation grid. The specified resolution of the DFAD data is comparable to map scales of 1:250,000 to 1:100,000. The specified resolution of DTED data is within a meter vertical resolution over a $100^2$ meter (3 arc sec) grid. A user can query into the DLMS database by pointing at a DFAD polygon superimposed on any image or map and retrieve the complete feature text description. A terrain package, ELEVATION, provides a transparent interface to the DTED database. Users can retrieve elevation information based on rectangular geodetic area, closest sample point to a geodetic point, or by weighted interpolation.

## 4.5. Conceptual Map Database

The map database component of MAPS, CONCEPTMAP, has been described in McKeown.[14] We will give a brief overview of the organization and concentrate on our new work in hierarchical organization and feature semantics.

### 4.5.1. Concept Schema

The basic entity in the CONCEPTMAP database is the concept schema. The schema is given a unique ID by the database, and the user specifies a 'symbolic' print name for the concept. Each concept may have one or more role schema associated with it. Role schema specify one or more database views of the same geographic concept. For example, 'northwest washington' can be viewed as a residential area as well as political entity. Another aspect is the ability to associate the same name to two different but related spatial objects. Consider the 'kennedy center' as a building and as the spatial area (ie. lawn, parking area, etc.) encompassing the building. The principle role of a concept schema indicates a preferred or default view. The CONCEPTMAP database is composed of lists of concept schema.

### 4.5.2. Role Schema

The role schema is a further specification of the attributes of the map feature. It contains the *role name* attribute (building, bridge, commercial area, etc.), a *subrole name* attribute (house, museum, dormitory, etc.), a *role class* attribute (ie., buildings may be *government, residential, commercial*, etc.), a *role type* attribute (ie. physical, conceptual or aggregate), and a *role derivation* attribute (ie. derivation method).

The role name, subrole, and role class attributes categorize the map feature according to its function. For example: this feature is a building, used as an office building, used for government purposes. The role type attribute describes whether the map feature is physically realized in the scene, or if it is a conceptual feature such as a neighborhood, political, or geographic boundary. The role type attribute also provides a mechanism to define the role schema as a collection of physical or conceptual map features. For example, the concept schema in MAPS for 'district of columbia' has a role type aggregate-conceptual, with aggregate roles, 'northwest washington', 'northeast washington', 'southwest washington', and 'southeast washington'. This mechanism allows the user to explicitly represent concepts that are strictly composed of other role schema. The role derivation attribute describes the method by which the role and its associated geodetic position description were added to the CONCEPTMAP database.

Each role schema contains a 3DID identifier that is used to access a set of CONCEPTMAP database files which contain geodetic information about the map feature. These identifiers can be shared when multiple roles have the same geodetic description, as in the previous example of 'northwest washington' viewed as both a residential and political area. The CONCEPTMAP 3D description allows for point, line, and polygon features as primitives, and permits the aggregation of primitives into more complex topologies, such as regions with holes, discontinuous lines, and point lists. Associated with each feature that was acquired from a image in the database is the generic name of the image. If the correspondence of the generic image changes due to the addition of more ground control points, or better a camera model, the position of the ground feature can be automatically recalculated.

The following is the set of files associated with each 3DID.

- [D3]  **3D geodetic location**
  - a set of <latitude/longitude/elevation> triples which define the geodetic position of the role
- [D3F]  **3D feature shape description**
  - metric values for length, width, area, compactness, centroid, fourier shape approximation etc.
- [EC]  **feature image coverage**
  - a list of generic images which contain this feature
  - image mbr and feature coordinates for each image
- [PROP]  **feature property list**
  - list of properties of the map feature
  - some general properties such as 'age', 'capacity', '3D display type'
  - feature type specific properties such as 'number of floors', 'basement', 'height', and 'roof type' for buildings

### 4.5.3. Database Query

CONCEPTMAP supports four methods of database query. The methods are *signal access, symbolic access, template matching* and *geometric access.* The following table gives a brief description of each query method.

- **signal access**
  Given a geodetic specification (point, line, area)[****], perform the following operations:
  - display all imagery at which contains point, line or area.
  - retrieve all map features within geodetic specification

---

[****] this specification may be in geodetic coordinates or require image-to-map correspondence

- retrieve terrain elevation
- **symbolic access**
  Given a symbolic name, such as 'treasury building' perform the following operations:
  - convert name into geodetic specification to perform signal access operations listed above
  - retrieve database description, facts and properties of the map feature
  - retrieve imagery based on symbolic (generic) name
- **template matching**
  Given a partial specification of symbolic attributes perform the following operations:
  - find all map features which satisfy the specification template and return their symbolic name
  - find all images and return symbolic (generic) name
- **geometric access**
  Given a geometric operation such as 'contains' and a geodetic specification perform the following operations:
  - find all map features which satisfy the operation performed over the geodetic specification and return their symbolic name.
  - find all image features and return symbolic name

These primitive access functions can be combined[14] to answer queries such as: 'display images of Foggy Bottom before 1977', 'what is the closest commercial building to this geographic point', and 'how many bridges cross between Virginia and the District of Columbia'.

### 4.5.4. Spatial Computation

CONCEPTMAP computes geometric properties based on the geodetic descriptions associated with each role schema in the database. A static description of all spatial relationships between map features for contains, subsumed by, intersection, adjacency, closest point, partitioned by is maintained in the database.

- **'contains'**
  - an unordered list of features which the map feature contains
- **'subsumed by**
  - an unordered list of features which contain the map feature
- **'intersection'**
  - an unordered list of features which intersect the map feature
- **'closest point'**
  - single feature which is closest to the map feature
- **'adjacency'**
  - an unordered list of features that are within a specific distance of the map feature
- **'partitioned by'**
  - the locus of points where two areal features share a common boundary.

If one or more of the map features in a spatial computation is a result of a dynamic query (and therefore not in the static database), these relationships are computed as needed. A simple 'memo' function is implemented to avoid recomputation of dynamic properties. The use of the static description can also be 'turned off' to evaluate hierarchical search as described in the following section.

The CONCEPTMAP database stores both factual and exact information describing the spatial relationship. For example, if two features intersect, the list of geodetic intersection points is stored, as well as the fact that they intersect at least once. This is necessary for queries which require the display of imagery containing a geometric fact, and may possibly be useful for describing the semantics of the intersection.

### 4.6. Toward Feature Semantics

The CONCEPTMAP database is used to build a *hierarchy graph* data structure, which represents the whole-part relationships and spatial containment of map feature descriptions.[13] This graph is used to improve the speed of spatial computations by constraining search to a portion of the database. Each node in the graph represents a map feature and has as its descendants those features that it completely contains in *⟨latitude/longitude/elevation⟩* space. The hierarchy graph is initially generated by obtaining an unordered list of features (containment list) for each map database feature.

We have begun to investigate the generation of map feature semantics directly from the hierarchical representation of the map feature data. A simple example is the semantic description of a bridge: the feature names and map locations that it connects as well as the names of the map features that it crosses over. Figures 2 and 3 show the result of applying a procedural description of the semantics of a bridge concept to calculate the 'connects' and 'crossover' relationship using the map feature descriptions of 'arlington memorial bridge' and 'theodore roosevelt memorial bridge'. These results are generated directly using the MAPS hierarchical organization for spatial data. We do not pose this as a theory of map feature semantics, but envision a set of feature specific procedures that can build these types of descriptions.

The procedure for bridge semantics is as follows: A bridge can be represented in the CONCEPTMAP database as a polygonal area, a list of linear segments, or as a geodetic point. The polygonal area arises when the bridge deck is represented, the list of linear segments approximates the center line of the bridge, and the point feature generally represents that the bridge is a landmark feature. No semantics are computed in the latter case. If the bridge is represented as a line, the end points are selected, otherwise the endpoints of the major axis of the bounding ellipse are retrieved from the feature [D3F] file. At some level of description, these endpoints define the 'connects' relationship, but this is not useful if we are envisioning generation of a reasonably complex symbolic representation.

The 'contains' relationship is applied to each endpoint using the hierarchical graph to order the search. As before, this search returns a list of features ordered by spatial

```
2 entries for 'contains' for 'querypoint 1'
entry 0:          'virginia'
entry 1:          'greater washington d.c.'
           ************ A N D ************
2 entries for 'contains' for 'querypoint 1'
entry 0:          'arlington memorial bridge'
entry 1:          'greater washington d.c.'

****************************************************
4 entries for 'contains' for 'querypoint 2'
entry 0:          'mall area'
entry 1:          'southwest washington'
entry 2:          'district of columbia'
entry 3:          'greater washington d.c.'
           ************ A N D ************
2 entries for 'contains' for 'querypoint 2'
entry 0:          'arlington memorial bridge'
entry 1:          'greater washington d.c.'

****************************************************
5 entries for 'intersection' for 'crossover'
entry 0:          'virginia'
entry 1:          'district of columbia' ·
entry 2:          'southwest washington'
entry 3:          'mall area'
entry 4:          'potomac river (Role: 0)'
****************************************************

2 entries for 'connects' for 'arlington memorial bridge'
entry 0:          'virginia'
entry 1:          'mall area'

1 entries for 'crossover' for 'arlington memorial bridge'
entry 0:          'potomac river'
```

**Figure 2:** MAPS: Semantic Computation from Spatial Data
Arlington Memorial Bridge

containment, and there may be several independent containment paths. Redundant paths are eliminated by examining whether the bridge is in the containment path. The first entry (0) in each of the remaining paths is one of the areas connected by the bridge. Using the 'contains' relationship, the other entries in the path are also valid connecting areas.

To compute the 'crossover' relationship, the 'intersection' relationship is computed for the bridge using the complete list of line segments or the polygonal description. A list of all the features that the bridge intersects is assembled. Entries in the intersection list are removed if they are also present in either of the 'connects' lists. The assumption is that those features that didn't contain a bridge endpoint, but intersected with the bridge description, are those features that the bridge crosses over. If there is sufficiently detailed elevation data for man-made features it should

```
2 entries for 'contains' for 'querypoint 1'
entry 0:              'virginia'
entry 1:              'greater washington d.c.'
        ************ A N D ************
2 entries for 'contains' for 'querypoint 1'
entry 0:              'theodore roosevelt memorial bridge'
entry 1:              'greater washington d.c.'

*****************************************************
3 entries for 'contains' for 'querypoint 2'
entry 0:              'northwest washington'
entry 1:              'district of columbia'
entry 2:              'greater washington d.c.'
        ************ A N D ************
2 entries for 'contains' for 'querypoint 2'
entry 0:              'theodore roosevelt memorial bridge'
entry 1:              'greater washington d.c.'
*****************************************************

5 entries for 'intersection' for 'crossover list'
entry 0:              'virginia'
entry 1:              'district of columbia'
entry 2:              'northwest washington'
entry 3:              'theodore roosevelt island'
entry 4:              'potomac river'
*****************************************************

2 entries for 'connects' for 'theodore roosevelt memorial bridge'
entry 0:              'virginia'
entry 1:              'northwest washington'

2 entries for 'crossover' for 'theodore roosevelt memorial bridge'
entry 0:              'theodore roosevelt island'
entry 1:              'potomac river'
```

**Figure 3:**  MAPS: Semantic Computation from Spatial Data
Theodore Roosevelt Memorial Bridge

be possible to compute semantics for 'passes over' and 'passes under' by calculating the feature elevation at the actual geodetic point of intersection.

## 5. Synthesis Tasks

In this section we will very briefly discuss three applications of the MAPS database to cartographic and image interpretation tasks. These tasks are 3D scene generation of views of Washington D.C.,[18] the use of the map database to guide image segmentation,[13] and some preliminary results on a rule-based system for airport scene interpretation.[19] Each task requires the capabilities of various aspects of the IMD model as implemented in the MAPS system. These applications pull together external and image/map databases, and are only possible using an integrated system that relates imagery, terrain, and map data through a unified cartographic representation.

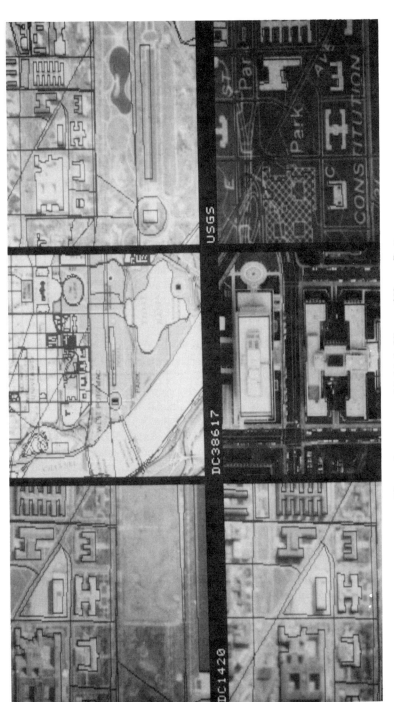

**Figure 4:** BROWSE: Multiple Views of Foggy Bottom

## 5.1. WASH3D: 3D Scene Generation

The first application of the MAPS database is in the area of 3D computer graphics for scene simulation and database validation. Computer graphics play an important role in the areas of image processing, photo-interpretation, and cartography. In cartography various phases of the map generation process use graphics techniques or source material analysis, transcription and update, and some aspects of map layout and production. However, many major steps in the generation of a cartographic product remain largely manual. One important step for which inadequate tools exist is the integration of terrain and cultural feature databases. This integration step is often used to verify the geodetic accuracy of natural and man-made features in the digital database prior to actual map layout and production. Another application is sensor simulation.[20, 21] Radar, visual, and multi-sensor scenes are digitally generated to verify the quality of digital culture and terrain databases or to determine the quality of the sensor model. Improvements to the level of detail contained in the underlying database can be subjectively measured in terms of the quality of the generated scene.

WASH3D[18] is an interactive graphics system that uses the MAPS system to integrate a digital terrain database, a cultural feature database, and the CONCEPTMAP database to allow a user to generate cartographically accurate 3D scenes for human visual analysis. WASH3D uses the coarse resolution DLMS database described in Section 4.4 to generate a baseline thematic map. The thematic map is a 2D image which is produced by scan conversion of the DLMS digital feature analysis database (DFAD) polygon database. We assign a color to each region polygon using the DFAD surface material code-- forest and park (green), water (blue), residential (yellow), and high-density urban (brown). DLMS terrain elevation data (DTED) is interpolated to determine ground elevations at each point in the 2D image. Since the resolution of the DFAD data is coarse, comparable to map scales of 1:250,000 to 1:100,000, we use the CONCEPTMAP database to provide high resolution 3D feature descriptions of buildings, roads, bridges, residential and commercial areas. The CONCEPTMAP database is derived from imagery with resolutions between 1:12000 and 1:36000, and the addition of these features effectively intensifies the perceived level of detail in the simulated scene, even though the base map is at a coarse resolution. Lukes[22] describes the utility of selective database intensification for tailoring standard database products to custom applications and for time-critical applications which cannot be handled by normal production schedules. Figure 5 shows a 3D scene of the Washington D.C. area generated by WASH3D.

## 5.2. MACHINESEG: Map-Guided Machine Segmentation

The second application of the MAPS database is in the area of map-guided machine segmentation. Users may specify a map feature from the CONCEPTMAP database or interactively generate a feature description using the SEGMENT program. In the case of a map database feature, MACHINESEG[23] uses an existing image coverage [EC] file (see Section 4.5.2) that specifies in which images the feature is found, and the feature location in the image. For interactive specification, an [EC] file is created dynamically by image-to-map correspondence using the image database. For each image, a high

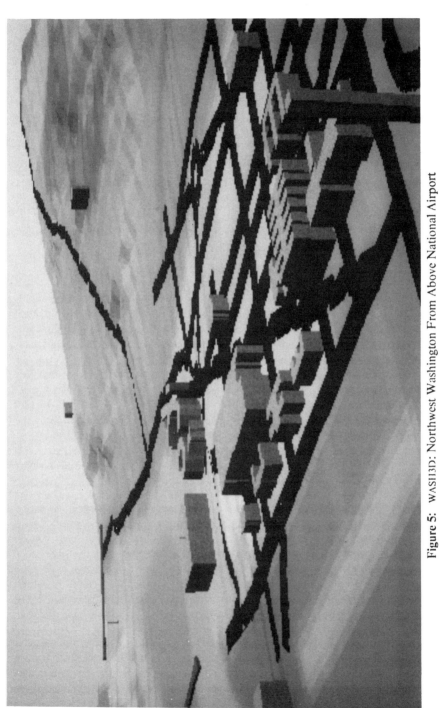

**Figure 5:** WASH3D: Northwest Washington From Above National Airport

resolution window containing the database feature is extracted and displayed. We expand the size of the image window to contain an area of uncertainty around the feature location. The expansion is currently based on the size of the feature, but we plan to incorporate correspondence error measures based on the quality of the camera model associated with each image. The image window is smoothed, and a segmentation is performed using a region-growing technique[24] which combines an edge strength metric and region merge acceptability based on spectral similarity to control region growing.

The significance of MACHINESEG is that it can search systematically for features in a database of images, an operation that is fundamental for change detection applications. It directly uses the map database description as an evaluation tool for image segmentation and interpretation. It also uses very general image processing tools to perform both segmentation and evaluation and is amenable to supporting other approaches to image segmentation and feature recovery. A further application of the MACHINESEG system is discussed in the following section.

### 5.3. SPAM: Rule-based System for Airport Interpretation

The third application of the MAPS system is in the investigation of rule-based systems for the control of image processing and interpretation with respect to a world model. In photo-interpretation, knowledge can range from stereotypical information about man-made and natural features found in various situations (airports, manufacturing, industrial installations, power plants etc.) to particular instantiations of these situations in frequently monitored sites. It is crucial for photo-interpretation applications that the metrics used be defined in a cartographic coordinate system, such as *⟨latitude/longitude/elevation⟩*, rather than an image-based coordinate system. Descriptions such as "the runway has area 12000 pixels" or "houses are between 212 and 345 pixels" are useless except for (perhaps) the analysis of one image. It is the case, however, that to operationalize metric knowledge one must relate the world model to the image under analysis. This should be done through image-to-map correspondence using camera models which is the method used in our system.

We have begun to build SPAM[19] to test our ideas in the use of the combination of a map database, task independent low-level image processing tools, and a rule-based system. SPAM uses the MAPS database to store facts about man-made or natural feature existence and location, and to perform geometric computation in *map space* rather than *image space*. Differences in scale, orientation, and viewpoint can be handled in a consistent manner using a simple camera model. The MAPS database facility also maintains a partial model of interpretation, separate from, but in the same representation as, the map feature database.

The image processing component is based on the MACHINESEG program described in the previous section. It performs low level and intermediate level feature extraction. Processing primitives are based on linear feature extraction and region extraction using edge-based and region-growing techniques. It identifies islands of interest and extends those islands constrained by the geometric model provided by MAPS and model-based goals established by the rule-based component. The rule-based component provides the image processing system with the best next task based on the strength/promise of expectations and with constraints from the image/map database system. It also guides the scene interpretation by generating successively more specific expectations based on image processing results.

## 6. Future Work

Our future work will be directed toward two research topics. First, we have only begun to explore the use of MAPS as a component of an image interpretation system. We will continue our work in the airport scene interpretation task, using the SPAM system as a testbed for integration of a rule-based system with the MAPS system. Second, there is much to do in expanding the CONCEPTMAP database to include more complex 3D descriptions, and in attendant issues of scaling and sizing to larger databases. Other tasks we will pursue are the evaluation of our hierarchical spatial representation to constrain search in large databases, general solutions to complex spatial queries for situation assessment applications, and the application of spatial knowledge to navigate through a map database.

## 7. Acknowledgements

The MAPS system is the result of much effort by several people. Jerry Denlinger implemented the BROWSE system and the MACHINESEG program. Wilson Harvey implemented the hierarchical graph generation and supervised much of the landmark database generation. Mike Matsko implemented WASH3D, the 3D scene generation system. Mark Nichols, John Pane, Jane Pate, and Dave Springer are responsible for various aspects of the image database generation and maintenance. The SPAM system is a joint collaboration with John McDermott. Raj Reddy has provided encouragement and support for this work.

## References

1.  Tatalias, Kosmo D., "Mass Data Base/Knowledge Base System," Tech. report DMA Technology Base Symposium, Defense Mapping Agency, August 1983.

2.  Nagy, G., and Wagle, S., "Geographic Data Processing," *Computing Surveys,* Vol. 11, No. 2, June 1979, pp. 139-182.

3.  *IEEE Workshop on Picture Data Description and Management,* IEEE Computer Society, Asilomar, Ca., August 1980.

4.  *IEEE Computer Magazine, Special Issue on Pictorial Information Systems,* IEEE Computer Society, November 1981.

5.  *Map Data Processing,* Academic Press, 1980.

6.  *Data Base Techniques for Pictorial Applications,* Springer-Verlag, 1979.

7.  Chang, N. S., and Fu, K. S.,, "A Query Language For Relational Image Database Systems," *Proceedings of the Workshop on Picture Data Description and Management,* IEEE, August 1980, pp. 68-73.

8.  Chang, N. S., and Fu, K. S.,, "An Integrated Image Analysis and Image Database Management System," Tech. report TR-EE-80-20, Electrical

Engineering Department, Purdue University, May 1980.

9.   Chang, N. S., *Image Analysis and Image Database Management*, UMI Research Press, Ann Arbor, Michigan, 1981.

10.  Samet, H., and Webber, R. E., "Using Quadtrees to Represent Polygonal Maps," *Proceedings of the IEEE Computer Vision and Pattern Recognition Conference*, June 1983.

11.  Rosenfeld, A., Samet, H., Shaffer, C., and Webber, R. E., "Application of Hierarchical Data Structures to Geographical Information Systems," Tech. report TR-1197, University of Maryland, 1983.

12.  Matsuyama, T., Hao, L. V., and Nagao, M., "A File Organization for Geographic Information Systems," *Proceedings of 6ICPR*, IEEE, Oct 1982, pp. 83-87.

13.  McKeown, D.M., "MAPS: The Organization of a Spatial Database System Using Imagery, Terrain, and Map Data," *Proceedings: DARPA Image Understanding Workshop*, June 1983, pp. 105-127, Also available as Technical Report CMU-CS-83-136

14.  McKeown, D.M., "Concept Maps," *Proceedings: DARPA Image Understanding Workshop*, Sept. 1982, pp. 142-153, Also available as Technical Report CMU-CS-83-117

15.  McKeown, D. M., and J. L. Denlinger, "Graphical Tools for Interactive Image Interpretation," *Computer Graphics*, Vol. 16, No. 3, July 1982, pp. 189-198.

16.  McKeown, D. M. and T. Kanade, "Database Support for Automated Photo Interpretation," *Techniques and Applications of Image Understanding III*, Society of Photo-Optical Instrumentation Engineers, Washington, D.C., April 1981, pp. 192-198.

17.  Defense Mapping Agency, *Product Specifications for Digital Landmass System (DLMS) Database*, St. Louis, Missouri, 1977.

18.  McKeown, D. M., and Matsko, M. S., "Urban Scene Generation for Cartographic Applications," Tech. report, Carnegie-Mellon University, in preparation, 1983.

19.  McKeown, D.M., and McDermott, J., "Toward Expert Systems for Photo Interpretation," *IEEE Trends and Applications '83*, May 1983, pp. 33-39.

20.  Faintich, M. B., "Digital Sensor Simulation at the Defense Mapping Agency Aerospace Center," *Proceedings of the National Aerospace and Electronics Conference (NAECON)*, May 1979, pp. 1242-1246.

21.  Faintich, M. B., "Sensor Image Simulator Application Studies," *Proceedings: International Conference on Simulators*, Sept. 1983, to appear

22.  Lukes, G. E., "Computer-assisted photo interpretation research at United States Army Engineer Topographic Laboratories (USAETL)," *Techniques and Applications of Image Understanding III*, Society of Photo-Optical Instrumentation Engineers, Washington, D.C., April 1981, pp. 85-94.

23.  McKeown, D. M., and Denlinger, J. L., "Map-Guided Feature Extraction from Aerial Imagery," Tech. report, Computer Science Department, April 1984.

24.  Yoram Yakimovsky, "Boundary and Object Detection in Real World Images," *Journal of the ACM*, Vol. 23, No. 4, 1976, .

EXPRIM : AN EXPERT SYSTEM TO AID IN PROGRESSIVE
RETRIEVAL FROM A PICTORIAL AND DESCRIPTIVE DATABASE

M. Créhange, A. Ait Haddou, M. Boukakiou,
J. M. David, O. Foucaut and J. Maroldt

*CRIN, BP 239, 54506 Vandoeuvre Cédex, France*

SUMMARY

The EXPRIM system (EXPert system to Retrieve IMages) is a young
project whose target is to manage and to interrogate a pictorial
base with a descriptive base attached. The hypotheses of work
are that the descriptive base is infinitely poor with respect to
the pictures themselves, so containing incomplete and imprecise
information, and that the requests may be not properly conceived
or formulated.
   The system processes interactively and by means of visualization devices and of an expert system playing the role of a
human expert in "fuzzy" retrieval (or recognition) in an environment of images. The successive phases of the process may be
roughly listed as follows, each of them being accomplished by
the user or by the system or by both interactively : putting requests to the descriptive base, possibly modulating these requests (elastic deformation), visualizing pertinent images or
samples of them, criticizing this result, using the criticism to
reformulate the requests, and so on.
   Such a system might concern inconographic retrieval, recognition aided by image, teaching of observation sciences, etc.

## 1. THE PROBLEMS CONCERNED

The reporter, the teacher, the publisher or anyone who needs to
illustrate a text or to reinforce an idea may have to choose
some pictures among a large collection from their descriptions.
Often this choice cannot be formulated correctly with words, and
is not even precise in the mind of the user. On the other hand,
even though one could formulate his or her request in some words,
it may happen that the answer would not be satisfactory ; one
essential reason may be that in many cases the description of a
picture is infinitely poor in relation to the large amount of
information in and about the picture. In consequence DBMS (Data
Base Management Systems) tools alone are not adequate to deal
with a "pictorial" database. Retrieval has to be somewhat fuzzy,
proceeding by hypotheses, trials and choices : so an expert system (4) (19) is strongly needed.

At the origin of the EXPRIM project (EXPert system to Retrieve IMages) is a press agency gathering a large collection of
photographs and wishing to develop automatized aid to image retrieval. An important contribution had already been made by our
laboratory to this action : the "Shapes and Images Recognition"
team had conceived a work station with a mosaic screen to visu-
alize a set of images together as a checkerboard. The aim of our
contribution was to help the user to formulate a request, and to
assist him in making it evolve to reach or pursue a satisfactory
selection. The underlying ideas are described in Hudrisier (16).

The system includes neither natural language interpretation
- at least in a first stage - nor image recognition. Its kernel
is an expert system using - possibly non traditional - access to
a traditional database (we call it the descriptive base) ; this
database contains information with respect to the various "dimensions" of the images : description of what is visible in each
of them, possibly ideas resulting from them, considerations
about style, details about events when the photographs were
taken, about people present, etc. Using this descriptive base,
the system guides the user as would a good image-documentalist
(an expert of visual documentation). In short : it aids the user
in having a first impact in the base and thus making a first selection of image references ; then it has tools, such as sampling, to select some views to be shown to the user ; the user
then says what are the selected views which are more or less pertinent for him and he can also formulate new ideas about the retrieval he is processing (image inference) ; then the system,
possibly interactively (if indeterminism is too strong), tries
to reformulate a new question (24) to the descriptive base, etc.

A second problem we are dealing with is to recognize a mushroom. This at first sight has no relation with the above. But
yet it consists in determining the nature of a mushroom by suc-

cessive phases of description (that is equivalent to a request),
selection, visualization, criticism, reformulation. And the system we call MYCOMATIC (20) plays the role of an expert of something like image-aided recognition. This second problem interests us in itself but also, for similarities and differences
with the first one, helps us in our reflexion.

We think that the two processes are pretty analogous, first
by the succession of their different phases, and even by the nature of the expertise they use : this we guess but are not yet
sure.

To sum up, we can define the kind of problem we are dealing
with by : interrogation of a pictorial base (7) (29) with a descriptive base attached, containing incomplete and imprecise information, the requests being possibly not properly formulated ;
and that interactively and by means of
    - an expert system playing the role of a human expert in
"fuzzy" retrieval or recognition in an environment of images ;
    - visualization devices.

In this paper, we shall first develop some of the semantics
of the EXPRIM project, give a commented example of a scenario of
usage and give an idea of our recent position about the rules of
the expert system. Then we shall show some more directions in
which we are working : specifying the system with abstract data
types, use of a relational database for successive non independent queries. This paper is not concerned with the description
of the MYCOMATIC system.

## 2. ARCHITECTURE AND BEHAVIOUR OF THE SYSTEM

### 2.1. Architecture

Figure 1 shows the different components of EXPRIM. We
explain the role of each of them.

## (a) The work station and the visualization manager

The work station is composed of a keyboard, an alphanumerical
screen and a pictorial screen with two user modes :
    - normal mode : the picture is viewed on full screen ;
    - mosaic mode : the screen is divided into n*m windows which
may be addressed by their reference numbers. After selection of
a certain set of pictures, the user may distribute them into
heaps, each heap corresponding to a window. The pictures within
a heap may be visualized one after the other in their window or
on full screen ; a picture can be copied from one heap to another. This visualization mode simulates an office desk allowing
sorting, composition and selection of pictures.

(b) The pictorial base

Pictures may be stored on different materials : numerical disk,
optical numerical disk, videodisk... In every case a picture may
be identified through its reference number, and the system includes a pictorial interface in order to access pictures from
the reference numbers given by the expert system.

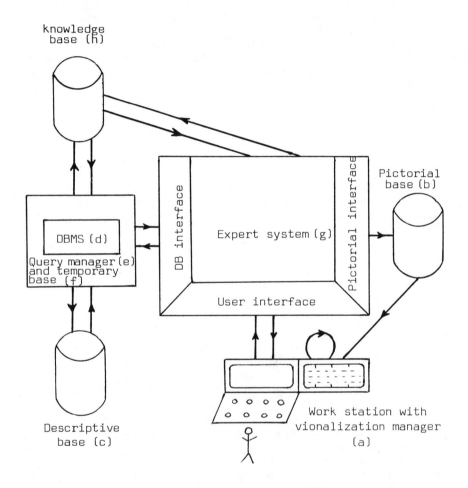

Fig. 1   The architecture of EXPRIM.

(c) The descriptive base

Pictures are described by alphanumerical information which permits their retrieval from user queries. It constitutes the descriptive base.

(d)(e)(f) The DBMS, the query manager and the temporary base

The descriptive base is managed by a DBMS which may be :
- a classical DBMS, relationnal or not (9) (11) ;
- a data base machine (2) (13) (21).
    The particularities of retrieval for descriptions of pictu-
res lead us to complete the DBMS by a tool which manages queries : the query manager. The main role of this tool is to keep
some intermediate results of queries in a temporary base during
a session in order to reuse them in the successive phases of a
query session (see also paragraph 4.2).

(g)(h) The expert system and the knowledge base

The expert system is the principal and original component of
EXPRIM. It performs all the functions we have presented in the
first part. We study it in chapter 3.
    It uses a knowledge base which contains :
- information about the vocabulary used to describe the pictures in the documentary base (neighbourhoods, generalisation,
and so on) ;
- information about the area illustrated by the pictures ;
- reasoning rules. We give in this paper a classification of
the rules and a few examples.

2.2. The principal functions of EXPRIM

In this paragraph we list the principal functions of EXPRIM
that have already been introduced in part one. Each function is
completed by important visualization functions.

Query initial formulation aid : this function consists in aiding
a user who is not familiar with the system or who does not know
precisely what he desires.

Query process : this function includes executing requests, but
also all that we may call the "elastic deformation" of queries.
It consists in flexibly interpreting the queries, as it is done
sometimes in documentary systems, using a structured thesaurus
(the more classical part of the knowledge base).

Query automatic (re)formulation : this function is concerned
with the analysis by the computer of the choice of pictures
made by the user at a visualization step. The role of the system is to try to discover in the set of descriptions of the
selected pictures some information which could permit the modification of the preceding query or the generation of a new one.
The function particulary includes picture sampling.

Query reformulation aid : when the system is not able to itself
reformulate a query, it proposes an aid to the user. This aid
consists in assisting the user in criticizing the set of displayed pictures, in suggesting to him different ways to complete
his retrieval or in putting queries in order to understand his
choice or his goal. This function is of the same nature as the
previous one (for instance it may consist in discovering common
features between different pictures) but it deals with visual
information while the previous one deals with descriptions. Both
may include inference, this function trying to stimulate human
inference from pictures and the previous one trying to do it by
itself from descriptions.

In the following paragraph we give an example of use of this
system. The example is not a real one but is caricatural, made
to illustrate briefly the different functions of the system.

## 2.3. Example

We describe here the example from an external point of view ; in
paragraph 3.3, we give for each step the rules used by the expert system to lead to the conclusions.

### The fact to illustrate

Mister X., not known to the public, becomes a minister. A
journalist has to write a paper about his surprising promotion
and wishes to illustrate it with some pictures of Mister X.
The successive steps of retrieval with EXPRIM might be as
follows :
- First step :
The journalist begins by the simple query "Pictures of Mister X.". The result is none : Mister X. is not known by the
system.
- Second step :
The system asks more details about Mister X. (residence, pro-
fession, political activities, etc.). The user answers that
Mister X. is a deputy mayor of Lorient. The system then propo-
ses about a hundred picture references concerning official
events at Lorient.
The user visualizes them and recognizes Mister X. on thirty
pictures.
- Third step :
The system, thanks to the descriptions in the descriptive
base, finds out that in a great number of selected pictures
there is a wellknown navigator, Alain Bombard.
The system considers the hypothesis that Mister X. and Alain
Bombard have common interests and continues by searching for

pictures of the navigator. The system then delivers about sixty
pictures among which about ten pictures are different from those
found at the second step and show Mister X.
- Fourth step :
    The user notices that one of the new pictures shows an ecolo-
gical association event and supposes that Mister X. could play
an outstanding part in this association. He gives a new request
to the system concerning this association and obtains a set of
pictures in which Mister X. appears.
- Fifth step :
    At this point the system proposes different research modes :
. further study of one of the partial results ;
. illustration of the subject by images related to the ground of
the research (i.e. the main underlying idea) ;
. one more visualization of the assembled documents.
    The user points out the second mode and indicates that he
wants to illustrate the sudden accession of Mister X. to the government. The system gives a new sample of pictures including an
airplane takeoff, a racing car on run, a bomb explosion. The
user points out the first one.
- Sixth step :
    The user asks to see again all the pictures included in the
visual file which he built up during the precedent steps and he
selects five pictures for his article. He also asks the administrator system to add the name of Mister X. to the lexicon and to
let it appear in the descriptions of the pictures on which Mister X. figures.

3. THE SEMANTICS OF EXPRIM

    3.1. Specificity of the visual information

We think that most of our reflexion is made necessary by one
particularity of the visual information : the fact that each
image is infinitely richer than any description we could give of
it. First, at the moment when the description is given, it is
impossible to describe every detail of the image (especially
when it is complex), every detail about the circumstances of
photography, ..., even if one would accept a bulky description.
But even if a description is not poor, it may happen that some
of the neglected elements of the image arise to interest ; for
instance when an unknown city or person becomes famous. However
this particularity is not specific to visual information, it is
available too for book indexing, music description, etc.
    Another particularity of visual information, more specific,
allows us to hope that our reflexions may lead to successful
solutions : the fact   that it is possible, by a very quick
glance at a set of images, to be able to distinguish those which

fit an aim and those which do not. So noise in descriptive retrieval is not a problem for us as long as it is not over-
whelming.

Another interesting specificity is the fact that a global
glance at a set of images is very suggestive and may provoke new
ideas in the mind of the user, stimulating his imagination : we
call this "image inference". This point will give richness and
power to our process.

### 3.2. The expertises

We have chosen to see the expertise in EXPRIM as being double :
    - that of an expert in "iconographic documentation" (we call
it EB : for "Basic") ;
    - that of an expert in the knowledge domain of the applica-
tion : for instance Art, or Sports, or Show business, etc. (we
call it ED : for "Domain").

Even if this distinction in somewhat strained, it seems to us
to be useful, and is not far from the real situation (documenta-
lists-specialists of domains).

We think that this case of two co-operative expertises is
frequent - for instance in computer aided teaching - and that it
would be a very fruitful way of research to study the different
ways for two expertises to work together : union of the two sets
of rules, but also rules calling for rules of the other expertise, etc.

EB will play roles at different steps of the process :
    - in non-visual retrieval : to make the request wider or to
make it sharper, in an "elastic" or non-elastic way, to help in
indirect retrieval (if we search A in the documents but A does
not exist in the lexicon or in any document, if B has some kin-
ship with A or is a part of A or is a property of A, then perhaps searching B will provide some images with A on them), to
deal with non-precise data, etc. ;
    - in the preparation of visualization : possibly to choose
sampling criteria, to organize the set of selected views into
stacks for providing the mosaic screen, etc. For the moment we
have distinguished three types of rules to use in this phase :
consistency rules (preventing the making of a priori fruitless
retrievals), sufficient accuracy rules (preventing the making of
non selective retrievals) and strategy rules ;
    - during visualization, perhaps ;
    - after visualization to deduce behaviour from the choices or
propositions of the user : to try to carry out a discriminant
analysis to discover some common features between the chosen
pictures or between the ones not chosen, in order to insert this
in a new request ; to help the user in discovering non described
common features, or in discovering fruitful ideas to complete

retrieval, etc. And to reformulate requests from this behaviour.

We can say that EB expertise will apply less to what is described in the descriptive base than to the "neighbourhoods" of it. In every case, the expert system will make the user interfere when indeterminism grows too high.

Up to now, we have studied what has to be expressed by rules, and this is not finished ; but we have not yet chosen a form for the rules and even a degree of richness. This will be done in a near future. To study the expertises, we will stay for some days in the press agency to observe experts working and to analyse their work ; and this observation will be continued from time to time afterwards.

For the moment, we think that for our present problem and more generally in documentation problems, EB expertise is somewhat a leader with regard to ED : strategies will probably be initiated with EB and then completed with ED. As for the problems of recognition or diagnostics, it is possible to consider them as particular cases of documentation : the description of one object to recognize may stand for a documentary request, the recognized object standing for the goal of retrieval. Using Mycomatic, we shall study if this parallel is reasonable or leads to too ineffective processes ; it is likely that for this kind of problems ED expertise would rather be the leader.

## 3.3. Some rules and their applications in a scenario

In this paragraph we present intuitively some general rules of both expertise levels of EXPRIM and their use in the example presented in paragraph 2.3. Note that we only give the used rules but many others may be candidates and may be tried. The EB level rules begin with B, those of level ED begin with D.

### Second step

B1 : If the searched object is unknown to the system, then ask for complements of information and infer from these complements using ED level rules.

To infer from "deputy mayor" and deduce "official event" the system uses the following rules amongst other candidates :

D1 : if Z is a deputy mayor then Z is a personality ;
D2 : if Z is a personality then Z appears on official event pictures.

### Third step

B2 : After the user's picture selection, try to generate a new request by making use of rules searching common points between pictures.

In order to generate the research for the name "Alain Bombard",
the system uses :
. the fact that a certain number of chosen pictures are indexed
by Alain Bombard ;
. and the rule :
  D3 : if the object of the research is a person and if the common descriptor D references persons then generate the request "D".

Note 1 : In the example, D stands for "Alain Bombard".
Note 2 : It is obvious that the rule D3 is completed by other rules like : an association references persons.
Note 3 : Rather than request "D", some more complicated rules may
provide request with D within a context deduced from the preceding request.

Fourth step

In our example the user himself infers from a particular picture
and deduces a new request ; but the system contains an analogous
rule applying to descriptions.

B3 : After a user's picture selection, try to generate a new request by using ED rules concerning the particularities of pictures.
  Example : In assuming that one of the selected pictures has
  been shot in an overseas department then the system would
  search other pictures with official events in this department
  by using the rule D4.
  D4 : if the searched object is a person having some role in
France and if a picture exists showing this object in an overseas department then look at official event pictures in this
department.

Fifth step

B4 : After picture selection, propose different modes of re-
search and then, depending on the selected mode, try to generate
a new request with ED level rules.
  To obtain the proposed sample (airplane takeoff, etc.) the
system uses the following rules :
  D5 : a person non indexed by the system is an unknown person.
  D6 : an unknown person who enters the government gets a very
quick promotion.
  D7 : a very quick promotion is an astonishing fact.
  D8 : a bomb explosion is often used to illustrate an asto-
nishing fact.
  D9 : a racing car at full speed gives an effect of rapidity.
  D10 : a very fast promotion is a brutal ascension.

<u>D11</u> : an airplane takeoff is a brutal ascension.

4. THE DIRECTIONS IN WHICH WE PRESENTLY WORK

We have undertaken a group of long-term actions which would con-
verge into the realization of the system but also are interesting in themselves :
- specifying the system with abstract data types ;
- study of the DBMS facet of the system ;
- study of the system as an expert system : we have already
briefly described this aspect in chapter 3 ;
- study of different modes of sampling a set of image descriptions : what partition (or equivalence relation) to choose
and what representatives to choose in every class of the partition ;
- realization of MYCOMATIC in PROLOG as programming language.
We give here an idea of the two first points.

4.1. Specifying a part of EXPRIM with abstract data types

(a) Why use abstract data types

The notion of abstract data type (AT) has the following properties which make them very effective tools for specification.

The constructive property

One of the principal types we have to specify is the type
"image" (for the description of a picture).
A picture may have several description modes and it is interesting to have mechanisms enabling progressive transition from
one mode to another. AT have a derivation property that allows
progressive construction of a type starting with another defined
type by simply adding :
- either operations (type enrichment) (31) (32) ;
- or new sets and new operations (type extension) ;
- and new axioms.
The constructive aspect will be very useful to us.

The structuring property

The AT approach leads to distinguish, in a given application,
the main object types used and to search for a specification of
the behavior of each of these object types, with respect to itself and to others. Hence this procedure leads to structuring
the application environment, in order to put in evidence and
locate its principal centers of interest and to isolate the most
interesting - or most delicate - operations. This structuring

aspect is essential in our project.

## Power of abstraction

The possibility of specifying objects and operations independently of their effective use and their representation is an important aid to the project design and implementation.

## Genericity

Another property of AT that is very interesting is the possibility of defining schemes of AT. This notion allows considerable economy in thinking in the sense that a specification may be used in different contexts (the construction of a stack of integers will be the same as the construction of a stack of characters or of other objects) (12) (14).

(b) An example of type specification : the type "image"

Let us give a possible specification of type "image" (many other specifications are possible (5)).

In this description mode, an "image" is represented by a set of descriptors each of which is a keyword or a keyword followed by a "nuance". There is no notion of dimension in this very simple version of the type.

To describe one type, we first give the name of the type (here "Image") followed by the names of the other types which take a part in its definition. Then we list the operations involving the type (their set defines the behaviour of the objects of the type) so as their profiles ; the names of these operations are written on the right and the profiles on the left ; the underlined operations imvide and ajdes are the "constructors" of the type "Image". Finally, we give the axioms which describe (here recursively) the operations of the type.

TYPE Image, Descripteur, Requête, Bool

OPERATIONS :

| | |
|---|---|
| ( ) -------> image : | imvide |
| (image,descripteur) -------> image : | ajdes, supdes |
| (image,descripteur) -------> bool : | presentdes |
| (image,descripteur,descripteur) -------> image : | modifiedes |
| (image,requête) -------> bool : | adequation |

AXIOMS :
Let $i \in$ Image ; $d_1$, $d_2$ $\in$ Descripteur
presentdes(imvide,$d_1$) = FALSE

$$\text{presentdes}(\text{ajdes}(i,d_1),d_2) = \underline{if}\ eg(d_1,d_2)\ \underline{then}\ TRUE$$
$$\underline{else}\ \text{presentdes}(i,d_2)$$
$$\text{supdes}(\text{imvide},d_1) = \text{imvide}$$
$$\text{supdes}(\text{ajdes}(i,d_1),d_2) = \underline{if}\ eg(d_1,d_2)\ \underline{then}\ \text{supdes}(i,d_2)$$
$$\underline{else}\ \text{ajdes}(\text{supdes}(i,d_2),d_1)$$
$$\text{modifiedes}(i,d_1,d_2) = \underline{if}\ \text{presentdes}(i,d_1)\ \underline{then}$$
$$\text{ajdes}(\text{supdes}(i,d_1),d_2)$$
$$\underline{else}\ i$$

Note : This rather simple specification of the type "image" well defines the objects manipulated as well as the principal operations that may be applied to them. The object "image" is perceived as a set of descriptors that the operation "ajdes" allows us to construct starting with an initial object "imvide" (empty). This object may evolve due to the operations "supdes" and "ajdes". "Presentdes" allows access to an object of the type.

Moreover, all the operations are completely defined, by recurrence on the constructors, for each object "image" of any size.

## Specification of the "adequation" operation

Interrogation of the descriptive base is done by requests having the form of boolean expressions. The atomic symbols of these expressions may be either descriptors (that is the case if the type "image" is the one specified above) or relations amongst these descriptors (as for other richer description modes) or even dimensions.

The possibility of defining schemes of AT naturally leads us to specify a parametrized type allowing the construction of a boolean expression over an arbitrary set of atomic symbols and the definition of the pertinence of an "image" for such a boolean expression.

$\underline{TYPE}$ expr(T),Facteur,Primaire,T,Image,Bool
  where T possesses an operation CONV the profile of which is :
  (image,t) : $------\!\!\rightarrow$ bool : CONV    (t $\epsilon$ T)

$\underline{OPERATIONS}$ :
(facteur,expr) $------\!\!\rightarrow$ expr :      $\underline{\cup}$
(facteur) $------\!\!\rightarrow$ expr :      o
(primaire,facteur) $------\!\!\rightarrow$ facteur : $\cap$
(primaire) $------\!\!\rightarrow$ facteur :      o'
(primaire) $------\!\!\rightarrow$ primaire :      $\daleth$
(expr) $------\!\!\rightarrow$ primaire :      {}
( T ) $------\!\!\rightarrow$ primaire :      o"

(image,expr) ————→ bool :
(image,facteur) ————→ bool :    } A
(image,primaire) ————→ bool :

AXIOMS :
Let i ∈ Image ; facteur ∈ Facteur ; primaire ∈ Primaire
A(i,∪(facteur,expr)) = A(i,facteur) OR A(i,expr)
A(i,∩(primaire,facteur)) = A(i,primaire) AND A(i,facteur)
A(i,⌐primaire) = NOT A(i,primaire)
A(i,{ expr }) = A(i,expr)
A(i,o(facteur)) = A(i,facteur)
A(i,o'(primaire)) = A(i,primaire)
A(i,o"(T)) = CONV(i,T) .

For all the interpretations of T, A(i,b), where b is a
boolean expression, means that the image i is pertinent for b.
Its recursive definition allows us to decompose the expression
down to the atoms ; we then substitute for A the operation
CONV. Here we give the following interpretations :
   T = descripteur
   A = adequation
   CONV = presentdes.
The above operations, adequation and presentdes, verify the
equations described in the part "axioms" of the type expr. Note
that the operation "presentdes" for an atomic request and an
image is – by the axioms of the type "image" – defined recursi-
vely from "imvide" by the constructors.

Note : This operation "CONV" is insufficient. It will be interesting to search in the neighbourhood of the descriptors and
hence broaden the notion of equality between request elements
and document elements (as in documentation systems). We will
have to quantify the separation between descriptors and hence
introduce a notion of distance. We will examine this important
problem in the future but, for the moment, we have specified in
three different ways the type "image" and the operation of "adequation" between a request and an image (5).

We are presently working towards specifications of the modulation of requests, of the broadening of the notion of equality
between request elements and document (image) elements, and of
the deductive aspect of the system.

4.2. The DBMS facet

(a) The problem of the choice of the DBMS

To manage the descriptive data base, we have a choice between
two kinds of systems :

- documentary systems like MISTRAL (22), SATIN (8) ; see also for instance (24), (26) or (10) ;
- relational systems like SYSTEM R (17), INGRES (28) or MRDS (15), or database machines like IDM500 (6), IDBP (23) or VERSO (2) ; see also (30).

At first sight it appears that a documentary system is closer to our problem than a relational DBMS. Presently studies are carried out about constructing effective documentary systems based upon database machines. Theses systems seem to fit especially well in the cases where the amount of information is large, as in our press application.

As all the database machines are relational we can see that, whatever the above choice would be, we need to introduce a relational approach for the descriptive database (11) (27), which we did.

(b) A possible relational realization of the type "image"

The specification we gave for image in paragraph 4.1 was very elementary for exposition reasons. But in the real models, that we did not completely choose yet, we shall at least introduce the notion of dimension, in the meaning given in the first part of this paper. Then a query will be a two-level boolean expression with a dimensions level and a descriptors level in each dimension.

In this case, the relational schema of the descriptive base could be written as follows :
IMAGE (IMNUM, AUTHOR, DATE, ...)
DESCRIPTION (IMNUM, DIMNAME, DESNAME, NUANCE)
with :
IMNUM : image number
DIMNAME : dimension name
DESNAME : descriptor name.

The constraint of the first normal form, supported by all the relational DBMS, leads us to this relation "DESCRIPTION" which surely will be of high cardinality ; that will notably damage the performance of the system.

In order to improve this performance we are studying a solution which is intermediate between documentary systems using inverted files and relational DBMS. This solution consists in completing the DBMS by a tool that we name : query manager. We very succinctly present its principal functions.

(c) The query manager

The query manager has three principal functions :
- query modulation ;
- query translation ;

- temporary results management.

## Query modulation

This function includes a syntax analysis of the query which generates a binary tree. This binary tree contains "modulation nodes"
which will be usefull for the "elastic deformation" mentioned in
paragraph 2.2 (query process) : a node of modulation is a landmark inserted by the analyser before each leaf of the tree. This
node may be used in two different ways :
   - as an access point for the query manager in order to substitute a neighbour descriptor to a given descriptor after consulting a lexicon ;
   - as an access point for a dialogue session with the user when
the lexicon consulting operation returns an empty or unsatisfactory result.
   Such modulation nodes can be attached also to non terminal
nodes or even to dimensions.

## Query translation

This task is to translate the internal representation of a given
query into a sequence of elementary queries expressed in terms
of the data manipulation language of a given DBMS.

## Temporary results management

We have written above that picture retrieval may need more than
one search in the descriptive database. The different successive
searches may differ just a little from their predecessors. So it
may be useful to save in a temporary database some results from
one request to the others ; for instance a sequence of every picture whose description contains the descriptor DES1 in the dimension DIM1 and the descriptor DES2 in the dimension DIM2. The
decision of which results to save, and how long, is carried out
by the expert system, which manages a history of the retrieval.
   Our reflexion about database management in EXPRIM is not yet
very deep. But before carrying on with this study we shall
observe the behaviour of the database system which will be implemented in the prototype that we shall realize very soon. It
will include an existing documentary system with inverted files.

## 5. CONCLUSION

The work we have presented here lies in the new trends of database research (3). By extending the field of the managed information so as to deal with pictorial information and related ones
(later on we will perhaps complete it by sound, either for TV

reporting or for computer aided teaching for instance) and by deeply appealing to artificial intelligence capabilities and being very interactive, the EXPRIM system extends the concepts of the classical DBMS but also their usage.

Amongst possible applications of this system, beyond the aid to the press agency and the MYCOMATIC system, we can imagine many possibilities : first, computer aided teaching or diagnostics in fields where visual information has great importance such as natural sciences, medicine, archeology, history of Art, but also visual retrieval for documentation purposes of burotics, etc.

We have presented the main ideas we have now in mind and hope to realize in a more or less near future. For the moment we have not yet written any program except for MYCOMATIC but we are going to begin and particularly to realize a prototype of the system. For this prototype we will write a query manager ; then, as soon as we have chosen an inference motor, we also shall write rules for the expert system. One emerging problem to solve is that of the language in which the user and the system will communicate ; we have some ideas and shall make them concrete soon.

We have still much to do to give life to our system but we think it is worth trying.

REFERENCES

1. Agence de l'Informatique (3, 4, 5 nov. 1982). Séminaire bases de données, Toulouse.
2. Bancilhon F., Scholl M. (1982). Le filtrage des données dans la machine base de données VERSO, 6èmes journées informatiques de Nice.
3. Agence de l'Informatique and INRIA (1983). Bases de données et nouvelles perspectives, Rapport of the group BD3.
4. Bonnet A. (1981). Applications de l'intelligence artificielle : les systèmes experts, Vol. 15, n° 4, pp. 325-341, RAIRO Informatique.
5. Boukakiou M., Créhange M. ( 1983). Un exemple de spécification à l'aide de types abstraits algébriques : le type "IMAGE" dans le système EXPRIM, Rapport CRIN 83-R-30.
6. Britton-Lee. IDM 500, Intelligent database machine, Product description, Britton-Lee, Inc, Los Gatos, Cal. USA.
7. Chang M.S., Fu K.S. (nov. 1981). Picture query languages for pictorial database systems, pp. 23-33, Computer.
8. Chouraqui E., Bourrelly L. Le système documentaire SATIN 1. Description générale et manuel d'utilisation, Centre de Recherche URADCA, Aix-Marseille.
9. Date. An introduction to database systems, Third edition, Addison-Wesley.

10. David J.M. (1981). Proposition d'un modèle de connaissances pour la documentation automatique, Vol. 15, n° 4, pp. 313-323, RAIRO, Paris.
11. Delobel C., Adiba M (1982). Bases de données et systèmes relationnels, Dunod Ed.
12. Derniame J.C., Finance J.P. (1979). Types abstraits de données, spécification, utilisation et réalisation, Ecole d'été de l'AFCET, Monastir.
13. Gardarin G., Bernadas P., Temmerman N., Valduriez P., Viemont Y. (sept. 1982). Sabre : a relational database system for a multiprocessor machine, 2nd Int. Workshop on database machine, San Diego.
14. Goguen J.A., Parsaye-Ghomi K. (1981). Algebraic denotational semantic using parameterized abstract modules, n° 107, pp. 292-309, Lecture notes in Computer Science.
15. Honeywell Information Systems (1980). Multics relational data store (MRDS) reference manual, Series 60 (level 68), AZ49, H. IS Waltham, Massachussetts.
16. Hudrisier H. (1982). L'iconothèque - Documentation audio-visuelle et banques d'images, Thèse d'Etat, La Documentation Française, Paris.
17. IBM (1981). SQL/data system general information, GH 24-5012-0, IBM Data processing division, White Plains.
18. Laurière J.L. (1982). Représentation et utilisation des connaissances. Les systèmes experts, Vol. 1, n° 1, Techniques et Sciences Informatiques.
19. Laurière J.L. (1982). Représentation et utilisation des connaissances. Représentation des connaissances, Vol. 1, n° 2, T.S.I.
20. Meunier B. (1983). Un exemple de système expert utilisant des données imprécises : MYCOMATIC, Rapport de DEA, CRIN.
21. Michel F. (1982). Le devenir des machines base de données, Convention Informatique.
22. CII-HB (1978). Mistral III/MISTRAL IV : guide de mise en oeuvre et guide de l'utilisateur, OOF3 FS11 REVO et OOF3 F466 REVO, CII-HB.
23. Morgan K. (1982). Database processor offers small system options, Mini-micro systems.
24. Naulleau D. (1973). Thesaurus conversationnel. Conception et réalisation d'un outil aidant à l'indexation et à la formulation de questions, Thèse de 3ème cycle, Paris VI.
25. Pinson S. (1981). Représentation des connaissances dans les systèmes experts, Vol. 15, n° 4, pp. 343-367, RAIRO Informatique.
26. Salton G. (1981). The SMART retrieval system : experiments in automatic document processing, Prentice-Hall Inc., Englewood Cliffs, New Jersey.

27. Schmidt J.W. and Brodie M.L., edited by, (1983). Relational database systems. Analysis and comparison, Springer-Verlag, Berlin.
28. Stonebraker M., Wong E., Kreps P., (1976). The design and the implementation of INGRES, Vol. 1, n° 3, ACM TODS.
29. Tang G.Y. (1981). A management system for an integrated database of pictures and alphanumerical data, n° 16, pp. 270-286, Computer graphics and image processing.
30. Université des Sciences Sociales de Toulouse (14, 15 feb. 1983). Conference about Design, implementation and use of relational DBMS on micro-computers.
31. Goguen J.A., Tatcher J.W., Wagner E.G. (1978). An initial algebra approach to the specification, correctness, and implementation of abstract data types, Acta Informatica.
32. Remy J.L. (1982). Etude des systèmes de réécriture conditionnels et applications aux types abstraits algébriques, Thèse d'Etat, INPL-CRIN, Nancy.

# MANAGING THE SEMANTIC CONTENT OF GRAPHICAL DATA

P. Brouaye, T. Pudet and J. Vicard

*Laboratoire de Formation, Centre Mondial Informatique et Ressource Humaine, Paris, France*

## INTRODUCTION

We present in this paper an interactive system for the management of graphics, where the semantic aspect, i.e. the meaning of the image, prevails over other considerations such as aesthetics, scale, or geometric features. The basic entities of the system are the semantic constituents of the images. This allows for a clear separation between the semantic and graphic representations, which make it possible to perform operations on the semantic representation before any physical representation of the image. Moreover, such an approach should yield noticeable gains in memory space and transfer times, which should make an implementation on microcomputers or small space computers feasible. Computer aided teaching, mathematical expression editing and any application asking for intelligent treatment of graphical entities are obvious candidates for such a system.

NEW APPLICATIONS OF DATA BASES
ISBN 0-12-275550-2

## 1.0 *INTRODUCTION*

In the field of image synthesis, the systems which permit
the acquisition, structuring and management of data are often machine and application dependent. This is mostly due to
the great variety of contexts, which makes it hard to find
a uniform representation. However, distinct applications may
require similar treatment. A computer-aided electronic card
design program and another program designed to help in learning the theory of queues are more alike than we may first
believe : the problem is, in the first case, to build a component network and, for example, to compute its transfer
function. In the second case, the problem is to define a
queuing network and to simulate it.

We have developed the core of a graphics system which allows the manipulation of several classes of images, each one
consisting of schematic graphical entities, that is entities
for which the semantic content prevails over the aesthetic
aspect and allows a simple graphical representation. The
building of elaborated images is done through a grammar characterizing the associated class. We thus define a uniform
representation of images which allows the user to work on
their semantic content and the system to take charge of the
graphical representation on any kind of physical machine.

Section 2 presents the low-level entities used by the system independently of the applications. Section 3 gives the
description of the tools which allow the application programm-
mer to define the images of a given context ; section 4 details the ordering of grammars which results from linking
images belonging to several contexts.

Section 5 discusses specific data base aspects, and section 6 defines two kinds of image animation, a formal one
and a more pragmatic one. Finally, we give some examples of
the applications implemented on the system.

## 2.0 *GRAPHIC EVALUATOR*

A single image has two distinct representations : an abstract one which contains its semantics, and a physical one
which contains all practical information required to draw
it. This latter section details the physical representation.

"Graphic evaluator" is a generic name that embodies two entities of the system : a graphic processor and a language evaluator. The graphic processor is able to draw specific data
called instances, some being acquired through an interactive
drawing module. A "mouse" allows the user to first select a
graphic tool (layout, colour, coordinate grid ...) and then
to build "by hand" the picture he desires.

It should be noted that the graphic processor cannot modify
an instance which is currently user defined (we shall see
that this user is in fact an application programmer). Therefore, the system retrieves and processes graphic data in an
independent manner thanks to a graphic language. This language is based on primitives which act on instances. Its syntax
is quite simple : a program is a sequence of instructions,
each consisting of a function name and a number of arguments.
    Example :

        (TRANS A p) (MAP B k) (CONCX A B)


Such a program (we call it a symbolic program) cannot be
evaluated because no binding occurs. We define a graphic expression (g-expression) as a formula that denotes an executa-
ble program. It binds the variables of the symbolic program
to real instances by the mean of an initial environment.
    Example :

        ((TRANS A p) (MAP B k) (CONCX A B)
        (A <an instance>) (B <an instance>)
        (p <a point>) (k <a real>)


The evaluation is further driven by the evalgraf function
which parses one instruction at a time, and reports successive side effects on the local environment. For instance, evalgraf would evaluate the previous program as follows : first,
translate instance A to point p, side effect on instance A,
second, map instance B with coefficient k, side effect on B,
third, join instances A and B along the x axis, side effect
on B.

This example shows only geometric primitives, but the language allows several others. The complete set is given in the
first appendix.

We now summarise the discussion in the following figure :

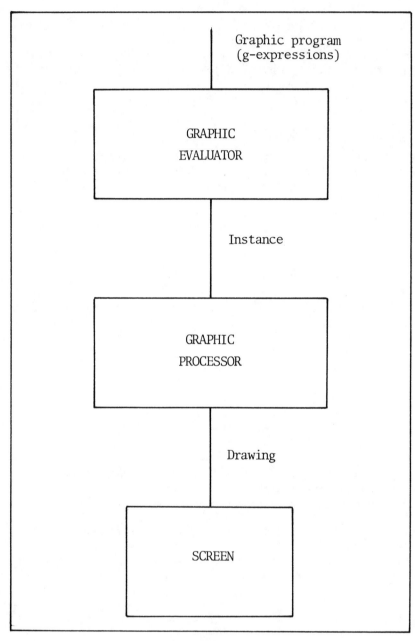

- Fig 1 -

## 3.0 *ELEMENTARY CONTEXT*

An elementary context defines both the abstract and physical representations of images in any given application. The first one is viewed through a functional language. The graphic processor is only able to manage instances and thus cannot understand this language. Consequently a context must also provide an image translator allowing the shift from an abstract representation to a physical one.

## 3.1 A Functional Grammar

The grammar G is a 3-tuple <T, N, P>. The set T of terminals is the union of three subsets : T = 0 + L + S. 0 is the finite subset whose elements are the names of basic objects. Each basic object has a physical representation (an instance) known by the system. L is a finite set of names of functions. Each name refers to a possible relationship between objects and is associated with a graphical expression with an empty environment. To adopt Lisp syntax, we add the set S= {(,)} of delimiters. N is the set of non terminals. P is the set of productions and is a finite set of rewriting rules. A **pro**duction rule is a pair (l,r), where l is a non terminal and r an element of (T + N)*.

Example : a grammar for electrical networks.

0={ R , S , C }; L={ serial, para }; N={ network }
P={ Rl , R2, R3, R4, R5 }

Rl: network --> (serial network network)
R2: network --> (para network network)
R3: network --> R
R4: network --> S
R5: network --> C

An abstract image could be for example (serial (para R C) (serial S R)). Thus it is a string of the grammar which we call an "abstract syntax tree".

## 3.2 An Instantiation Function

The next step is now the transformation of this abstract representation into a physical representation. For this purpose we define a graphical instantiation function "ig",which operates on the abstract syntax tree t, and returns an instance. It is a translation function *"trad"* followed by an execution function.

*Exec.*

The syntactic conventions and the definition of production rules entail the following characteristics for the abstract syntax tree :
- the leaves are terminals of O.
- the nodes are terminals of L.

Example: t =

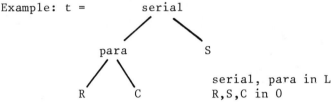

serial, para in L
R,S,C in O

The evaluation of "*trad*" consists of a recursive postfix traversal of t. If u is in O then *trad*(u) = rep(u), where rep(u) is the instance associated with u , otherwise u is in L and *trad*(u) = p(u), where p(u) is the graphical expression refering to the relationship u.

Example: t =

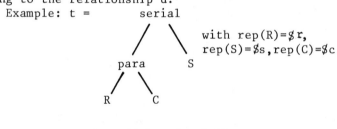

with rep(R)=$r,
rep(S)=$s,rep(C)=$c

and trad(t)= p(serial)

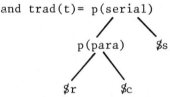

The internal nodes of *trad*(t) are g-expressions whose initial surrounding is given by the sons of v. Thus *trad*(t) is a graphical program and *exec* recursively defines its execution. In fact the evaluation of *exec* consists of a postfix traversal. If w is a leaf of *trad*(t) then *exec*(w)=w otherwise *exec*(w) = evalgraf(a(v)), where a(v) is the tree with root v.

Example : looking at the previous image we obtain
exec(trad(t))=evalgraf( p(serial) )

where RES1=evalgraf( p(para) )

RES1 is an  instance that represents a resistor and a capacitor in parallel.
Finally, evalgraf( p(serial) )=RES is an instance.

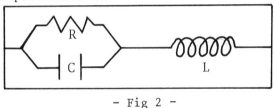

It is processed by the graphical processor and gives the
following representation:

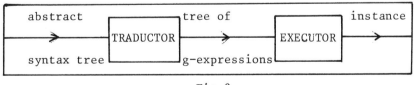

- Fig 2 -

The following diagram summarises the transformation of the
abstract representation into a physical representation.

| abstract | | tree of | | instance |
|---|---|---|---|---|
| → | TRADUCTOR | → | EXECUTOR | → |
| syntax tree | | g-expressions | | |

- Fig 3 -

The *exec* level links this scheme with the previous one, and
realizes the graphical evaluation of the g-expression tree.

In summary, in a given context, the system transforms a
well-formed expression of the grammar (abstract syntax tree)
into a tree of graphical programs (tree of g-expressions).
This last tree is recursively evaluated by the graphical

evaluator. The evaluator is thus a compiler: it generates a
graphical code (an instance) from a program written in a
high-level language (the language of the context grammar).

## 4.0  *HIERARCHICAL CONTEXTS*

We now tackle the following problem: how can we build elaborated images incorporating the low-level images defined in
a former, more elementary context ? For example, how can we
build an interconnection network above switching nodes,which
are images of the elementary context "queuing network" ? We
thus want to create a context "interconnection network",
whose "basic forms" are the images created in the context
"queuing networks".

### 4.1 Nested Grammars

The former remark leads to a more general notion of context
This generalised context is still defined by a functional
grammar, which differs from that of elementary contexts in
the definition of the set T of terminals: The set 0 of basic
object names is no longer associated with a fixed set of names and their graphical representations, but to one or several names of predefined contexts. The set 0 is then the set
of the names of images already existing in the specified
"sub-contexts", and an interpretation of their semantics
yields their graphical representations, as formerly. The objects of a generalized context thus differ from those of an
elementary one in that they use images defined in lower-level
contexts.

Such a definition produces a natural order on contexts :
$G1 > G2$ if some of the images of $G2$ are terminals of $G1$.

We may define a "graphical editor" context, which would be
greater than any other context, and would be called on when
editing the images of the database.

As an example of what structured contexts mean, let $G0$ and
$G1$ be two contexts, and assume we want to define a context
$G2$ which uses images of $G0$ and $G1$.
The grammar of $G2$ is $(T2,N2,P2)$, where

$T2 = 02 + I(G0) + I(G1) + L2 + S2$ :

- 02 is the set of basic forms belonging only to $G2$

- I(G0) and I(G1) are the sets of existing images which belong to the contexts G0 and G1.

- P2 is the set of production rules.
  It incorporates rules of the following type ( case of a link of degree two ):
  NT --> (1 a b ) where :
  a and b are in NT2 + 02 + ( I(G0) , I(G1) ).

For example, if a = I(G0) and b is in 02, this is a short way of writing all the rules of the kind: NT--> ( 1 i0 b ) where i0 is any one of the images of G0.

This partial order between contexts allows us to easily define hierarchical contexts, from simple ones to more complicated ones, as well as to build images step by step. More over, we can also consider abstract images at different levels.

## 4.2 Partial Rewriting

Let us return to the former example. We notice that the abstract image ( 1 i0 b ), where i0 is an image of the low-level context G0 and b a basic form of G2, may be written in a different way, by describing the abstract tree of i0. Depending on the desired approach, it may be more interesting to focus on just one of the representations. Such a "semantic zoom" may be extremely useful for a user approaching the data base without knowing its contents.

## 4.3 The Task of the Application Programmer

Contexts are created by the application programmer. To define a context, we must first consider the sets of object names, link names and non-terminals and a production system. These four sets define the high-level language and the abstract representation of the images. To generate images, the programmer adds the set of instances associated with basic objects and the set of graphical expressions associated with links. As an example, we give in appendix 1 a simplified definition of the context : "electrical networks".

## 5.0 *DATABASE ASPECTS*

The dual representation of images helps to clarify some of the usual problems in the management of graphic entities :

most of the image processing is concerned only with the semantic content of the images.

## 5.1 Contexts

A context is characterized by the set of sub-contexts it
imports (which may be empty), the grammar <T,N,P>, the graphical programs corresponding to links and the instances corresponding to the (possibly empty) subset of the basic objects of T. These data, which constitute the context, do not
take us much space, which allows for their, and the data pertaining to sub-contexts, residing permanently in central memory during a user session. In the case of a very high-level
context, it might be necessary to use a virtual memory system.

## 5.2 Images

A set of abstract images is associated with each context.
Each image is defined by a phrase of the grammar and its low
memory requirement allows it to be stored as a character
string. However, visualisation calls for a graphical instantiation phase. This gives rise to a trade-off between memory
space used and processing time required.

## 5.3 Access to Data

The user starts a session with a database composed of
several contexts, the content of which are not necessarily
known. It is thus necessary to provide a "fly over"
functionality which reviews the distinct contexts and some
examples of the images. This allows for the choice of a working
context kept in central memory. The user then has access to
image manipulation functions, some of which are typical of
graphical processing: colouring, zooming, editing, and others
more database-oriented.

## 5.3.1 Creation –

The user writes a string of the context grammar, which is
just writing a "program". Nevertheless, for very complicated
images corresponding to long sentences, the user builds the
image "step by step". As an example, let us assume the desired graphical representation is the following :

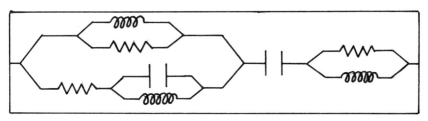

- Fig 4 -

The associated abstract representation is then :

(serial (para (serial R (para C L)) (para L R))
        (serial C (para R L)))

The user would write first


I  < -- (para L R)

        then


I' < -- (para C L)


I' < -- (serial R I')


I  < -- (para I I')

I' <-- (para R L)

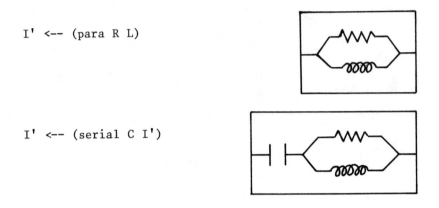

I' <-- (serial C I')

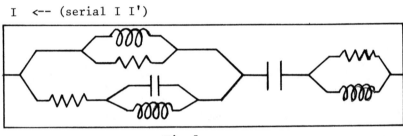

I  <-- (serial I I')

- Fig 5 -

Such a method allows for extreme flexibility in the construction of the image. It frees the user from the management
of the graphical representation, and provides him with a simple way of identifying distinct components of the same type.

### 5.3.2 Modification

A modification is likewise limited to the abstract image.
It translates into a substitution inside the abstract tree.
This allows for inserting or deleting components of an image.
Moreover, we can then mix several already existing images of
a given context.

### 5.3.3 Search

In a given context, searching is done on the semantic content of the images. The user specifies an abstract syntax
tree and it is up to the system to look for this pattern in
the set of the images of the context. The comparison operator

consists then of unifying the abstract image and the given pattern.

As an example let us consider the following database:

```
1: (para (serial R L) C)
2: (serial (serial R L) C)
3: (serial   R C)
```

We want to know if there is an image of the database inclu- ding a resistor and a inductor in serial. We write this query as follows :

```
        motif=(serial R L)
answer : matching image 1, image 2
```

We then modify the query by looking for images including a resistor in serial with another component. The scheme beco- mes (serial R x) where x is a variable and the answer is :

```
        matching image 1, x=L

        matching image 3, x=C
```

We then look for images including components in serial with a capacitor. The associated scheme is (x y C) and the answer :

```
        matching image 1, x=para, y=(serial R L)
        matching image 2, x=serial, y=(serial R L)
        matching image 3, x=serial, y=R
```

The abstract representation of images thus allows for high level queries on the database, and for a natural language user interface written in a programming language such as PROLOG, which is a natural candidate since we need to include unification.

## 6.0 *ANIMATION*

There are some applications for which we need more than the static image from the graphical processor. For example, the interest of a graphical representation in computer aided learning stems more from the modifications of the image than from the image by itself: animation helps make visible the qualitative aspects of the studied object.

The animation of an image is usually modelled by a sequence
of physical images: (IP)i. In the following, we restrict ourselves to two kinds of animation: the adding or subtracting
of an element to the image, or a change of nature in one of
the components of the image. We therefore choose two methods:
terminal multiplication and superimposition, each associated
with one of the kinds of animation.

Terminal multiplication associates one distinct terminal of
the functional grammar with each state of a basic object. If
an application consists of n objects and each object Oi may
be in Pi distinct states, the total number N of terminals of
the grammar will be :

$$N = \sum_{i}^{n} Pi$$

Thus, a sequence IPi of graphical instances generated by
the graphical instantiation is associated with the sequence
IAi of abstract images generated by the application program.

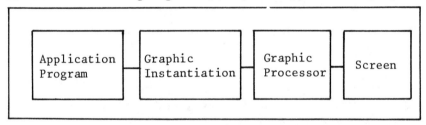

- Fig 6 -

We plan to do the following optimization: given two consecu-
tive abstract images, find the common part of the two trees
and submit to the graphical processor only the part to be
modified. Unification algorithms would be appropriate for
such a task.

$$(IA)i+1=sigma((IA)i) \text{ where } sigma= R/para$$

$$\begin{array}{cc} / & \backslash \\ R & C \end{array}$$

This method may be used without modification to the system defined above where the number of states of any given object is small. When the number of distinct states and objects grows there is a need for two optimizations, of the graphical instantiation (compiler optimization) and the graphical processor, which has to generate an instance quickly (large scale integration of the processor).

Superimposition is the pragmatic approach used in the second kind of animation and is characterized by a movement of elements on an invariant topography (background). The elements are independent of the topography (for example, the way a pawn moves on a chessboard is not related to the graphical representation of the chessboard). We will treat separately the background (this is done once at the beginning of the animation) and the elements. A graphical interface coupled with the application program helps in moving the elements on the background. To do this, we need the three graphical primitives CREATE, MOVE and DESTROY. These affect the elements, and the positions of the logical components of the background (sub-forms). These positions are supplied by the evaluator to the interface during the graphical generation of the background.

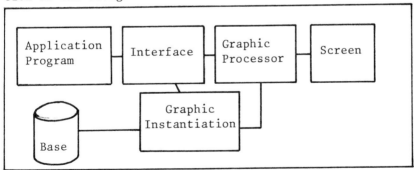

- Fig 7 -

In summary, we may notice that, even if the second kind of animation is quicker to implement on given examples, the first one forms a basis for a more powerful and formal model for abstract image animation.

## 7.0  *APPLICATIONS*

We discuss in this section some examples of application.

### 7.1 Queuing Networks

To demonstrate visually a computer performance and through-put simulation, a context "queuing network" has been develo-ped on the system. The concerned networks have one entrance and one exit, or can be closed. The grammar is as follows:

$$G = ( T , N , P ) \text{ where}$$
$$T = 0 + L + S$$
$$0 = \{ \text{queue delay} \} ;$$
$$L = \{ \text{serial parallel retro-connected feed-back} \} ;$$
$$S = \{ (,) \} ;$$

The terminal called "queue" is a basic object referring to a one server queue. "Delay" refers to a queue with an infi-nite number of servers. A customer entering a delay sees only a slowdown that is independent of other customers, and no queue. These two terminals being basic objects, their graphi-cal representations are constructed by the application pro-grammer with the help of an interactive drawing program. These representations are given below.

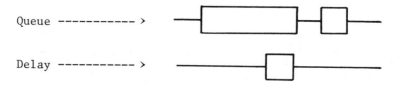

Queue ----------- >

Delay ----------- >

- Fig 8 -

The elements of the subset L (links) are the various connec-tion possibilities between networks. The set N of non termi-nals consists of the single element "network". The set P con-tains the following production rules :

        network --- >  (serial network network)

        network --- >  (parallel network network)

        network --- >  (retro-connected network network)

        network --- >  (feed-back network)

```
network ---> (queue)
network ---> (delay)
```

At this point, the application programmer specifies the programs interpreting the links in terms of primitives, whose
descriptions are given in appendix 1.

Example

The following abstract image is built under the context
"queuing networks" :

```
(feed-back (serial (parallel queue delay)
(retro-connected queue (feed-back delay))))
```

and has the following graphical representation :

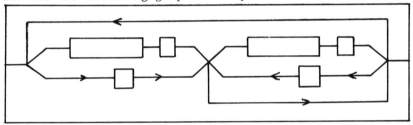

- Fig 9 -

A graphical simulation program for queuing networks has also
been developed, which shows the movement of customers in the
network.

Other possible applications are :

- Mathematical expressions.

The set T of terminals would contain alphanumeric characters
and mathematical operators like integral, summation, and
root symbols.

- Games.

For instance, chess played by an application program generating abstract image sequences.

## 8.0 *CONCLUSION*

The major influence behind the system design was the distinction between the semantic contents of the images and
their graphical representations on various devices (graphical terminals, plotters, hardcopy ...). This distinction allows us to operate on abstract representation stored in the
database, rather than on physical representations. We think
it allows new possibilities for graphics on cheap and low
memory capacity computers. Also under consideration is the
development of a generalised mailing system (text and images)
on a local network between microcomputers.

## 9.0 *APPENDIX 1 : AN ELECTRICAL NETWORKS CONTEXT*

The system monitor drives the definition of a context. In
the following example, it prompts the ">" sign before any
message.

```
        (define network)

>give the sequence of object names

(R  L  C)

>give the sequence of link names

(serial para)

>give the production rules

>rule 1

(network (serial network network))

>rule 2

(network (para network network))

>rule 3

(network R)

>rule 4

(network L)
```

>rule 5

(network C)

At this point, the application programer uses the drawing module to specify the shapes of the different objects that belong to the context.
>give R shape

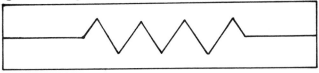

- Fig 10 -

>give L shape

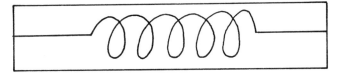

- Fig 11 -

>give C shape

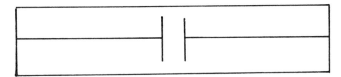

- Fig 12 -

>give serial translation

(CONCX a b)

>give para translation

(set res (CONCY a b))

(set p (queue (div (vl res) 2)))

```
(SUBST res (INFX a) p)

(SUBST res (INFX b) p)

(set p (queue (div (v2 res) 2)))

(SUBST res (SUPX a) p)

(SUBST res (SUPX b) p)
```

The following figure shows the side effect on two resistors.

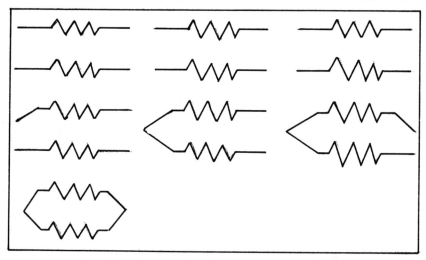

- Fig 13 -

11.0

BACKUS J. Can programming be liberated from the von Neumann style ? A functional style and its algebra of programs. Commun. ACM 21,8 (August 1978), pp 613-641.

BURGE, W.H. Recursive Programming Techniques. Addison-Wesley. Reading, Mass. 1975.

CHAILLOUX J.,HULLOT J.M.,LEVY J.J.,VUILLEMIN J. Le Système Lucifer d'aide à la conception de circuits Rapport de recherche NO 196 Inria, March 1983.

CHANG S. K., KUNII T. L. Pictorial Database Systems. Computers, vol 14. num 11, 1981

FU K. S. Syntactic Methods in pattern recognition. Academic Press, 1974.

FEINER S.,NAGY S.,VAN DAM A. An experimental system for creating and presenting interactive graphical documents. ACM transactions on graphics, vol 1, num 1, Jan 82 pages 59-77.

GRAVE M., OUANOUNOU G. Etude d'opérateurs sur objets graphiques élémentaires. Congress AFCET, Nancy, Nov. 1980.

MAGNENAT-THALMANN N., THALMANN D. GRAFEDIT. Computer graphics, vol 6, num 1, 1982, pages 41-46.

QUINT V. Un système interactif pour la production de documents mathématiques. T.S.I. vol 2, num 3, 1983.

TANIMOTO S. L. Hierarchical picture indexing ad description. Asimolar workshop on picture data description and management, Aug 1980.

ULLMAN J.D. Principles of Database Systems. Computer Science Press, Potomac, Md.,1980.

VOIROL W. GRED. Conference Science Press, Potomac, Md., 1980.

WELLER D., WILLIAMS R. Graphic and relational data base support for problem solving. Proceeding of the 3th annual conference on computer graphics, interactive techniques and image processing. Siggraph 1976.

YAMAGUCHI K., KUNII T. L. PICOLLO. IEEE transactions on computer vol c 31, num 10, Oct 1982.

# Textual Data Bases

MANAGING TEXTS AND FACTS IN A MIXED
DATA BASE ENVIRONMENT

F.Bancilhon and P. Richard

*INRIA, BP 105, 78153 Le Chesnay Cédex, France*
*LRI, Bât 490, Université Paris-Sud, 91405 Orsay, France*

# 1. INTRODUCTION

Relational Data Base Management Systems are now available as software products. Even though they offer simple data defininition languages and powerfull query languages and offer a high degree of data independance they are essentially meant for management type applications.

New types of applications are now emerging that require large amounts of data to be stored, fetched and updated : office automation, information systems, computing aided teaching, software engineering are examples of such areas.

For such applications : a relational system is not in general a sufficient tool ; It lacks the ability to manage new types of data : not only factual but also textual, vocal and pictorial. Therefore there is a need for new systems that would allow the declaration and manipulation of these various types of data.

In this paper we address the problem of managing factual and textual data in the same system. The problem is essentially a data model problem : EF Codd has defined in 1970 a neat model to declare and manipulate factual data ; we are faced now with the problem of defining another "data model" that will allow both factual and textual data.

We think that a basic assumption should be taken in designing such systems : the relational model is currently the best model to describe factual data, therefore the new system should at least include the functions and capabilities of relational systems. Taking this assumption into account two reasonable approaches are taken in the litterature :

## (1) -  Augmenting the relational data model :

Starting from a relational system, we can extend it to offer textual capabilities. Such extension can include the possibility of having "textual type" attributes on which specific operations can be done, or the introduction of "complex objects" in the system. Example of this approach is the Haskin - Lorie suggestion of system R extensions [HASK 82] . The main advantage of such an approach is the possibility of rapidly developping a new system from a classical relational DBMS. One of the drawbacks is that the new system might be complex and look like a "patched up" relational model.

## (2) -  Designing a new data model :

In order to avoid the patched up system one could think of developping a new data model. This approach has been taken by a number of researchers working in the office automation area [JOLO 82, CRAMP 82] . These data model accept various types such as documents texts, etc. In general they include the entity relationship model rather than the relational model as a factual model. While this approach offers the advantage of a complete clean data model it has the drawbacks of implying the development of completely new systems and of generating "yet another data model".

We believe that both approaches are worth investigating and that only the result of the ongoing experiment will designate the winner.

In this paper we suggest a third approach that has the advantages of

   (1)   incorporating a relational DBMS in the new system without any changes

   (2)   offering a complete environment in which the user will be allowed to manipulate facts in a relational database and text in a textual database.

In this approach, the user sees two distinct data bases : a textual one and a factual one, he can query both data bases, he can also transfer data from one data base to the other : through text interpretation he can generate relations from texts and through text generation he can generate texts from relations

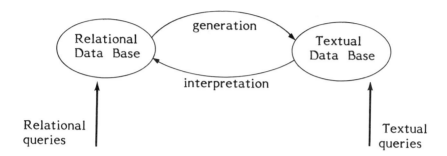

To manage such a system, we need for each data base a data definition language and a query language, we also need a text generation language and a text interpretation language.

For the relational system we can use a classical relational DDL and any relational query language (QUEL, SQL, QBE,...), therefore any relational DBMS will do.

For the textual system we need a text definition language (TDL) and a text query language (TQL). And finally we need a means to translate texts into relations and conversely.

In this paper, we first present a text definition language (TDL) that describes the hierarchical structure of a text, then we define a text query language (TQL) that can query texts from their structure and finally we describe the two way translation process between texts and relations. TDL and TQL define a textual data base system. In order to clarify what we mean by such a system let us first discuss the overall structure of a textual data base.

## 2. LEVELS OF TEXT DATA BASE SYSTEMS

It is now widely accepted that a factual database includes three levels : physical, conceptual and external. System integration is done at the conceptual level, while application programs are implemented on top of the external level.

The question arises whether in a textual database we should have the same hierarchy. One major difference is that we shall not have the integration problem in textual data bases : there is no reason for different application programmers to

integrate their diverse visions of the same text (as they have
to integrate their visions of the same facts that come from
the real world) : each application programmer will simply have
his own texts (even if they can share some of these texts in
common).

This simply comes from the facts that texts are real objects
while relations are just a representation of real world facts.

Let us therefore restrict our attention to one single text. We
can have different visions of this text.

(1) -   The first vision is external, it is the physical
        appearance of the text on a CRT screen or on a piece
        of paper. This external level deals with spaces between
        lines, justification, and position of each word of the
        text on the page or the screen. It is specifically the
        level of text edition and manipulation.
        For instance at this level a letter is seen as having a
        date written in the upper right corner, the sender
        address under that date and sendee at the same level
        on the left of the page and so on.

(2) -   The second vision is conceptual, it only deals with the
        structure of the text. It sees the text as constituted
        of specific elements, each element in turn consisting of
        smaller atoms. But at this level there is no need to
        know how that structure is going to be mapped onto a
        screen or a piece of paper.
        For instance the letter is constituted of a date, a
        sender, a sendee, a body, a signature and a
        postcriptum. Each of these elements in turn can be
        described : the "sender" includes a name and an
        address etc...

(3) -   Finally the third vision is internal or physical. This is
        the internal representation of the text structure and is
        fully dependant on the implementation (using pointers
        or tags for instance).

This paper only deals with level (2) i.e. with the structure of
the text. Many operations such as queries and updates can be
defined at this level and need not be done at the external
level : if we want to know when our last letter to Smith was
sent the only information we need to define the query is the
structure of letters. Similarly to make a change of address it
is sufficient to know that in the text "letter" there is an
address component. The text definition, query, generation and
interpretation will therefore be defined at the conceptual level.

## 3. TEXT DEFINITION

Consider for instance a library. It consists of a set of items that can be either books or periodics. A periodic consists of a header (title and date) and a sequence of articles ; each article in turn consists of a header (title and authors names) and a body that is a sequence of paragraphs.

A book also consists of a header (title and author) followed by a sequence of chapters ; each chapter in turn consists of a header (chapter number and title) and a body that is a sequence of paragraphs.

Such a structure can be represented by the following structure tree.

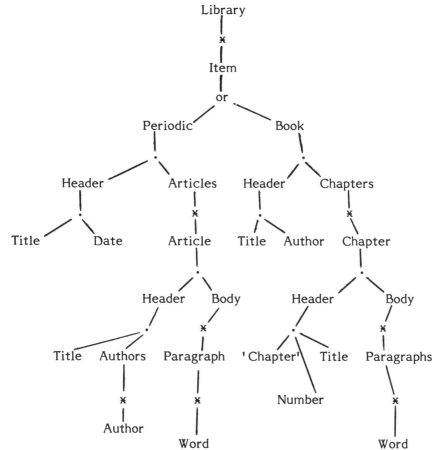

**Figure 3.1.**

In this structure tree, iteration is represented by a x-node, concatenation by a .-node and alternative by an or-node.

Constants are written between quotas (for example 'Chapter') and all terminals (Title, Date, Author, etc.) are assumed to be of the string type.

To declare such a tree we use a PL/1 or Pascal like syntax. The formal BNF description of this syntax is given in appendix as we assume that the example presented in Figure 3.2 is self explainatory.

The tree of Figure 3.1 is called the <u>structure tree</u> of the text. Each node in that tree can be given a unique name that consists of the sequence of node names starting from the root and leading to that node. For instance the node corresponding to the title of a periodic has unique name Library.Item.Periodic.Header.Title.

(This unique naming assumes, of course, that all the sons of a node have distinct names).

In general it is not necessary to give the entire sequence of nodes and we can take the shortest sequence leading to the node that satisfies the prefix property, to uniquely identify the node. We shall call this shortest sequence the UID of the node. For instance the UID of the node corresponding to the title of a periodic is

Periodic.Header.Title

while the UID of the title of a chapter of a book is

Chapter.Header.Title

```
Library is sequence of
   Item is one of
      begin
         periodic is
            begin
               header is begin
                              Title is string
                              date is string
                     end
               articles is sequence of
                  article is
                     begin
                        header is begin
                                    Title is string
                                    Authors is sequence of
                                       Author is string
                              end
                        body is sequence of
                           paragraph is sequence of
                              word is string
                     end
            end
         book is
            begin
               header is begin
                           Title is string
                           Author is string
                     end
               chapter is sequence of
                  chapter is
                     Begin
                        Header is begin
                                    'chapter'
                                    number is string
                                    title is string
                              end
                        Body is sequence of
                           Paragraph is sequence of
                              word is string
                     end
            end
      end
```

**Figure 3.2.**

## 4. AN INFORMAL DESCRIPTION OF TQL

TQL is a language that allows to query texts from their structure. The user will be able to extract some parts of the texts that satisfy some conditions. The language is SQL-like and uses variables and qualifiers. A BNF description of the syntax of the language and a formal definition of its semantics are given in [Ban 82a] . In this section we simply describe TQL through some example queries.

This description shall use the two following example structure trees :

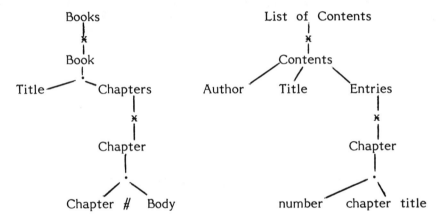

The basic notion in TQL is that of a <u>cursor</u> : a cursor is essentially a pointer that designates a structure in the text. For instance the query :

      x <u>cursor</u> <u>on</u> Book <u>in</u> Books
      <u>select</u> x. title

creates a cursor x on the UID "Book" in the "Books" text. The select clause just asks to output the title part of that book. The result of that query is the sequence of titles of the Books text.

To print all the chapters of all the books we could use :

      x <u>cursor</u> <u>on</u> Book <u>in</u> Books
      <u>select</u> x.chapter

The <u>in</u> clause will be forgotten when no confusion is possible. Of course several elements can be printed by the same select clause

> x <u>cursor</u> <u>on</u> Book
> <u>Select</u> x.title, x.chapter #

will print for all books their title followed by the <u>list of</u> chapter numbers. It is also possible to print constants within the text, thus :

> x <u>cursor</u> <u>on</u> Book
> <u>select</u> 'title', x.title

will insert the word "title" before each title. the next powerfull construct of TQL is the <u>where</u> clause that allows us to qualify cursors. For instance

> x <u>cursor</u> <u>on</u> Book
> <u>Select</u> x
> <u>Where</u> x.title = 'Kidnapped'

will just print the entire book 'Kidnapped'

> x <u>cursor</u> <u>on</u> Book
> <u>Select</u> x.title
> <u>where</u> x.chapter # = '15'

will print the title of all books having a chapter number 15. Note that "where x.chapter # = '15'" is interpreted as "<u>there exists a chapter # equal to 15</u>". Of course more complex expressions can be constructed such as

> x <u>cursor</u> <u>on</u> Book
> <u>Select</u> x.title
> <u>Where</u> x.chapter # = '15'
> <u>and</u> x.title ⊃ 'man'

will give the title of all books having at least 15 chapters and having 'man' in their title. We shall not elaborate here on the necessary comparison operators.

A reasonable set might be :

$$=, \neq, >, <, \geq, \leq, \supset, \subset, \underline{near}$$

Where <u>near</u> is a proximity operator defined by "equal up to a misspelling". At the level of detail of this paper it is only important to know that such a set could be defined.

When we want to compose one text from two texts it will be necessary to use two cursors. The first trivial example is that of concatenation :

>       x cursor on Books
>       y cursor on List-of-Contents
>       select x,y

will print the sequence of all books followed by the list of contents.

A more complex operation will insert the author's name into the book text :

>       x cursor on book
>       y cursor on contents
>       Select x.title, y.author, x.chapters
>       Where x.title = y.title

This operation is very similar to that of relational join. Note however that in the answer the set of books is ordered in the same way as in the book text. This is because in TQL we order terms lexicographically as in the original texts. Semi-join operations could also be defined by printing all books that are mentionned in the list of contents.

>       x cursor on Book
>       y cursor on Contents
>       Select x
>       Where x.title = y.title

The main difference between TQL and relational calculus comes when we want to do "nested" joins : for instance, list for all books the sequence of chapters with their titles and numbers

>       x cursor on Book
>       y cursor on Contents
>       x' cursor on x.Chapter
>       y' cursor on y.Chapter
>       Select x'.chapter #, y'.chapter title, x'.body
>       Where x.title = y.title
>       and x'.chapter # = y'.number

In this query four cursors were created but they were "linked" by the fact that an occurence of cursor x' is generated by an occurence of cursor x and same for y and y'.

Finally the last feature of TQL is the ability to create cursors that represent queries. Consider for instance the query

Q(x,y) :

> x' <u>cursor</u> <u>on</u> x.chapter
> y' <u>cursor</u> <u>on</u> y.chapter
> <u>Select</u> x'.chapter #, y'.chapter title, x'.Body
> <u>Where</u> x'.chapter # = y'.number

it is a query having x and y as "free cursor variables", we can define a new cursor say z and attach it to Q(x,y).
Thus giving :

> x <u>cursor</u> <u>on</u> Book
> y <u>cursor</u> <u>on</u> Contents
> z <u>cursor</u> <u>on</u> Q(x,y)
> <u>Select</u> x.title, y.author, z
> <u>Where</u> x.title = y.title

which represents the complete "join" of the two structures.

## 5. TEXT INTERPRETATION

Text interpretation consists in building a relation or a set of relations from a text. We are not all concerned here with complex operations such as text understanding i.e. artificial intelligence type operations. Our main concern is with simple operations that use the syntactic (and not semantic) structure of the text.

**Definition 5.1.**

An <u>interpreter</u> of a structure tree is a pair of functions I=(D,C) where

> - D associates with each node UID of the tree a relational descriptor D(UID)
>
> - C associates with each non terminal UID of the tree a relational expression that computes the value of the descriptor of that node from the values of the descriptors of its son nodes.

**Example :**

> Consider the following structure tree

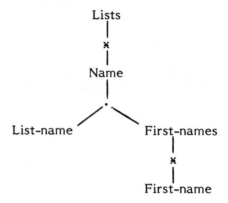

(In french speaking countries, people have an unbounded number of first-names).

A possible interpreter of this tree is $I_1$ :

Lists $< R_5(N) = U \ R_4(N) >$

Name $< R_4(N) = R_3(N) \cup R_2(N) >$

Last-name $R_3(N)$

First-names $< R_2(N) = U \ R_1(N) >$

First-name $< R_1(N) >$

Another possible interpretation is $I_2$ :

List $< R_5(LN) = U \ R_4(LN) >$

Name $< R_4(LN) = R_3(L) \times R_2(N) >$

Last-name $R_3(L)$

First-names $< R_2(N) = U \ R_1(N) >$

First-name $< R_1(N) >$

Note that in the case of x-nodes the associated function must be compatible with iteration (for instance union or intersection).

Let us now turn to the interpretation of a text : given a structure tree an interpreter (D,C) for this tree and a text that satisfies the structure tree, we can associate with the text its syntax tree according to that structure. For instance consider the following text and its associated syntax tree :

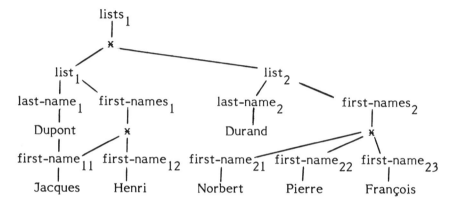

We have given subscripts to nodes of the syntax tree that have the same UID.

**Definition 5.2.**

Let ST be a structure tree, let I = (D,C) be an interpreter of ST. Let T be a text satisfying ST. The <u>interpretation</u> of T by I is the relation R defined as follows :

    - R is the descriptor of the root

    - the value of R is computed as follows :

We consider the syntax tree of T. Let $n_i$ be a node of this tree. We associate with this node the descriptor D(n) (n is the corresponding UID in ST) and we assign it a value by applying the following rules :

    - if $n_i$ is a node whose son is a leaf $\ell_i$, then the value of D(n) is $\{\ell_i\}$.

    - else, the value of D(n) is computed from the value of the sons by applying the relational expression C(n).

□

We illustrate this definition on example 5.3.

The interpretation of the tree according to $I_1$ is :

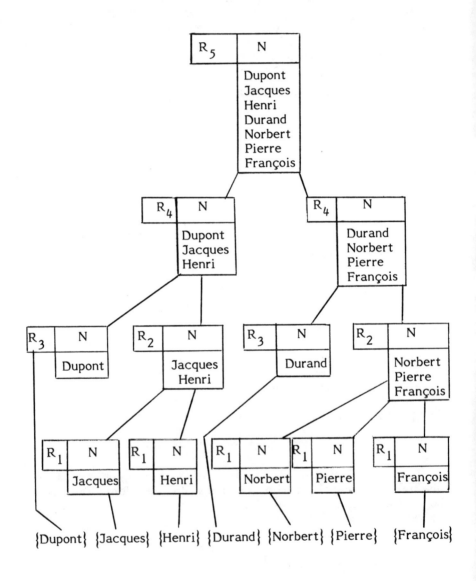

While interpretation with respect to $I_2$ is :

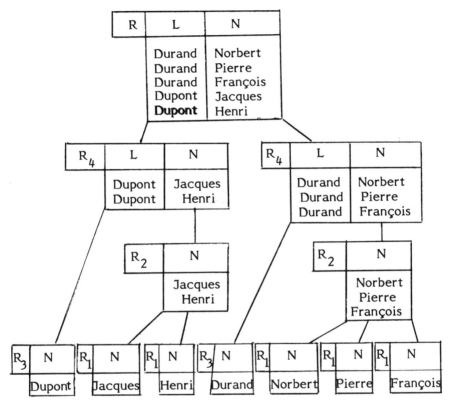

Looking at these two examples one can see that $I_1$ interprets the text by the list of names in the text and that $I_2$ constructs the R(First-Name, Last-Name) relation. The interpretation $I_2$ seems to be the "natural" interpretation.

We formally define the natural interpreter of a text.

**Definition 5.3.**

Let ST be a structure tree.

The <u>natural interpreter</u>    $I_N = (D, C_N)$ is defined as follows :

- for each UID n in ST, $D_N(n) = R_n$ (<u>atset</u>(n))

- for each leaf A in ST, atset(A) = A

- for :    A        atset(A) = atset(B)

           |
           ✗        $D_N(A) = R_A(atset(A))$
           |
           B        $C_N(A) = "U\ R_B(atset(B))"$

                                   K
- for :    A        $atset(A) = \underset{1}{\overset{K}{U}}\ atset(B_i)$

           |        $D_N(A) = R_A(atset(A))$
          ╱•╲
    $B_1$........$B_K$   $C_N(A) = "R_{B_1}(atset(B_1))\ x...x\ R_{B_K}(atset(B_K))"$

                                                                    □

In the above definition, we used UID's instead of nodes names (non terminals). If we had used non terminals to define attributes names, we would have been faced with a now classical problem in relational theory : that of overloaded attributes [FAGI 82] . For example, the nodes title in the library text can represent either a periodic title or a novel title or a chapter title. There is no ambiguity in the structure tree, but we can be lead to overloaded attributes if we do not define the mapping D over UID's.

## 6. TEXT GENERATION

In this section, we concentrate on the generation of texts in our textual data base from relations in the factual data base. We wish to construct from a relation and a structure tree a text satisfying the structure tree. In order to define the generation process, we associate to each structure tree a regular expression that involves the leaves of the tree such that texts satisfying the structure tree are sentences of the language generated by the regular expression.

**Example 6.1.**

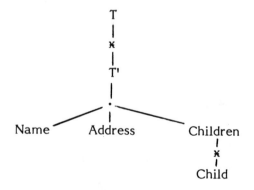

The regular expression is $(Name,Address(Child)^x)^x$. In what follows, we shall assume that the structure tree according to which we generate a text from a relation, is such that each leaf is an attribute name. We define some restrictions on the acceptable regular expressions.

**Definition 6.1**

The <u>acceptable</u> regular expressions are recursively defined as follows :

- if $\mathcal{C}_1^x, ..., \mathcal{C}_p^x$ are acceptable then so is :

$$\mathcal{C}_1^x \cdot \mathcal{C}_2^x \cdot \, ... \, \cdot \mathcal{C}_p^x$$

- if $\omega_1, ..., \omega_{p+1}$ are subsets of a set of attributes U, (at least one of them being non empty), and if $\mathcal{C}_1^x, ... \mathcal{C}_p^x$ are acceptable, then so is :

$$(\omega_1 \, \mathcal{C}_1^x \, \omega_2 \, \mathcal{C}_2^x \, ... \, \mathcal{C}_p^x \, \omega_{p+1})^x$$

- no other regular expressions are acceptable.

■

This definition restricts to the set of regular expressions from structure trees. For example, we do not accept expressions like : $(A^x B^x)^x$ or $AB^x$ since we do not know how to generate a text from a relation $R(AB)$ according to these expressions.

In defining the generation step we use the following notation [DELO 78] . Let $R(U)$ be a relation, and X, Y two subsets of U. Let $R(X)$ be the projection of $R(U)$ on X, then $\forall \, x \in R(X)$, we define $R(x,Y) = \{y \in R(Y)/xy \in R(XY)\}$. Thus $R(x,Y)$ is the set of Y-values associated to a given X value x in $R(XY)$.

**Definition 6.2.**

We define the <u>generated text</u> according to an acceptable regular expression E from a relation $R(U)$ as the result of the recursive procedure $Gen(R(U),E)$ :

- if E : $\mathcal{C}_1^x \; \mathcal{C}_2^x \; ... \; \mathcal{C}_p^x$ and $\mathcal{C}_i$'s are defined over $U_i$'s subsets of U, then :

$$Gen(R(U),E) = Gen(R(U_1), \mathcal{C}_1^x)Gen(R(U_2), \mathcal{C}_2^x)...Gen(R(U_p), \mathcal{C}_p^x)$$

- if $E = (\omega_1 \mathcal{C}_1^x \ \omega_2 \mathcal{C}_2^x \ ... \ \omega_p \mathcal{C}_p^x \ \omega_{p+1})^x$, where $\omega_i$'s are subsets of $U$ such that $U\omega_i = X$ and $\omega_i$'s are defined over $U_i$'s, then :

$$Gen(R(U),E) = x_1 [\omega_1] \ Gen(R(x_1,U_1), \mathcal{C}_1^x)x_1 [\omega_2]$$

$$Gen(R(x_1,U_2), \mathcal{C}_2^x) \ ... \ x_1 [\omega_{p+1}] \ x_2 [\omega_1] \ Gen(R(x_2,U_1), \mathcal{C}_1^x)$$

$$... \ x_2 [\omega_{p+1}] \ ... \ x_n [\omega_1] \ Gen(R(x_n,U_1), \mathcal{C}_1^x) \ ... \ x_n [\omega_{p+1}] .$$

where $R(x) = \{x_1,x_2,...,x_n\}$ and $x_j [\omega_i]$ is the projection of t-uple $x_j$ on $\omega_i$.      ◻

This definition is an application of the compacting process defined in [VERSO 82] .

An important point is the problem of ordering. Texts are ordered structures while relations are sets. In the generation process of definition 6.2, we have implicitly supposed that "something" picks up the tuples of R(X) in a given order. In the real world, our feeling is that the user may choose the ordering used for generating the text (for example, lexicographic order, on the key of the relation).

But he also can leave the choice to the generation procedure. In this case (following the choice axiom) we assume that we can use a choice function that gives us a tuple of R at each step. We illustrate on an example the result of Gen. Let us consider the following relation :

| R | Name | Address | Child |
|---|---|---|---|
| | Joe | Paris | John |
| | Paul | Toulouse | Jean |
| | Joe | Paris | Eva |
| | Henri | Lille | Pierre |

We generate a text according to the expression :

$$(Name,Address(Child)^x)^x$$

The result text given a particular choice function (here, lexicographic order on the key "Name Child") is :

T = "Henri Lille Pierre Joe Paris Eva John Paul Toulouse Jean"

Text interpretation and text generation may seem at first similar to the operations "Nest" and "Unnest" defined in [SCHE 82] . However, there are important differences, "Nest" (resp "Unnest") transforms a relation in 1NF (resp. in $NF^2$) into a $NF^2$ relation (resp 1NF). On the other hand, texts in our work are ordered hierarchical structures, thus very different from a relation in $NF^2$ or in any other normal form, that is why unlike for "Unnest" and "Nest" [JAES 81] interpretation is not inverse to generation. Furthermore, TQL is not an attempt to extend the relational model to unformatted data, but is a tentative formalization of the notion of text.

## CONCLUSION AND FURTHER RESEARCH

Even though the language might seem a bit complicated at first, experiments on a number of examples, have shown it is a fairly powerful and a simple tool. The interpretation of texts in terms of relations naturally leads us to define some notion of completeness of TQL. Shortly, we would like the following diagram to commute.

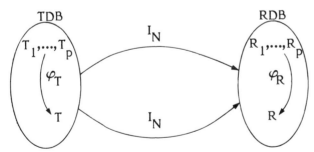

That is, every relational query over the interpretation of a set of texts can be expressed by means of a TQL query on this set followed by the interpretation of the result text : some attempts have been made to show it [BAN 82b] and some partial results have been proved, but the problem is still open. TQL was designed with the idea of being used in an environment where a hardware filter can process large amounts of data sequentially [VERSO 80] . We believe that most of the operating can be done in linear time.

## REFERENCES

[ADIB 82]    M. Adiba, C. Delobel, V. Joloboff, Private communication.

[BAN 82a]    F. Bancilhon, P. Richard, "TQL a textual query language", Research report n° 145, INRIA France.

[BAN 82b]    F. Bancilhon, P. Richard, "TQL : A look at text interpretation and completeness", Working seminar on database machines, Gressoney St Jean, February 22-27, 1982.

[BOGO 82]    G. Bogo, H. Richy, I. Vatton, "Proposition de modèle pour la manipulation de documents", Rapport de Recherche TIGRE n° 4, CII Honeywell Bull, Grenoble, Novembre 1982.

[BRUA 81]    M.F. Bruandet, "Notion de concept pour la construction automatique d'un thesaurus evolutif", Congrès AFCET, Nov. 81.

[CHRI 82]    C.Y. Chrisment, J.B. Crampes, M. Zina, "Les bases d'information généralisées", Projet BIG Lab. CERFIA. Université Paul Sabatier - Toulouse.

[CRAM 82]    Crampes et Zina, "BIG : production de documents mixtes : image, texte, données", convention informatique Sept. 82.

[DELO 78]    C. Delobel, "Normalization and hierarchical dependencies in the relational data model", ACM Trans Database Systems, Vol. 3, N° 3, Sept. 78.

[FAGI 82]    R. Fagin, A. Mendelzon, J. Ullman, "A simplified universal relation assumption and its properties", ACM trans. on Data Base Systems, Vol. 7, N° 3, Sept. 82, pages 343-360.

[HASK 82]    R.L. Haskin, R.A. Lorie, "On Extending the Functions of a Relational Database System", Proc. of ACM-SIGMOD 82, June 2-4, Orlando, Florida.

[JAES 81]    G. Jaeschke, H.J. Schek, "Remarks on the algebra of non first normal form relations" in Principles of Database Systems, ACM SIGACT-SIGMOD, Los Angeles, March 82.

[JOLO 82]    V. Joloboff, S. Kowarski, M. Lopez, "Projet de bases de données textuelles", Rapport de recherche IMAG N° 273, Grenoble, Fev. 1982.

[RICH 82]    G. Richter, "IBM inscribed nets modeling text processing and data (base) management systems", VLDB 81 Cannes, Sept. 9-11, France.

[SCHE 82]    H.J. Schek, P. Pistor, "Data Structures for an integrated data base management and information retrieval system", in proc. of 8th VLDB, Mexico city, Sept. 82.

[STON 82]    M. Stonebraker, H. Stettner, J. Kalash, A. Guttman, and N. Lynn, "Document Processing in a Relational Data Base System", Memorandum N° UCB/ERL MB2/32. Electronics Research Laboratory, University of California, Berkeley, May 1982.

[VELE 82]    F. Velez, "LAMBDA : un langage de définition et de manipulation de base de données généralisées", Séminaire base de Données, ADI, Toulouse, Nov. 1982.

[VERSO 80]    F. Bancilhon, M. Scholl, "Design of a Back End Processor for a Data Base Machine", Proceedings of ACM-SIGMOD, Los Angeles, 1980, pp. 93-93g.

[VERSO 82]    F. Bancilhon, P. Richard, M. Scholl, "On line processing of compacted relations", Proc. of the 8th VLDB Mexico, Sept. 82.

## APPENDIX.

BNF description of TDL.

```
Declaration-statement = identifier : declaration
declaration =iteration
            | concatenation
            | alternative
            | constant
            | string
iteration = is sequence of declaration-statement
concatenation = is begin d-list end
alternative = is one of begin d-list end
constant = 'string-of characters'
d-list =declaration-statement
       | d-list declaration-statement
```

# FIRST STEPS TO ALGEBRAIC PROCESSING OF TEXT

T.H. Merrett

*School of Computer Science*
*McGill University, Montreal*
*Quebec, Canada   H3A 2K6*

We are working to establish fundamental principles of the
nature and manipulation of text data.  Our concern is with
text data that is on secondary storage because it is big or
permanent.  Great success has been achieved in the modelling
and processing of formatted data, notably through the relational model and the operations that have been defined for
relations.  Little of similar fundamental nature is known
about text data.  We emphasize algebraic operations on data
because of the algebraic requirement of *closure* - that the
result be of the same type as the operand(s).  This paper
investigates operations on text data and uses the investigation to indicate suitable abstractions of text for which
useful algebraic operations may be definable.

## 1.  SECONDARY STORAGE

Secondary storage, such as magnetic disks, video disks,
magnetic bubbles and magnetic tape, has two attributes which
distinguish it from random access memory (RAM):  size and
permanence.  Most text data of interest must persist longer
than the duration of a single program run, and so require
secondary storage.  The "permanence" involved may be long
term, as in a library, or it may need to accommodate only
the persistence required for a receiver to acknowledge a
message sent to him on an electronic mail network.  Much
text data is larger than can be held at once in RAM of a
typical workstation - a 500 page book needs about 1.5 mega-
bytes of character data alone.  It is important therefore
to design text processing systems which incorporate access
to secondary storage and which accommodate the peculiarities

of data transfer to and from secondary storage.

The price we pay for the cheapness per bit of massive
secondary storage is in the access/transfer ratio, the
relative time it takes to *find* a sequence of data compared
with the time it takes to *transfer* the data to RAM. This
ratio is on the order of $10^4$ for magnetic disks of all
generations [Merrett, 1983], as opposed to an access/trans-
fer ratio of 1 for RAM. This high ratio requires that data
on secondary storage be *blocked* and this in turn requires
that we take special care to *cluster* the data so that logically related items are found, if possible, on the same
block [Blasgen and Eswaran, 1977]. This is a consideration
of major importance in the design of systems using secondary storage. One of the little-recognized triumphs of
the relational algebra [Codd, 1971] is the extent to which
it takes into account this consideration of blocking and
clustering on secondary storage, while providing great logical flexibility and processing power.

## 2.  ALGEBRAIC PROCESSING

The aspect of the relational algebra that allows us to optimize our use of each block of data as it is transferred,
without having to access it repeatedly, is that it treats
relations as *atomic* objects, undecomposable into individual
tuples. It is inherent in algebraic systems to make this
kind of abstraction: mathematical algebras, such as group
theory, do not investigate the internal structure of their
elements but deal with their formal properties relative to
the operations defined on them. A group element, for
instance, might be a permutation, which if carried out in a
warehouse would require the services of a fork-lift truck:
none of this concerns the algebraic study of permutation
groups. This is the first important aspect of the relational
algebra, which at once treats formatted data and the operations on it at a suitable level of abstraction, and at the
same time permits implementations to make optimum use of the
secondary storage on which all data of concern to database
research and practice must be kept.

The second important aspect of the relational algebra,
and a second inherent characteristic of algebraic systems,
is *closure*. Algebraic systems must be closed under their
operations: the result of an operation is of the same type
as the operand(s) and so can be operated on again. In a
computer system, algebraic closure is a simplifying principle
of great import. If I operated on a normalized relation and
got something else as a result - say an unnormalized relation

or a multiset with duplicate elements – then either I could
not be able to manipulate the result further, or I would
have to learn a whole new set of operations or at least of
special cases. This violation of closure either restricts
me or complicates my life.

3. OPERATIONS ON TEXT

We thus advocate algebraic processing because of its double
advantage of providing data objects at a suitable level of
abstraction and of requiring closure of the operations on
those objects. For formatted data, the relational algebra
embodies these advantages ideally. For text data, we are
still in a state of unenlightenment. In this section we
summarize some investigations we have made into the kinds of
operations that are made on text in practice. We take a
broad view of text so as to include as many different
aspects as possible. Thus we have looked into editing, formatting, concordance and index building, dictionary searching,
style editing, statistical analyses, cryptography, classifying and abstracting. Some common aspects appear, which
lead to suggestions for abstractions and possible operations
in subsequent sections.

*Editing*

A text *editor* is necessarily an interactive process giving
the user a fine control over insertions, deletions and
changes to the text. It appears hard to reconcile this with
the atomic aspect of the algebraic approach, which would
avoid decomposing text into individual lines and characters,
or sentences and words. The same difficulty was solved in
the case of a relational editor [Merrett and Chiu, 1983] by
introducing a two-faced operator which on one hand is algebraic, producing a new relation by editing an old (details
not specified), and on the other hand provides an interactive
syntax for specifying the details of the edit. We find in
text processing a number of applications of this approach
(which could be called the Janus approach, after the two-
faced god of Roman doorways, if the name had not been first
claimed by a text formatting system).

*Formatting*

Formatting is the process of arranging text on pages, or
wherever it is going to appear. Recent examples of formatting systems are $T_EX$ [Knuth, 1979] and GML [Goldfarb,

1981].  $T_EX$ is an example of a procedural formatter, which
specifies in fine detail how the text is to be laid out.
GML takes the descriptive approach, identifying in a "markup" process the various structural components of the text,
such as chapters and paragraphs.  Routines independent of
the text are used to specify the detailed layout of these
structural components.  Both $T_EX$ and GML are batch systems.
Several other systems, such as Etude [Hammer et al., 1981]
emphasize interactive formatting, and JANUS [Chamberlin
et al., 1981] considers the inclusion of images and other
non-sequential material following the way that publishers in-
terpolate such matter into the galley proofs.

*Indexing*

The compilation of a concordance from a text is a relatively
straightforward process that can easily be automated.  Such
a process can easily be algebraic in the first requirement,
that of atomicity.  The second algebraic requirement, that
of closure, is harder to satisfy, because the concordance
could be seen as formatted data (e.g., a relation) while
the operand is text.  An *index*, on the other hand, is much
more intricate to build than a concordance.  A concordance
is just a list of words and indicators of their context (or
it might be a KWIC index, with the context explicit) while
an index is a list of *ideas* and must include synonyms,
antonyms, groupings, subdivisions, cross-references, must
resolve ambiguities, etc. [Collision, 1969].  This requires
a skilled indexer, although an interactive machine could be
an indispensable tool.

*Dictionary Searching*

Many applications of computers to text are word-oriented,
like indexing, but require *dictionary look-up*.  Word-transliteration is an example, a prelude to machine translation.
A number of indexing requirements, such as consistency of
spelling and use of singular or plural, looking up synonyms
and antonyms, resolving ambiguities, etc., can require
searching an appropriate dictionary or thesaurus.  This can
be seen as an algebraic operation for which text and formatted data are the operands.
    *Style editing* could use dictionary search to check
spelling, but can go much farther, such as offering to
change suspicious occurrences of "which", to "that", of "may"
to "can", "might" or "is permitted to" [Walker, 1981].
*Tag editing* can be a combination of interactive and auto-

matic processes, in which words of text are tagged with syntactic or semantic attributes for use in linguistic analysis, information retrieval or abstracting [Inman, 1981].

## Statistical Analysis

Most of computerized *linguistic analysis* of text involves counting ratios such as word type to word token, noun to article, etc. This involves identifying parts of speech by dictionary lookup or tagging, and then doing arithmetical counts. More sophisticated applications of word frequency analysis identify "aberrant vocabulary" in parts relative to a corpus of work, or measure co-occurrences of words [McKinnon, 1983].

## Cryptography

The *enciphering* and *deciphering* of text are operations mostly at the level of characters rather than words. *Cryptanalysis* requires statistical information on the frequencies of letters, digrams (pairs of letters) and trigrams (triples of letters) [Denning, 1982].

## Abstracting

The process of extracting sentences automatically from a text and combining them suitably into an *abstract* of the text has been investigated by e.g., Rush, Salvador and Zamora [1971] and Mathis, Rush and Young [1973]. A great deal of empirical input about what is required in an abstract goes into the automation of this process, and their work is apparently restricted to scientific papers as texts. An interesting conclusion is that word frequencies alone do not helpfully indicate the content of a document but are rather detrimental to the production of good abstracts.

## Classifying

A fundamental operation in information retrieval is the classification of the documents in a set. *Clustering* is often used, based on *term vectors*, which give essentially the frequencies of words or their presence or absence in a text, and on *similarity matrices*, which measure closeness of the term vectors [Salton, 1983].

*Searching*

Finally, of course, we can *search* text for the occurrences
of given patterns: either strings of characters or words
that occur anywhere in the text, as in the linear algorithms
of Knuth, Morris and Pratt [1970] and Boyer and Moore [1977];
or strings that occur starting at predefined places in the
text, as in PATRICIA [Morrison, 1968]; or general patterns
including strings, free matches, alternatives, conjunctions,
etc.

## 4. OPERATIONS ON SEQUENCES

Given this diversity of operations and processes on text,
we wonder what abstraction can model text in general and
what algebraic operations can be defined on this abstraction
to enable us to do all the useful things described in the
last section. The most obvious abstraction is that text is
a *sequence*, if not a *hierarchy of sequences*: a text is a
sequence of sections, a section is a sequence of paragraphs,
a paragraph is a sequence of sentences, a sentence is a
sequence of words, a word is a sequence of characters. We
can contrast a sequence with a relation, which is just a set.
In a sequence, order is important, and duplicate elements
are allowed, distinguished from each other by their position
in the ordering. In a set, neither of these is true.
   When we come to define operators on sequences, based on
the processes described on text in the last section, we
encounter difficulty, however. First, the operators will
have to mix types, as in the case of compiling a concordance,
which is a relation - a set of entries - rather than a
sequence - from a text, which is a sequence. Second, the
operations are not closed, as in the case of a dictionary
lookup in a word-transliteration application: the
dictionary may have several alternatives (in French, say)
for a word (in English), and the transliteration will have
to give them all in the absence of syntactic or semantic tags
to resolve the choice presented to the human translator.
Thus the result is not a simple sequence, but something more
general, a *sequence of sets*. (Similarly in some graphics
applications which we do not pursue here, we can define
realistic operations on sequences which yield *sets of sequence*.)

## 5. REPRESENTING SEQUENCES AS RELATIONS

While sequences thus do not seem to form a powerful enough

abstraction, we notice that relations - or at least formatted
data - are involved in a number of the results.  We wonder
if we can obtain an at least temporary solution by treating
the whole problem as an application of relations.  We observe that a *sequence can be represented as a relation* - a
set - by making a tuple of each element in the sequence
together with a *sequence number*.  Then the ordering of the
sequence is carried in the sequence number, and there are no
duplicates because the sequence number forms a key.  (If the
sequence is not simple, like a sequence of sets, the sequence
number will repeat for each alternative in a set, and so is
not a key.  This just shows that the generalization, sequence
of sets, is easily handled by the same representation.)

   We pursue this approach now in a little more detail, considering first the simplest model of text, either as
sequences of words or as sequences of characters.  The relational representation relaxes our concerns about algebraic
closure somewhat, since we will use the full relational
algebra and insist only that relations result.  Some rather
nice results appear, which are encouraging.  For instance,
if we represent a text as a relation holding a sequence of
words, the *text is its own concordance*, since the only
difference between text and concordance lies in the ordering
of the tuples which is, of course, irrelevant in a relation.
If we represent a text as a relation holding a sequence of
characters, the cryptological distinction between *transposition* and *substitution* enciphering becomes symmetrical
and quite revealing.  Here are some details.

*Concordance Building*

A text is its own concordance in the representation we are
discussing, but we can refine it somewhat by removing "stop"
words, i.e. words that are too common in a given language
to carry any significant meaning or to be worth indexing.
In Figure 1 we show the text "I was coming to the Computing
Centre because the computer was being comical about my code",
the list of stop words and the concordance built using the
difference join operation of the relational algebra,
CONCORDANCE ← ENGLISH djoin STOP.  (For a summary of all
operations in this section, see the Appendix.  For precise
specifications, see Merrett [1983].)  Figure 1 also shows
an index that was built using Collison's [1969] twenty rules:
the antonym rule gave the entry "code *vs* free access", which
seems to capture the sense of the text very nicely.  The
index was, of course, built manually, and is included only
to indicate that automation has some way to go.

| ENGLISH (EWORD | SEQ) | STOP (EWORD) | CONCORDANCE (EWORD | SEQ) |
|---|---|---|---|---|
| about | 14 | about | coming | 3 |
| because | 8 | because | Computing | 6 |
| being | 12 | being | Centre | 7 |
| Centre | 7 | I | computer | 10 |
| code | 16 | my | comical | 13 |
| comical | 13 | the | code | 16 |
| coming | 3 | to | | |
| computer | 10 | was | | |
| Computing | 6 | | | |
| I | 1 | | | |
| my | 15 | | | |
| the | 5 | | | |
| the | 9 | | | |
| to | 4 | | | |
| was | 2 | | | |
| was | 11 | | | |

An index:   calculator   *see computer*
code *vs* free
   access     16
computer     10
Computing
   **Centre**     6
       *see also code*

Figure 1   Automatic Concordance Building, Manual Indexing

*Dictionary Searching*

With text represented relationally as a sequence of words, looking up its words in a dictionary is simply a matter of joining the text with the relation containing the dictionary. If we have an application such as the transliteration problem shown in Figure 2, every word in the text must be looked up and, from what we said about clustering in Section 1, it is apparent that a merge - the most obvious implementation of the join operations - is the most efficient way to do the lookup. So efficiency accompanies simplicity. The relational algebra to do the transliteration in Figure 2 uses the "left join", which transmits the entire text to the result even if there is no match. The first line is an expression of the *domain algebra* and just says that the English word should be used in the result if there is no matching entry in the dictionary. Figure 2 shows the dictionary, extracted from the 1960 edition of Larousse's Dictionnaire Moderne, the two lines of program, and the resulting transliteration in text form with alternatives shown. The English

text is ENGLISH from Figure 1 and a translation into French
is "Je venais au service d'informatique parce que
l'ordinateur avait un comportement bizarre à propos de mon
code". Our efforts are not meant to be representative of
the state of the art in machine translation.

DICT
(EWORD      FWORD)

| EWORD | FWORD | | EWORD | FWORD |
|-------|-------|---|-------|-------|
| about | autour de | | my | ma |
| about | parmi | | my | mes |
| about | vers | | the | le |
| about | en | | the | la |
| about | sur | | the | les |
| about | concernant | | to | à |
| because | parce que | | to | de |
| centre | centre | | to | sur |
| centre | cercles | | to | avec |
| code | code | | to | pour |
| comical | comique | | to | a part |
| I | je | | to | contre |
| my | mon | | to | selon |

let TRANS be if FWORD = $\mathcal{DC}$ then EWORD else FWORD
FRENCH ← TRANS, SEQ in ENGLISH ℓjoin DICT

$$"je \ was \ coming \begin{Bmatrix} à \\ de \\ sur \\ avec \\ pour \\ a \ part \\ contre \\ selon \end{Bmatrix} \begin{Bmatrix} le \\ la \\ les \end{Bmatrix} Computing \begin{Bmatrix} Centre \\ Cercles \end{Bmatrix}$$

$$parce \ que \begin{Bmatrix} le \\ la \\ les \end{Bmatrix} computer \ was \ being \ comique \begin{Bmatrix} autour \ de \\ parmi \\ vers \\ en \\ sur \\ concernant \end{Bmatrix}$$

$$\begin{Bmatrix} mon \\ ma \\ mes \end{Bmatrix} \begin{Bmatrix} code \\ chiffre \end{Bmatrix}"$$

Figure 2   Word Transliteration Using a Dictionary Search

*Cryptography*

Given a plaintext message, MSG(PT,PS) represented as a sequence (seq. no. PS) of characters (PT), the two classes of
cipher are:  tranposition ciphers, which compute a new PS;
and substitutuion ciphers, which compute a new PT.  For
instance, the matrix transposition cipher reads a message
such as RENAISSANCE into the rows of a H × W array (say
3 × 4) and reads it out in column order, obtaining
RINESCNSEAA.  The new sequence numbers are CS, shown in
Figure 3, and defined by the domain algebra expression

  let CS be PS ÷ W + H × (PS mod W).

A substitution cipher, on the other hand, gives new characters, CT defined by

  let CT be chr(f(ord(PT)-65)+65

where chr and ord are functions that map from the ASCII
ordinal position to the character and inversely.  For the
Caesar cipher, CT is shown in Figure 3 using

  $f(x) = (x + 3) \mod 26.$

All the ciphers given by Denning [1982] are variations of
these transformations on either CS or CT.

| MSG(PT | PS) | CS | CT |
|--------|-----|-----|-----|
| R | 0 | 0 | U |
| E | 1 | 3 | H |
| N | 2 | 6 | Q |
| A | 3 | 9 | D |
| I | 4 | 1 | L |
| S | 5 | 4 | V |
| S | 6 | 7 | V |
| A | 7 | 10 | D |
| N | 8 | 2 | Q |
| C | 9 | 5 | F |
| E | 10 | 8 | H |

Figure 3   Transposition (CS) and Substitution
(CT) Ciphers

*Linguistic Analysis*

We can look at two of the many types of statistical analysis
that linguists and other researchers like to apply to text.
The *type/token ratio* is a measure of richness of vocabulary:
type is the count of the number of different words used in
a passage, while token is the total number of word occurrences.  Figure 4 shows the domain algebra statements needed
to compute TT, the type/token ratio, and the result for
ENGLISH of Figure 1.

| ENGLISH (EWORD | SEQ) | EN | EWORD | SEQ | EN |
|---|---|---|---|---|---|
| about | 14 | 1 | Computing | 6 | 9 |
| because | 8 | 2 | I | 1 | 10 |
| being | 12 | 3 | my | 15 | 11 |
| Centre | 7 | 4 | the | 5 | 12 |
| code | 16 | 5 | the | 9 | 12 |
| comical | 13 | 6 | to | 4 | 13 |
| coming | 3 | 7 | was | 2 | 14 |
| computer | 10 | 8 | was | 11 | 14 |

```
let EN be fcn + of 1 order EWORD
let TYPE be red max of EN      << 14 >>
let TOKEN be red + of 1        << 16 >>
let TT be TYPE/TOKEN           << .88 >>
```

Figure 4    Type/Token Ratio

*Range coocurrence* is a measure of associations of different words - if two words occur near each other sufficiently
frequently, they may be hypothesized to represent concepts
the author wishes to link together.  The following exercise
partitions the text into groups of three words and measures
word coocurrence within these ranges.  (A more usual exercise is to use sentences as the ranges, which is just as
easily done assuming the sentence structure is supplied in
the text relation.)  Using an abstract version of ENGLISH,
in which words are represented by letters (and from which
stop words may have been removed), we find the range and,
incidentally, the count of the number of occurrences of each
word (Figure 5).  To measure coocurrences, we must find all
pairs of words in each range.  This is achieved by a natural
join of ENGLISH with itself on RANGE.  We then count the
number of coocurrences, COO, of each pair of words:  thus
words A and C occur jointly twice, in ranges 1 and 4.  A

final refinement is to eliminate the spurious coocurrences of
words with themselves:   only C occurs twice in one range; all
other correlations of C with itself result from its four
occurrences in the text.  Figure 6 shows part of the natural
join, with some of the values for COO and the final coocurrence, COOC.  This attribute is actualized in a relation
COOCURRENCE which can be shown as a matrix:

|   | A | B | C | D |
|---|---|---|---|---|
| A | 0 | 4 | 2 | 2 |
| B | 4 | 0 | 4 | 2 |
| C | 2 | 4 | 2 | 0 |
| D | 2 | 2 | 0 | 0 |

ENGLISH

| (EWORD | SEQ) | RANGE | COUNT |
|--------|------|-------|-------|
| A  | 1  | 1 | 4 |
| B  | 2  | 1 | 5 |
| C  | 3  | 1 | 4 |
| D  | 4  | 2 | 2 |
| A  | 5  | 2 | 4 |
| B  | 6  | 2 | 5 |
| C  | 7  | 3 | 4 |
| C  | 8  | 3 | 4 |
| B  | 9  | 3 | 5 |
| A  | 10 | 4 | 4 |
| C  | 11 | 4 | 4 |
| B  | 12 | 4 | 5 |
| B  | 13 | 5 | 5 |
| A  | 14 | 5 | 4 |
| D  | 15 | 5 | 2 |

let RANGE be ceil(SEQ/R) <<e.g., R=3>>
let COUNT be equiv + of 1 by EWORD

SIDE1[WD1,RG,S1,CT ← EWORD,RANGE,SEQ,COUNT]ENGLISH
SIDE2[WD2,RG,S2 ← WD1,RG,S1]SIDE1

Figure 5  Range Coocurrence

```
SIDE1 ijoin SIDE2
(RG   WD1   WD2   S1   S2   CT)   COO   COOC
  1    A     A     1    1    4     4     0
  1    A     B     1    2    4
  1    A     C     1    3    4     2     2
  1    B     A     2    1    5
  1    B     B     2    2    5
  1    B     C     2    3    5
  1    C     A     3    1    4
  1    C     B     3    2    4
  1    C     C     3    3    4
  2    D     D     4    4    2
  :
  2    A     A     5    5    4     4     0
  :
  4    A     A    10   10    4     4     0
  4    A     C    10   11    4     2     2
  :
  5    A     A    14   14    4     4     0
  :
```

let COO be equiv + of 1 by WD1,WD2          << not all >>
let COOC be if WD1=WD2 then COO-CT else COO  <<  shown  >>
COOCURRENCE ← WD1,WD2,COOC in SIDE1 ijoin SIDE2

Figure 6   Range Coocurrence (concluded)

*Statistical Analysis, Classifying, etc.*

Space does not permit mention of the straightforward expressions for frequency analysis, word clustering, term
vectors, similarity matrices, etc., using the relational and
domain algebras.

## 6.  TEXT AND DOCUMENTS

The above illustrations are limited to simple sequences,
either of words or of characters.  Text has a more elaborate
structure, which is usually a hierarchy - say of letters,
words, sentences, paragraphs, etc.  The lower structure of
text - letters, words and sentences - can be represented as
an easy extension of the above simple sequences.  The higher
structure can be represented as an essentially binary relation which gives the relative positions of nodes in the
hierarchy:  a sentence is contained in a paragraph, a list
is nested inside another list, a program block contains

statements, etc. For natural language text, we are attracted
by the descriptive approach of GML [Goldfarb, 1981], which
enables a user to define his own structure and which makes
formatting and layout an automatic consequence of this
structure, specified by a programmer/typesetter. Our
structural representation accommodates the descriptive syntax
for GML, as well as the syntax of programming languages.

   *Documents* are still higher level structures which incorporate text, tables, diagrams, footnotes, bibliographies,
etc., and cross-references within and among all these.
Tables are relations, footnotes and bibliographies are text,
and we are working on relational/sequential representations
of diagrams. Thus our approach bears the seed of an integrated treatment of documents as well as of the individual
components.

## 7. SUMMARY

The search for a model of, and algebraic operations on, text
has not yet led to a suitable abstraction for text alone, but
we can use the relational and domain algebras profitably for
a wide range of desirable operations on text.

## APPENDIX

### *The Extended Relational Algebra*

We outline the operations of the extended relational algebra
used in Section 5. Further details are given by Merrett
[1983]. We perceive relational operations as generalizations
of set operations, just as relations are generalizations of
sets. Set operations come in two flavours: the family
(union, intersection, etc.) of binary operations on sets which
produce sets; and the family (superset, subset, etc.) of
binary operations on sets which result in logical values.
These generalize, respectively, to the $\mu$-joins, which operate
on relations $R(X)$ and $S(Y)$ to give a relation $T(X \cup Y)$; and
to the $\sigma$-joins, which operate on relations $R(X)$ and $S(Y)$ and
result in a relation $T(X + Y)$. (Where X and Y are sets of
attributes, $\cup$ is the union operator and + is the symmetric
difference operator.) Codd's [1971] operator natural join is
one of the $\mu$-joins, while his division and natural composition
are $\sigma$-joins. Apart from set complementation, there are no
unary operators on sets: relations require projection and
selection operations, which can be combined in the T-selector
and generalized (by adding quantifiers) to the QT-selector.
This gives three classes of operations on relations, con-

stituting the extended relational algebra.  In addition, it
is useful to define some classes of operations on attributes,
which result in new attributes, constituting the "domain
algebra".

Section 5 of this paper makes use of the μ-joins and T-
selectors and of four of the classes of domain algebra
operators, which we now proceed to describe.  We start with
relational *assignment*, an important operation whenever we
have a closed set of operators which make expressions
possible.  Assignment can assume a simple form, as in

CONCORDANCE ⟵ ENGLISH djoin STOP,

in which CONCORDANCE inherits the attributes of the expression on the right, namely {EWORD,SEQ} ∪ {EWORD}.  It can be
used in a more complex form to rename attributes by position,
as in

SIDE2[WD2,RG,S2 ⟵ WD1,RG,S1]SIDE1,

which makes SIDE2 the same relation as SIDE1, but with WD1
renamed WD2 and S1 renamed S2.

The *T-selector*,

TRANS,SEQ <u>in</u> ENGLISH <u>ℓjoin</u> DICT

extracts the attributes TRANS and SEQ from the relational expression ENGLISH ℓjoin DICT and creates the projection of
this expression on those attributes:  in this form, it is
simply relational projection.

The μ-*joins* generalize the set operators ∪, ∩, - and + to,
respectively, <u>ujoin</u>, <u>ijoin</u>, <u>djoin</u> and <u>sjoin</u>.  Codd's natural
join is <u>ijoin</u>, the "intersection join":  it is easy to see
that the natural join of two sets, R(X) and S(X) (which are
written as relations but are just sets over the same domain,
X) is the intersection R ∩ S.  The other set operations can
be generalized in exactly the same way that ∩ generalizes to
<u>ijoin</u>.  In addition to the four μ-joins listed, we also need
<u>ℓjoin</u> and <u>rjoin</u>, which specialize to the left and right
identity operations on sets.  Informally, if we define
(2) ≙ R <u>ijoin</u> S, (1) ≙ those tuples of R which do not participate in R <u>ijoin</u> S, (3) ≙ those tuples of S which do not
participate in R <u>ijoin</u> S, we have:

R <u>ujoin</u> S ≙ (1) ∪ (2) ∪ (3)     R <u>ℓjoin</u> S ≙ (1) ∪ (2)
R <u>djoin</u> S ≙ (1)                 R <u>rjoin</u> S ≙ (2) ∪ (3)
R <u>sjoin</u> S ≙ (1) ∪ (3)

(If R has the attributes X and Y and S has the attributes Y
and Z, the result relations have the attributes X, Y and Z:
in practice we make an exception for djoin, which results in
only the attributes X and Y.  Further refinements are in
Merrett [1983].)

The domain algebra operates on attributes to give attributes (and is not called the "attribute algebra" only for
reasons of euphony).  It is deliberately independent of the
relations on which the attributes are defined, and so results
in "virtual attributes", which must be "actualized" in some
particular relation.  This is done by renaming the virtual
attribute in some relational algebra expression, usually projection.  Thus the domain algebra follows a philosophy of
lazy evaluation – domain algebra statements are macros, and
can be called "virtual relations".

The most obvious use of the domain algebra is to create
new attributes by arithmetical combinations of other attributes.  Thus

> let TT be TYPE/TOKEN

is a domain algebra expression defining an attribute TT as
the ratio of attributes TYPE and TOKEN.  This extends to the
class of *horizontal* operations, which includes arithmetical
expressions and any calculation for which, in each tuple, a
value can be calculated for the new attribute without
accessing other tuples.  Thus

> let TRANS be if FWORD = $DC$ then EWORD else FWORD

is a horizontal operation.

The remaining classes of domain algebra operation all process several tuples to arrive at a result:  they are
"vertical" operations.  The first class extends the notion
of *totalling* the values of an attribute.  Totalling uses the
arithmetical operator, +.  Other operators can also be used,
but they must be commutative and associative, otherwise the
result depends on the order of the tuples, which violates
the definition of a relation.  Thus

> let TYPE be red max of EN

is a legitimate *reduction* (red) operation, which finds the
maximum value of the attribute EN.  The operation of *counting*
can be derived from reduction on a *constant attribute*:

> let TOKEN be red + of 1.

A close relative of the class of reduction operations is the class of *equivalence reduction* operations, which includes *subtotalling*. Equivalence reduction groups tuples into equivalence classes, each with the same value of some attribute or set of attributes, and finds the total or maximum or whatever of another attribute within each equivalence class. A statement which counts the number of tuples for each value of the pair of attributes, WD1 and WD2, is

<u>let</u> COO <u>be</u> <u>equiv</u> + <u>of</u> 1 <u>by</u> WD1,WD2.

Another class of vertical operators is *functional mapping*, which can be used for a cumulative sum of one attribute according to an ordering defined by another attribute:

<u>let</u> EN <u>be</u> <u>fcn</u> + <u>of</u> 1 <u>order</u> EWORD

counts the number of different values of EWORD. It gives the number of *different* values because the <u>of</u>-attribute is assumed to be functionally dependent on the <u>order</u>-attribute, and the result attribute is also fixed as a function of the order-attribute: the operation is a *functional* in the mathematical sense of a function whose argument and result are themselves functions - such as an indefinite integral. The arithmetical operator (+ in the example) is not constrained to be associative or commutative because of the ordering imposed by the order-attribute.

The final class of domain algebra operators, *partial functional mapping*, which is related to functional mapping as partial integration is related to integration, or as equivalence reduction is to reduction, is not used in this paper.

ACKNOWLEDGEMENTS

I would like to thank the members of my Winter 1983 course on Information Systems, who participated in the formulation of these thoughts about text: Ines Anderson, Roger de Peiza, François Dongier, Brenda Fayerman, William Fok, Valentine Ihebuzor, John Kirkpatrick, Frank Lok, Eddie Mok, Nina Moliver, Felix Nevraumont, Ilario Pedron, Nicholas Rallis. David Diamond also participated. Lynda Pilkington typed the paper, with accuracy under pressure. I am grateful to the Fonds Formation de chercheurs et actions concertées of the Province of Québec for a research grant.

REFERENCES

1. M.W. Blasgen and K.P. Eswaran, 1977. Storage and access in relational databases. IBM Syst.J. 16 4(1977)363-77.
2. R.S. Boyer and J.S. Moore, 1977. A fast string searching algorithm. CACM 20 10(Oct. 1977)762-72.
3. D.D. Chamberlin *et al.*, 1981. JANUS: an interactive system for document composition. Proc. SIGPLAN/SIGOA Symposium on Text Manipulation, Portland, Oregon (8-10 June, 1981) SIGPLAN Notices 16 6(June, 1981)82-91.
4. E.F. Codd, 1971. Relational completeness of data base sublanguages in R. Rustin ed. Data Base Systems, Prentice Hall (1972)65-98.
5. R. Collison, 1969. Indexes and Indexing. Benn (1969).
6. D.E. Denning, 1982. Cryptography and Data Security. Addison-Wesley (1982).
7. C.F. Goldfarb, 1981. A generalized approach to document markup. Proc. SIGPLAN/SIGOA Symposium on Text Manipulation, Portland, Oregon (8-10 June, 1981) SIGPLAN Notices 16 6(June, 1981)68-73.
8. M. Hammer *et al.*, 1981. The implementation of Etude, an integrated and interactive document preparation system. Proc. SIGPLAN/SIGOA Symposium on Text Manipulation, Portland, Oregon (8-10 June, 1981) SIGPLAN Notices 16 6(June, 1981)137-46.
9. E.E. Inman, 1981. TAGEDIT: a computer tool for literary and linguistic research in P.C. Patton and R.A. Holoien eds. Computing in the Humanities. D.C. Heath & Co., Lexington, Mass. (1981)145-53.
10. D.E. Knuth, 1979. $T_EX$ and METAFONT New Directions in Typesetting. Digital Press. American Mathematical Society (1979).
11. D.E. Knuth, J.H. Morris, Jr., and V.R. Pratt, 1970. Fast pattern searching in strings. SIAM J. Computing 6 2(1970)323-50.
12. B.A. Mathis, J.E. Rush and C.E. Young, 1973. Improvement of automatic abstracts by the use of structural analysis. J. Am. Soc. for Information Sci. 24 2(March-April, 1973)101-9.
13. A. McKinnon, 1983. The Shape of Authorship. To appear.
14. T.H. Merrett, 1983. Relational Information Systems. Reston Publishing Co., Reston, Va. (1983).
15. T.H. Merrett and G.K.-W. Chiu, 1983. MRDSA: full support of the relational algebra on an Apple II. Journées sur la Conception, l'Implantation et l'Utilisation de SGDB Relationnels sur Micro-Ordinateurs. Toulouse (14-15 February, 1983).

16. D.R. Morrison, 1968. PATRICIA: practical algorithm to retrieve information coded in alphanumeric. JACM 15 (1968)514-34.
17. J.E. Rush, R. Salvador and A. Zomora, 1971. Automatic abstracting and indexing II Production of indicative abstracts by application of contextual inference and syntactic coherence criteria. J. Am. Soc. for Information Sci. 22 4(July-August, 1977)260-74.
18. G. Salton and M.J. McGill, 1983. Introduction to Modern Information Retrieval. McGraw-Hill (1983).
19. J.H. Walker, 1981. The document editor: a support environment for preparing technical documents. Proc. SIGPLAN/SIGOA Symposium on Text Manipulation, Portland, Oregon (8-10 June, 1981) SIGPLAN Notices 16 6(June, 1981)44-50.

# A MODEL FOR WORD PROCESSING SYSTEMS

M.R. Laganà\*, E. Locuratolo\*\*, R. Sprugnoli\*\*

*\*Dipartimento di Informatica, Università di Pisa, Italy*
*\*\*Istituto di Elaborazione dell'Informazione del CNR,*
*Pisa, Italy*

## 1. INTRODUCTION

In the present development of office automation systems the most important roles are played by data base management, from one side, and "text (or word) processing systems" (WPS) from the other. Large data bases containing textual data are to be organized for sharing and disseminating information, in the form of letters, reports, articles and so on. Hence, two main problems arise: first, how to access easily and efficiently to the information pieces of the data base, and second, how to achieve the best formal accuracy in the content and a fine printing of every single piece. Word processing systems are devoted to the latter point and in the present paper we propose a general model of such systems and sketch the implementation of a particular system derived from the model.

## 2. THE MODEL

Our model of a "word processing system" consists mainly in three components, which we call T (for "text"), S (for "screen") and D (for "dictionary"); so we shall refer to the model as to the "TSD model".

The first component T represents the text, as it is stored in the computer memory. T is a sequence of items, some of which are "words" and others are "commands". A "word" is a triple $(w, d, \sigma)$ where w̲ is a sequence of letters, i.e. a word in the usual sense of the term. Uppercase letters are not considered, since the form of the word is specified by the specifier $\sigma$; it indicates whether the word w̲ contains no uppercase letters, begins by an uppercase letter or it is formed up by uppercase letters only. These are the three major cases occurring in the practice and correspond generally to common names, proper names and abbreviations. To take into account other possibilities, $\sigma$ may assume a forth value indicating that w̲ is a "special word", possibly composed of digits and special characters. The d̲ is the "delimiter", that is how the word is closed in the text, e.g. by a space, or a comma followed by a space, or a full stop, or something else. Note that this is a "logical" representation of the words occurring in a text; both d̲ and $\sigma$ can be easily codified since they can take up only a very limited number of values.

A command̲ is a couple $(c, p)$, where c̲ is the name of the command and p̲ is the list of the parameters relative to that command. Commands can be specified at a low or at a high level; a low level command may be "begin underlining" or "write a blank line"; a high level command may be: write the following words in the font corresponding to "chapter heading". A discussion of these forms for commands can be found in (3); in our opinion, the high level approach is to be preferred.

The second component, the screen S, represents the form in which text is introduced in the computer memory and is displayed every time the user needs to see the content of the text. Formally, S is a sequence of characters whatsoever, specifically àll the characters which can be displayed on the particular device the user is working at. In a high level approach to WPS's, many editing features are not directly specified by the user, but are inferred by the system in accordance to the form in which the user types his text on the "screen"; other commands needs to be specified explicitly. Anyhow, there exists a function $t:S \quad T$ converting the screen to the internal format of the text; displaying of the text requires another function s:T $\rightarrow$ S acting as inverse of $\underline{t}$. Actually, $\underline{s}$ is not really an inverse; in fact $\underline{t}$ operates some sort of normalization, so that $s(t(S)) \neq S$ but $t(s(t(S)))=t(S)$. To be precise, both $\underline{s}$ and $\underline{t}$ depend on the particular device on which S is displayed, however the internal text should be device independent, that is, for every device $\Delta$, $\Delta'$ we have: $t_\Delta(s_\Delta(t_\Delta(S)))=t_{\Delta'}(s_{\Delta'}(t_\Delta(S)))$; for the sake of simplicity, we shall suppose that the device $\Delta$ is fixed.

The third component, the dictionary D, is a set of triples $(w,\sigma,i)$, where $\underline{w}$ is a word, $\sigma$ is a specifier, as it was defined for T. The dictionary is the set of the "correct words", that is the words that can appear in the text. Its aim is to allow the user to have an indication of possibly mispelled words, and hence to correct them. The specifier $\sigma$ denotes the "usual" form of the word: no uppercase letters, initial uppercase, all uppercase, special word. Note that a common word in the dictionary may be, in the text, specified as "no uppercase letters", or "initial uppercase" (at the beginning of a sentence), or "all uppercase" (appearing in a chapter heading). A simple set of rules R° applies to a word $\underline{w}$ in the text and the corresponding word in the dictionary:

1) if $\underline{w}$ is specified as "no uppercase" in the dictionary, it should be specified as "no uppercase" or "initial uppercase" or "all uppercase" in the text;
2) if $\underline{w}$ is specified as "initial uppercase" in the dictionary, it should be specified as "initial uppercase" or "all uppercase" in the text;
3) if $\underline{w}$ is specified as "all uppercase" in the dictionary, it can be specified only as "all uppercase" in the text;
4) if $\underline{w}$ is specified as "special word" in the dictionary, it should be specified in the same way in the text.

Finally, the indicator $\underline{i}$ signals the "degree of stability" of the word; some words should always appear in the dictionary; other words appear only for a limited period of time (for example, the names of occasional customers); others are relevant for a single session (e.g. a foreign word). Several degrees may be considered and maintained.

The dictionary should not contain "all the possible"

words;  on the contrary it ought to be as limited as possible, in order to signal the highest number of possible errors.  As for the text T,  our dictionary is a "logical" component; systems exist possessing a "virtual" dictionary, that is a hash table (1) from which it is possible to infer whether a word is correct with a very high probability. From a modeling point of view, our system models also these systems,  in which,  however,  it is actually impossible to maintain the specifier $\sigma$ and the indicator $\underline{i}$.

Now we can define our TSD model of a WPS as a 7-tuple $(T, \{S_\Delta\}, D, \{t_\Delta\}, \{s_\Delta\}, v, O)$,  where $T, S_\Delta, D, t_\Delta$ and $s_\Delta$ are defined as above (depending on the device $\Delta$) and $\underline{v}$ and $\underline{O}$ are to be defined now.  $\underline{O}$ is the set of the operations of the system;  every $\underline{h}$ in $\underline{O}$ is a function transforming a triple $(T, S_\Delta, D)$ in another triple $(T', S'_\Delta, D')$,  as we shall see in the next section;  $\underline{v}$ is a predicate $\underline{v}:T\times D \to \{0,1\}$, where $v(T,D)=1$ if and only if the word in every triple in T is also contained in a triple of D and the corresponding specifiers satisfy the rules $R°$.

Now we can define a <u>state</u> of te TSD model as a triple $(T, S_\Delta, D)$,  where T,  S$_\Delta$ and D are as above;  furthermore a <u>consistent</u> <u>state</u> is any state $(T, S_\Delta, D)$ for which $v(T,D)=1$, $T=t_\Delta(S_\Delta)$ and $T=t_\Delta(s_\Delta(T))$.

## 3. OPERATIONS

The set O contains the operations defined in our TSD model;  every operation should transform a consistent state $(T,S,D)$ (the device $\Delta$ will be understood) in another consistent state $(T',S',D')$,  where,  possibly,  T=T',  S=S' and D=D'.  This latter case is typical for the operation f in O corresponding to the <u>formatting</u> phase of a WPS,  that is the output of the text T on the final device,  such as a printer or a photo-typesetting machine.  For most WPS's, f is a function of T only and does not depend on the output device;  in the interesting system of Reid (3),  there are many functions $f_{\delta\tau}$ in O,  where $\sigma$ is the output device and $\tau$ is the type of the document (a letter,  a report, a chapter in a book, and so on).  So, we have different $f_{\delta\tau}(T)$ and the high level commands embodied in T act differently in accordance with the capabilities of the device $\delta$ (e.g. many character fonts, spacing capabilities, and so on) and the conventions relative to the type of the document. Actually, the data base contains a file of "templates" $\mathcal{J}_{\delta\tau}$, each containing the formatting rules for $\delta$ and $\tau$, so that $f_{\delta\tau}(T)=f^\circ(\mathcal{J}_{\delta\tau},T)$ and a single program $f^\circ$ can perform the various functions $f_{\delta\tau}$. Finally, $f^\circ$ (or the $f_{\delta\tau}$'s) can generate a set of working files $\{F_i\}$ (as a consequence of suitable commands in T) to be able to prepare automatically the general index, an author index, a subject index, and so on, whenever they are required.

From our point of view the formatting operation(s) is(are) not particularly interesting, since we are more concerned with the editing capabilities of WPS's. Here we must limit ourselves to a few examples, which, we hope, will be sufficiently meaningful. Let us begin by the following definition: a breakpoint in a screen S is any decomposition S=S'S" such that t(S'S")=t(S')t(S"). Breakpoints can be easily recognized from a syntactical point of view; we do not give a formal definition of S by a context-free grammar, but it can be easily understood that typical breakpoints are the beginning of a word or of a command. In particular, as a text is introduced in the computer memory, we can decide when the last breakpoint appears; it delimits the last word or the last command introduced. Let us suppose that a word has been added to the screen, so that the system has to perform the operation in O inserting the new word in the text T. The first example will discuss the actions required to execute the operation.

First of all, the characters added to the previous screen are analyzed to create the triple $(w,d,\sigma)$ which should be inserted in the text: the delimiter $\underline{d}$ is easily recognized; unless the word on the screen contains special characters, unexpected combinations of lower and uppercase letters (in which case $\sigma$ has to reflect the case), $\underline{w}$ is set to lower case letters and $\sigma$ is set to the proper value. Then $\underline{w}$ is searched for in the dictionary D; if a triple $(w,\sigma',i)$ is found such that $\sigma$ and $\sigma'$ satisfy the rules $R^\circ$, everything is all right and the procedure is over;

if σ and σ' do not satisfy R° an error procedure is
entered. When w is not found in D, the fact is signalled to
the user and a question is asked whether w is mispelled or
it is a new word to be introduced in the dictionary;   in
this latter case also the indicator i is required; for some
users it is set to a default value,  but for more skilled
users the system asks for it and,  anyhow,  adds the new
triple to D.

We remark that the insertion operation transforms a
consistent  state  (T,S,D)  in  another  consistent  state
(T',S',D')  and  it  is  this  very  fact  to  direct  the
formulation of the procedure performing the operation.  The
same objective is pursued for the other operations, such as
deleting or correcting some words or commands,  add an
existing file of text, move part of the text from some zone
to another zone, and so on.

For what concerns deletions and changes,  we can sketch
here  some  point  to  clarify  the  behaviour  of  these
operations.

When we wish to delete some part of the text, we have to
look for it on the screen S,  since in the text T words are
set apart one from another in the triples,  and punctuation
is hidden  in  the  delimiters.  However,  deletions must
reflect on the text T as well,  and in some cases also on
the dictionary.  In fact,  while stable words cannot be
erased from the dictionary, non-stable ones can be deleted,
if required by the user.  For example,  mispelled words (if
erroneously accepted at a first moment) have to be erased
from the dictionary, but if the user changes a word to some
synonim,  it can be maintained in the dictionary for future
use.

Modifications can be seen as deletions followed by new
insertions, and there is no new problem.

Note that if we wish to delete or modify a single,
complete word,  it may be easier to look for it in the text
T,  rather than on the screen S.  Although this is not the
usual case, we shall see that it is important in our system
derived from the model (see section 4).

## 4. A SYSTEM FROM THE MODEL

From our TSD model we have derived a particular WPS and now we wish to sketch the main features of this system.

For what concerns the commands, we have adopted a philosophy analogous to (3) and relative to a high level approach. Although interesting, however, commands are a secondary aspects of our WPS and we focused our attention on the internal structure of the three components T, S and D. Contrary to most systems in which T=S and our distinction appears to be a logical consideration rather than a practical one, in our WPS the text T assumes a special compact form, especially suitable for being stored on secondary memory and passed among different computers.

Let us begin by the screen S; it has no special form and represents the interface between the system and the user; the input and the modifying phases are accomplished by means of S. In order to save space, S does not correspond to the whole text introduced in the computer; although virtually the functions s and t are completely defined, in practice they have only partial arguments; this does not at all influence the system.

The text T is a sequence of three byte groups; every group may represent one of three components: a word, a command, a connector (to be defined in a moment). The three components of a word are coded in the following way: the word is symbolically represented into two bytes; the specifier occupies only two bits of the third byte and other five bits are dedicated to the delimiter. We use only 4 specifiers (as remarked in section 1) and less than 32 delimiters. Actually, the last bit of the third byte can be used as a flag: a 0 indicates a group corresponding to a word, a 1 denotes a command or a connector. The representation of a word is simply the address (to be discussed later) of the word in the dictionary D.

A command is identified by the flag 1 in the third byte, plus another flag 0 in another bit of the same byte. The remaining 6 bits of the byte denote the command; our system is not particularly complicated; so we have only about 40 commands, and their parameters are coded in the first two

bytes of the group. Because of our high level approach, we
do not use complex parameters.

Two flags set to 1 indicate a <u>connector</u>; connectors have
not been introduced in the model since they are related
only to implementation; the first and most important kind
of connector is used to insert text inside an existing
text. Instead of shifting some part of the old text, we
insert a connector, whose first two bytes point to the end
of the text. Here we insert the new text, and finally we
add a new connector pointing back to the continuation in
the old text.

Another use of connectors is to delete part of the text.
In fact, we change the first triple of the deleted text
into a pointer to the continuation, and set to zeros all
the other triples. A modification to the text is treated
accordingly; if the modified part contains less triples
than the original, we "delete" the extra triples;
otherwise, we write a continuation connector when no more
triples are available, and continue at the end of the text
as in the case of insertions.

When the text is recorded on secondary storage, only
words and commands are stored in their proper order, and
connectors are lost.

The dictionary D is realized by means of a set of tables
and binary trees. Stable words are recorded in alphabetical
order in tables, a table for any possible length of the
words. So we have a table for 1 character words, a table
for 2 characters words, and so on. Words longer than 15
characters are grouped in a single table. Fast access is
obtained by binary search and the words are compressed to
five bits for character. Non-stable words form the dynamic
part of D, so they are stored in binary trees (also
according to their length), which can be intermixed in
every way. Obviously, new words are added to the
appropriate tree. Words with the special specifier cannot
be compressed and they are maintained in a separate tree.

This structure allows us to maintain the dictionary D in
central memory; since we use 2 bytes for the address of a
word in T, we are limited to 64 kbytes for D. However, a
dictionary of 10,000 stable words with an average length of

8 characters (stored in 5 bytes after compression) occupies only 50,000 bytes. If more memory is necessary, we use the convention that addresses are relative to even numbered locations; hence, every item has to start at an even location and some space is lost (on the average, half byte for every word), but we can address up to 128 kbytes. Analogously, in T the connectors can refer only within 64 kbytes; however, if we address the group instead of the byte, the available address space is increased up to 192 kbytes.

Now let us sketch some points on the behaviour of our system. First of all, we remark that the screen S is easily obtained by the text T by means of the dictionary D; the function s simply scans the groups in T, converts the commands, and, for what concerns the words, can find directly their content using the address in the first two bytes of the group and fetching them from D. The function t is realized simply as the characters are input from the keyboard or from a file.

If we have to look for a word w in the text we should proceed in the following way. The screen contains only a small part of the whole text; on this part of the text we can perform any sort of searching, as we discussed in section 2. However, if we wish to search w in the whole text, we first look for w in the dictionary, determine its address A and then we perform a linear searching for A in the triples of the text. For a sequence of words we proceed analogously. Note that in the same way we can look for words "beginning by" some sequence "y" of characters, performing a parallel search with the addresses $A_1, A_2, \ldots, A_K$ of the words in the dictionary beginning by "y".

A more difficult problem is to look for a string "contained" in some word; this can be done only on that part of the text which is "translated" into the screen S. This however, is a minor limitation of our system and we can simply recommend the user not to try it.

The rather complex structure of the dictionary D is due not only to the problem of space saving, but also to the following fact. The main use of the dictionary is to detect possible errors, that is words not contained in it. There exist (see (2)) algorithms to try to correct automatically a mistaken word, looking for items which are "near" to the mispelled one. Here "near" means that a character was wrong, or two characters were swapped, or one character was missing from or added to the word. This limits searching to words with the same length $r$ or length $r\pm1$, and such a procedure is speeded up by our structuring of D. As an ending remark, we note that adding a new component to the elements in D, it is easy to maintain references to the synonims of the words, which is done by some WPS.

## 5. REFERENCES

1. Dodds, D.J. (1982). Reducing dictionary size by using a hashing technique. *Comm. ACM*, 25, 6, 368-369.

2. Peterson, J.L. (1980). Computer programs for detecting and correcting spelling errors. *Comm. ACM*, 23, 12, 676-687.

3. Reid, B.K. (1980). A high level approach to computer document formatting. *Conf. Rec. of the 7th Annual ACM Symp. on Princ. of Program. Lang.*, 24-31.

# High Level Interfaces

# A TOOL FOR FORM DEFINITION IN OFFICE INFORMATION SYSTEMS SPECIFICATION

F.Barbic, M.Carli, B.Pernici and G.Bracchi

*Dipartimento di Elettronica, Politecnico di
Milano, Piazza Leonardo da Vinci, 32
20133 Milano, Italy*

ABSTRACT

FDS is an interactive tool developed for supporting form
type specifications in office information systems. Forms definition takes separately into consideration logical aspects
and physical aspects. This subdivision simplifies the form
definition process through isolation of semantic characteristics from implementation details.

The interactive tool is subdivided into different environments, intended for the description of different logical and
physical aspects and for the specification of aids for the
end-user of the form.

FDS has been specifically designed to support the form-
definition step in the office information system design process: however, it provides a basis also for the subsequent
design steps, since it allows specification of views, of
logical constraints and of automatic filling in procedures.

## 1. INTRODUCTION

The recent years have seen a growing attention towards projects for developing systems for information management in
the office environment. In fact forms constitute a powerful
way of representing meaningful groups of data (such as documents) both as a communication tool for the end user and as
an internal data structure for office information systems,

NEW APPLICATIONS OF DATA BASES
ISBN 0-12-275550-2

since most operations on data that are executed in the office
may be seen as manipulations of forms (4).

These considerations have stimulated a considerable number of office research activities centered on form management (1,2,3). Forms are seen as the office element through
which most office functions are executed, such as data manipulation and retrieval, electronic mailing, data processing,
message handling, and so on. A number of advanced prototypes
for form management already exist, where forms are utilized
from different view points. Some of them, such as OFS (10)
and Officetalk-D (2), propose solutions for an integrated
office project involving all the different aspects of office
work, as text management, data communications, and information storage. These prototypes include office models based on
information flow that describe the office in terms of informative units moving through the different parts of the office. Hence, in these systems forms constitute the vehicle
through which office procedures are performed and information is transferred. A different approach is followed, on the
other hand, by systems like OMEGA (1) in facing form management: they provide sophisticated tools that support functions such as defining, filling in, storing and retrieving
from a database different types of forms on an office workstation.  Another well-known implementation is the OBE
system (11) based on an extension of the QBE database query
language, that constitutes a tool allowing to perform all
the main functions of form manipulation.

In any form management system a module dedicated to the
definition of the forms to be subsequently managed must be
present. However this module is developed in a incomplete
way in the above mentioned prototypes. In fact, such systems
point their major emphasis on the functions to be performed
on forms during office activities, while little attention
is devoted to the definition of forms, that are seen as
simple elements of the system containing information. However, many semantic aspects that are specific to various
types of forms can be captured during their definition. For
instance, integrity constraints on the value of their attri
butes and access rights to the various parts of the forms.

In this paper the Form Definition System (FDS), a tool

for the definition of form types based on a Form Definition
Language (FDL), will be illustrated.

FDL and FDS have been developed by the Politecnico di Milano Office Systems research unit, in cooperation with the
IBM Scientific Research Center of Rome, where FDS has been
implemented. FDS is intended to provide consistent definitions of all the different aspects of the forms.

Its main purpose is to support the definition phase of
structured forms, separating logical components from physical components of the form. Logical components consider the
form attributes with their semantic aspects and deal with
problems of data correctness and data protection. Physical
components consist instead of a serie of interfaces, named
templates, that present the form to the user on different
output devices.

FDL is a high level language used by FDS for supporting
the creation of form types. It allows explicit definition of
several aspects of forms which in other systems are usually
specified outside to form definition, although being strictly connected with the form type. The possibility of specifying form type characteristics, like constraints, users'
views and templates, directly at the form definition stage,
also simplifies subsequent definitions of the form manipulation operations, that have not to be concerned with the mana
gement of basic aspects that are directly embodied in the
form definition (3).

An innovative concept in FDL is the possibility of
defining different logical views of the same form. In the
same way as in database design the same data may be seen from
various viewpoints by users (8) also in office system design
it is useful that the same form may be seen in different
ways, through views, by users having different requirements,
and by different activities making available at each time
only the data to which the user is authorized to have access
and that are pertinent to the activity itself.

Section 2 of this paper will discuss the main aspects of
form definition activities in FDS. Section 3 will specifically illustrate the architecture of the FDS form definition
system, while Section 4 will introduce the main characteristics of the FDL language.

## 2. ASPECTS OF FORM DEFINITION IN FDL

The Form Definition Language FDL, in addition to the descrip
tion of all elements that are present in conventional forms,
such as fields and graphic elements, emphasizes the specification of semantic aspects of forms and provides utilities
to make form manipulation easier. Before describing the
fundamental elements on which the FDL approach is based, it
is useful to define some terms that will be used in the
paper.

A form type X is a set of attributes $X_0$, $X_1$,...$X_n$, where
$X_0$ is the identifying attribute. Each attribute is described
by its name and by a set of properties on its content.

A form view X' of a type X is a subset of attributes $X_0$,
$X_1$,... $X_n$; each view is associated with a group of users.

A form template X" of a view X' is the graphical represen
tation of a form view on a particular displaying device. For
each form view many form templates may exist, corresponding
to different device types, such as video displays, printers,
etc.

A form instance x of a type X is a set of values $x_0$, $x_1$,
...$x_n$ corresponding to the attributes $X_0$, $X_1$,... $X_n$. The
value of each attribute may be assigned by the user or automatically by the system.

The structure of form specification in FDL is summarized
in Fig.1.

In the logical component the characteristics of the form
attributes must be defined. FDL allows to define, for each
attribute of the form, a set of controls and of constraints
that will be activated during the form manipulation process.
In this way, it is possible to reduce both the filling in
errors and the work to be manually performed.

It is useful to further distinguish the static and the
dynamic components. In the static component the form name,
the attribute names and static properties and the view names
and attributes are defined. The dynamic component includes
instead the description of those aspects that are associated
with the execution of an operation on the form (data insert
ion, modification, etc.); in this component the following
information is described:

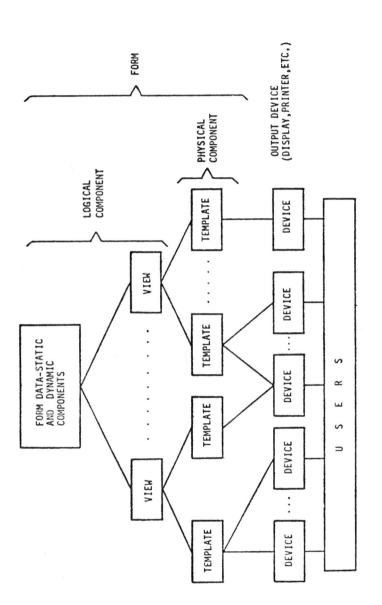

Fig. 1 - Form structure in FDL.

a) Data constraints that must be satisfied to ensure data in
tegrity. Constraints are enforced by functions operating
on the values of the associated attributes. When the value of an attribute is inserted, all corresponding constraints are checked.

b) Privacy rules, that ensure the protection of private data.
Using these rules it is possible to grant the access to
reserved attributes to a predefined class of users only,
and to restrict the possibility of attribute values modification.

c) Automatic filling in procedures, that allow to automatically derive some attribute values from other attribute
values. In fact, forms often contain attributes whose
values are dependent on other attribute values in the
form instance. This solution increases both filling in
speed and also correctness in generating form instances,
since values obtained through this type of automatic pro
cedures are consistent with those already present.

Two types of automatic filling in procedures are defined:
algorithmic procedures and retrieval procedures operating
on a relational database.

Algorithmic procedures produce certain attribute values
through the execution of an algorithm and using, as arguments, values of other attributes. The use of retrieval procedures involves instead the existence of a relational Data
Base used by the office information system. The aim of these
procedures is to interact with the external Data Base Management System to extract the desired data, basing the
request on some attribute values in the form.

Different views of the same form can be defined, since
users interested in different subsets of attributes of the
same form type may co-exist. Views provide several advantages: first of all, the user can manipulate only the data
under his power, so making the filling in process simpler
and faster; in fact, the user does not have to take care of
data that are not related with him. Moreover, communications
through the office are more efficient, since the quantity of
transmitted data is reduced. The use of logical views also
allows to treat data security problems, enforcing isolation
of information.

The <u>physical component</u>, that is represented by a set of
form templates, implements the graphic aspect in which form
logical views are seen on different communication devices,
such as video displays or printers. The purpose of templates
is to establish a graceful interface between form views and
users through a particular device. In this way it is possible to interact with objects similar to traditional forms.
Users can see the form in its final graphical aspect, and
insert each value in its correct position.

<u>Filling in aids</u> are finally provided, in addition to the
form creation facilities, in order to help the naif user in
system's use. It is important to define, for each form type,
templates containing example values of the attributes
constituting the form, explaining notes associated to certain attributes and including information for correct attrib
ute filling in, and diagnostic messages to be displayed in
case of error. Users may have access to these help facilities during the forms filling in process.

3. THE FDS ARCHITECTURE

In this section the structure of the form definition tool
FDS, that is based on the high level Form Definition Langua
ge (FDL), will be illustrated. FDL allows the user to work
at an abstraction level, without being concerned with
storage structures details. Choices involved in the definit
ion process are solved by means of appropriate menus; the
interactive orientation of the system and the presence of
menus ensure guidance of the user and strict control of the
correctness of his activities (9).

To obtain a good modularity, FDS is structured into
environments (see Fig. 2), that allow to face the definition
of different aspects in an uniform manner. Environments are
hierarchically structured. In each environment a single
aspect of the form type to be defined is specified.Language
commands are specified in terms of displayed questions and
user answers. The syntax used in the different environments
is homogeneous, so that it is possible to define different
aspects of a form using a common approach.

The form definition process starts with the specification

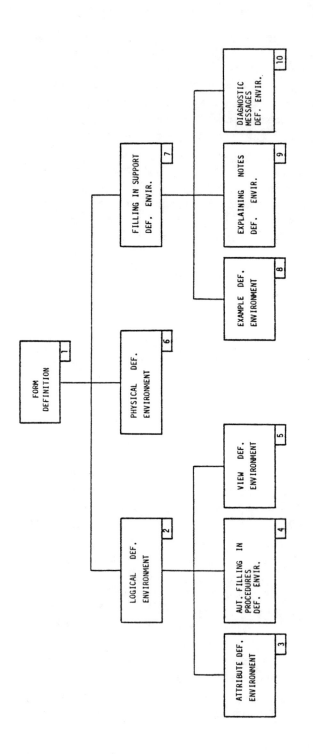

Fig. 2 - *FDS environments.*

of the form type name. It is necessary to build a data
structure that is dynamically enriched during all the definition activities that are carried out; this data structure
is obtained visiting in advanced order the definition schema
(ascending numeration in Fig. 2). This solution involves a
certain rigidity in the definition process, but allows a
careful control on form specification and imposes a reasonable sequence of activities from a conceptual point of view.
The FDS interactivity allows immediate validity controls on
the form components under specification. Two types of validity controls exist: the correctness of single instructions
(attribute definitions, view definitions, etc.) is tested
first, and at the end of the definition process a series of
controls are then carried out to verify the consistency of
the entire data structure.

Fig. 2 shows the different FDS environments.

In the logical definition environment the logical form
component is described considering static and dynamic
aspects. This environment is partitioned into three sections:
a) Attribute definition environment
b) Automatic filling in procedure definition environment
c) Logical view definition environment

In the physical definition environment templates are described for each logical view and for each output device.

The filling in support definition environment finally
contains information that provide explanations useful for a
correct form filling in.

In the next section, for each environment its most impor
tant features will be described, and the general syntax of
FDL will be presented.


4. THE FDL LANGUAGE SPECIFICATIONS

In this section the basic constructs of FDL will be described, outlining their semantics and motivating the
language design choices. Some examples will also be provided
to illustrate the most significant features of the language.
Keywords will be underlined on the syntax specifications,
while brackets will indicate elements that may be present a
specified number of times.

## 4.1. The Logical Definition Environment

*The attribute definition environment.* Attribute definitions
consist of the specification of static and dynamic aspects
of attributes. Static aspects are the same for all types of
attributes: name, type and format. Through dynamic information, that is instead different for each attribute type, it
is possible to represent the features of all types of
attributes that are present on forms and to define the operations that may be executed on them: for instance, not all
attributes may be updated, once a value is provided.

Most of the attributes present in conventional paper
forms can be completely described by their name, format and
if necessary, by constraints on their values. However, some
attributes may require a more complex definition due either
to their important meaning in the form (like, for instance,
signatures) or to their internal structure. Particularly
relevant are the fields representing authorizations, because
they give official validity to a form instance. Only certain
users can have a write access to them, and it is then
necessary to provide some access control to forbid unauthor-
ized accesses.

Sometimes some parts of a form may have a variable
structure. A variable structure is a set of attributes
partitioned into subsets, only one of which must be filled
in, depending on an attribute value. A particular attribute,
named "root" of the variable structure, determines through
its value which subset of attributes must be filled in for
completing the form instance. For example, only if the
attribute MARRIED contains the value YES it is necessary to
fill in the attributes concerning the wife/husband.

A particular type of attributes are those containing free
text parts; these attributes are very different from ordina
ry attributes, since their size cannot be established at
the form definition time. Other types of attributes having
a particular structure are those to which more than one
value may be associated. Such attributes are often grouped
together and represented on forms as tables. For instance,
in an order form, since many items may be ordered, the attributes ITEM DESCRIPTION, PRICE, etc. constitute a group of

these attributes (repeating group). For completeness, it is
necessary to point out that non conventional elements such
as pictures, diagrams, etc. are often present in forms. In
this paper they will not be considered, since their management involves sophisticated user interfaces and recording
tools.

Each form attribute is defined using the following general syntax:

ATTRIBUTE          : < attribute name >
TYPE               : < type >
{ SUBTYPE          : < subtype > $\}_0^1$
  FORMAT           : < format description > $\}_0^1$
MODALITY           : < modality description >
{ SPECIAL CLAUSE   : < clause description > $\}_0^n$

The structure of the attribute definition depends on the
attribute type specification. The chosen type actually
involves the presence of some of the subsequent specifications and determines the format of the "special clause".
According to the previous discussions, four types of attributes exist in FDL: STANDARD, PROTECT, ROOT, TEXT. Each of
them can also be part of a REPEATING GROUP.

STANDARD attributes refer to usual fields of a form for
which it is sufficient to describe name, format and possibly
one or more constraints (for instance, an employee salary).

PROTECT attributes are used to handle authorizations and
all attributes needing particular access controls.

ROOT attributes control variable structure parts of a
form. Their value determines the logical structure of the
form instance.

TEXT attributes allow to consider free text parts, impos
ing no constraint on their content and their format.

REPEATING GROUPS are useful because they allow to treat
groups of multivalued attributes, so that a unique name
issued to refer to an entire matrix of values.

The presence of a subtype is subordinated to the attribute type; the subtype is used for example to distinguish
the numeric or alphabetic nature of an attribute.

The format description is optional and is used to
describe the maximum length of attribute values. For TEXT
attributes the maximum size of text is dependent on the

available space on the templates.

Modality description allows to control the insertion and
update operations that can be performed on the attributes.
This ensures also that certain attributes are inserted in a
mandatory way. In fact, forms instances may often be considered complete only if a set of significant attributes has
been filled in. In addition, since many users may manipulate
the same form instance, it is sometimes useful to prevent a
user from updating certain attribute values that were
previously filled in by another user.

The attribute types refer to very different concepts; the
fundamental features of each attribute type are expressed
through the particular structure of the special clause. For
STANDARD attributes some constraints may be imposed on their
possible values. Constraints, that are functions operating
on the attribute values, allow to check data validity
during the updating of a value. It is so possible to verify
the correctness of a single attribute and the consistency
of an attribute value with respect to other previously
inserted values.

In the definition of a PROTECT attribute it is necessary
to specify the list of users that are allowed to manipulate
the attribute. In the definition of ROOT attributes it is
instead requested to list, for each permissible value of
the attribute, the subset of attributes that must be filled
in. TEXT attributes, being free from any control on their
content, do not need the specification of any special clause. The definition of the clause for a REPEATING GROUP
consists in listing the set of attributes that constitute
the group and in specifying those attributes that identify
an occurrence of the group.

Some simple examples of attribute definition are the
following:

a) ATTRIBUTE   : PRICE
   TYPE        : STANDARD
   SUBTYPE     : CHAR
   FORMAT      : LENGTH x=5
   MODALITY    : MANDATORY, UPDATABLE
   CONSTRAINT  : RANGE (100, 10.000)

b)  ATTRIBUTE     : MEANS-OF-TRANSPORT
    TYPE          : ROOT
    MODALITY      : MANDATORY, NOT UPDATABLE
    CASE
      MEANS-OF-TRANSPORT = PERSONAL-CAR : COVERED-MILES,
                                          PETROL-COST
      MEANS-OF-TRANSPORT = PUBLIC SERVICE:TYPE-OF-TRANSPORT
      END                                 TICKET-COST

*Defining automatic filling in procedures.* When the attributes specification phase is completed, automatic filling
in procedures, if applicable, are specified. Through these
procedures it is possible to obtain some attribute values
using functions operating on other attribute values. For
instance, it is convenient to automatically fill in the
"total" attribute of some "cost-items" applying a sum algorithm, or else the personal data of an employee can be
derived from his code with the system performing an automatic retrieval function from a Data Base. Each procedure is
triggered when all its arguments have an assigned value. The
syntax for automatic filling in procedures specification is
the following:

PROCEDURE    : < procedure name >
FUNCTION     : < function name >
ARGUMENTS    : < argument list >
RESULT       : < result description >

In defining a procedure it is necessary to specify the
name of the function corresponding to the desired procedure;
it is possible to use pre-specified functions, or else to
define them according to the particular needs, writing
specific procedures. The arguments of the selected function
may be fixed parameters, or attribute names whose value will
be considered. Examples of these procedures are the following:

        PROCEDURE    : SUM
        FUNCTION     : SUM
        ARGUMENTS    : COST 1, COST 2
        RESULT       : TOTAL-COST

        PROCEDURE    : GET
        FUNCTION     : GET

ARGUMENTS ___        : PERSONAL-DATA, EMPLOYEE $H$
RESULT ___           : SALARY, SKILLS

GET is the Data Base retrieval function; PERSONAL-DATA
refers to the DB relation that has to be searched; EMPLOYEE
$H$ , key of the relation, identifies a tuple.

The value of SALARY and SKILLS are then extracted from
the correct tuple and are inserted in the form when the GET
function is executed.

*The view definition environment.* Views are defined using the
following syntax:

VIEW ___             : < view name >
IDENTIFIERS ___      : < identifier list>
{ ATTRIBUTE      : < attribute name >;
{ MODALITY       : < modality description> $\}_0^1\}_1^n$

A view definition begins with the specification of its
name and of the identifiers list (i.e. the list of users
that are associated to the logical view). The set of attributes constituting the view is then listed. For each attribute, it is possible to indicate a modality different from
the one declared in the attribute definition, provided that
it is consistent with the previous definitions. This enables
expression of particular controls on operations performed
on the form through the view. For instance, an attribute,
that has been declared as updatable in its definition, may
be made non-updatable in a particular view.

After defining every view of the form, it is necessary to
describe the logical filling in sequence that exists among
the views. In fact, a form instance is always originated
with a specified view, named beginning view. When the beginning view has been completely filled in, the immediately
following views can be used, and so on iteratively. The view
logical sequence is represented using the following syntax:

BEGINNIGN VIEW       : <  beginning view name >
{ CURRENT VIEW     : <  view name >;
  GENERATED VIEWS: <  view list >$\}_0^n$

After specifying the name of the beginning view, for each
view the list of subsequent views is given. An example of
view definition is shown in Fig. 3, in which two views on

```
{FORM DEFINITION FORM 'EXAMPLE'}
                    .
                    .
                    .
    ATTRIBUTE : TYPE-OF-REQUEST
    TYPE      : STANDARD
    SUBTYPE   : CHAR
    FORMAT    : LENGTH X = 6
    MODALITY  : MANDATORY, NOT UPDATABLE
    CONSTRAINT: ENUM (FEES, REFUND, LOAN)

    ATTRIBUTE : NOTE
    TYPE      : TEXT
    MODALITY  : NOT MANDATORY, UPDATABLE
                    .
                    .
                    .
{VIEW DEFINITION FROM FORM 'EXAMPLE'}
    VIEW       : REQUEST
    IDENTIFIERS : DEPARTMENT-A , DEPARTMENT-B
    ATTRIBUTE : NAME
    ATTRIBUTE : ADDRESS
    ATTRIBUTE : TYPE-OF-REQUEST
    ATTRIBUTE : NOTE
    ATTRIBUTE : DATE 1

    VIEW       : AUTHORIZATION
    IDENTIFIERS : SMITH
    ATTRIBUTE : NAME ; MODALITY : READ-ONLY
    ATTRIBUTE : ADDRESS ; MODALITY : READ-ONLY
    ATTRIBUTE : TYPE-OF-REQUEST ; MODALITY : READ-ONLY
    ATTRIBUTE : NOTE ; MODALITY : READ-ONLY
    ATTRIBUTE : DATE 1; MODALITY : READ-ONLY
    ATTRIBUTE : SIGNATURE
    ATTRIBUTE : DATE 2

    BEGINNING VIEW : REQUEST
    CURRENT VIEW : REQUEST ; GENERATED VIEWS : AUTHORIZATION

{TEMPLATE OF VIEWS FOR FORM 'EXAMPLE'}
```

```
REQUEST                          AUTHORIZATION

NAME ......................      NAME............. ADDRESS....................
ADDRESS...................       TYPE OF REQUEST............... DATE...........
TYPE OF REQUEST ...........      NOTE...........................................
NOTE .....................       SIGNATURE         DATE OF AUTHORIZATION
DATE .....................       .............     ...........................
```

Fig. 3 - *Examples of view definition.*

same form are defined. Two corresponding templates are also
represented, in order to provide a graphical idea of this
definition. Referring to the example, all employees of
departments A and B may have access to the REQUEST view,whi-
le only Mr. SMITH can have access to the AUTHORIZATION
view; the AUTHORIZATION view logically follows the REQUEST
one. The attribute values inserted in the REQUEST view
cannot then be manipulated in the AUTHORIZATION view.

## 4.2. *The Physical Definition Environment*

In the physical definition environment templates are
specified. A template is a graphic element corresponding to
a logical view of a form, having a  fixed format, and where
values of attributes can be inserted only in particular
input areas. A template is defined, for each view and for
each communication device, using the following syntax:

>   TEMPLATE   : < template name >
>   VIEW       : < view name >
>   DEVICE     : < device type >

The FDL interpreter interfaces with the graphic editor
ZEDG (7), that allows creation of graphic elements such as
lines and rectangles, and insertion of headings and word-
ings. The template drawing yields a graceful aspect of the
view. In this way the user may interact through an easy to
understand representation with the logical structure of
the view. An accurate allocation of graphic elements and a
correct choice of headings can make the template more readable.

In Fig. 3 two templates were shown in their final aspect.

## 4.3. *Specifying Support Functions*

In addition to the logical and physical components that
constitute the form, some filling in supports can be
defined. FDL statements are provided to specify examples of
filled in templates, that are produced by filling in empty
templates of the specified type with typical example values.
It is also possible to create explaining notes that contain
information for correct filling in: each of them is associa

ted with attributes showing some filling in difficulties. Finally, diagnostic messages may be specified; they are phrases displayed to the user when a filling in error occurs. The user can have access to external support functions at any stage of the filling in process in order to obtain the desired explanations.

## 5. CONCLUSIONS AND RECOMMENDATIONS

FDS constitutes a tool for defining the different aspects that are present in a form. The FDL high level form definition language allows a consistent translation of conventional paper forms to an electronic system, and it makes possible a control of the data information content, to ensure a good correctness level of the forms.

The interpreter of FDL is implemented on a VM/370 System under VM/SP Operating System, and is written in the REX language (5). Templates and external supports definition is obtained using the ZED and ZEDG editors (6,7).

FDS represents only a starting, although crucial, point of an integrated form management system: many other tools , such as a form manipulation language and an electronic mail system, will utilize the FDS form definition system as a foundation for performing office functions.

## ACKNOWLEDGEMENTS

The authors are grateful to Drs. L. Lippi, G. Pala and G. Sommi of the IBM Scientific Center of Rome for the support received in defining the FDL language and in implementing the corresponding functions.

## REFERENCES

1.  Attardi G. and Simi M. (1981). Consistency and completeness of OMEGA, a logic for knowledge representation. *In* "Proc. 7th International Joint Conference on Artificial Intelligence". Vancouver.
2.  Ellis C.A. and Bernal M. (1982). OFFICETALK-D: An experimental office information system. *In* "Proc.SIGOA

Conf. on Office Information Systems". Philadelphia.

3.  Ferrans J.C. (1982). SEDL - A language for specifying integrity constraints on office form. *In*"Proc. SIGOA Conf. on Office Information Systems". Philadelphia.

4.  Gehani N.H. (1982). The potential of forms in office automation. *IEEE Transactions on Communications*, Vol. COM-30 N. 1.

5.  (1981). IBM Tutorial. "REX: Reformed Executor".

6.  (1981). IBM Tutorial. "ZED: Editor".

7.  (1981). IBM Tutorial. "ZEDG: Graphic Editor".

8.  Pelagatti G., Paolini P., and Bracchi G. (1978). Mapping external views to a common data model, *Information Systems*, Vol. 3, N. 2.

9.  Rohlfs S. (1980). Linguistic considerations for user interface design. *In* "Integrated Office Systems", Naffah (ed.).

10. Tsichritzis D.C. (1980). OFS: an integrated form management system. *In* "Proc. VLDB 80". Montreal.

11. Zloof M.M. (1982). Office-by-Example: A business language that unifies data and work processing and electronic mail, *IBM Systems Journal*, Vol. 21, N. 3.

A NATURAL LANGUAGE FRONT END TO DATABASES
WITH EVALUATIVE FEEDBACK

B. K. Boguraev and K. Sparck Jones

*Computer Laboratory, University of Cambridge,
Corn Exchange Street, Cambridge CB2 3QG, England*

## ABSTRACT

We describe a natural language front end to databases. The system
has been designed to promote portability and to facilitate
interactive natural language feedback with the user. The operation
of the system is illustrated by examples.

## 1. INTRODUCTION

It has been argued that the utility of natural language front
ends to databases is self-evident, in the sense that such front
ends will increase the accessibility of structured data to
infrequent (and possibly naive) users, who otherwise would be
unwilling (or unable) to learn specialised languages and protocols
for access to the information they desire. The convenience of,
and specifically the freedom of expression allowed by, natural
language, has been the rationale for the active research in the
last few years in the design and construction of natural
language interfaces to database systems ((5), (7), (8), (16)).

There are nevertheless those who are doubtful about the
real utility of such interfaces. For example Shneiderman (12)
comes to the conclusion that natural language possesses certain
undesirable properties as a medium for communication with
structured formal objects, and argues that a formal language is
much better suited to such a purpose. Furthermore, there are
objections to the extensive buffering between the user's
(possibly erroneous) view of the domain world and the
administrative structure of the database which natural
language interfaces imply: it has been argued that the layers of
question translation and interpretation software may introduce
incorrect interpretations of the input which will retrieve wrong
information from the database (wrong in the sense that it is not
<u>exactly</u> what the user wanted, but likely, as it is offered as an

answer without any qualification, not to be perceived as wrong).

To make a better, and indeed the real, case for natural language interfaces to databases, it is necessary to look at such front ends not as 'passive' programs, limited to operational responses to individual commands, but as cooperative agents engaged in active dialogue with the user. Natural language front ends to databases will become really useful only after they have won the user's confidence by displaying powerful capabilities for justifying and allowing the user to monitor their operations, including allowing the user to validate the answers to questions, which may have been derived not simply by direct retrieval of information stored explicitly in the database, but indirectly, as the result of a deductive chain of reasoning constructed by applying a set of common-sense or domain-applicable inference rules to intermediate data extracted from the database. Clearly the capabilities of such interfaces must extend well beyond the straightforward and limited interpretation of an input question sufficient to generate a formal query for the back-end database management system (DBMS), with the system's responses confined to those of the database system itself, or to crude error messages indicating that the input question could not be interpreted.

The remainder of this paper decribes a system for natural language access to structured databases being developed in Cambridge. The system is characterised by modular design; an extensive use of general, as opposed to domain-specific, semantics; and the exploitation of natural language not only for system use but for system construction; and is aimed at the use of natural language not only for questioning but for feedback. The short-term development objective of the work has been a transportable system, but the system has been designed with the long-term objective of extension to include cooperative capabilities. Our view is that modularity is an important design principle not only because it promotes transportability, but also because it allows for the incremental development of a cooperative front end.

Section 2 discusses the constraints imposed on the design of a natural language interface to databases by the requirement for transportability, and in the light of these presents an overview of the Cambridge system architecture. The following three sections give a detailed account of the system in its current state. Sections 3 and 4 describe the system's two main components, for analysis and translation. Section 5 concentrates on the cooperative, 'evaluative feedback', capabilities of the interface, i.e. the system's means of showing the user, in natural language, for his evaluation, its interpretations of the input question. The final section, 6, reports on the current status of the system testing in relation to back-end databases, indicates the planned future directions of the work, and summarises the main points of comparison between the Cambridge and other database front end systems. Most of the general aims of our work, for example transportability, are common to natural language interface projects. However our exploitation of general semantics is individual, and the details of the Cambridge system differ from those of others.

## 2. SYSTEM OVERVIEW

In order to maintain ease of transportability of a natural language front end to databases across different domains, database structures and DBMS query languages, it is essential to approach its design with several crucial issues in mind.

First, the natural language analyser must utilise a general syntactic grammar of English; in addition, semantic processing of the input must be motivated as far as possible by the general semantics of ordinary language, and should not depend entirely on the specifics of the database domain. Second, in order to reconcile the user's view of the information stored in the database with the actual administrative structure of the formatted data within the framework of a transportable system, which implies a well-defined gateway to the DBMS proper, a DBMS-independent abstraction of the input question is required; this then has to be translated against the database schema to derive the actual DBMS search query. Finally, as the front end is being moved to different domain and/or DBMS environments, the questions of acquiring a new lexicon, a new schema, and (possibly) a new low-level query language, have to be solved.

Our design tackles these problems by carefully identifying the different types of knowledge required in the process of interpreting a natural language question to derive a search query, separating domain-independent from domain-dependent knowledge, and also domain knowledge from database administrative knowledge, in all stages of processing. Transportability is further enhanced by keeping the central, linking, domain-specific knowledge in declarative form.

In order to achieve this, as well as to provide a good platform for that domain-dependent processing of the input which is necessary, initial linguistic processing is carried out by a powerful non-domain-dependent semantic analyser: this delivers rich, explicit and normalised semantically-based meaning representations for questions which are more convenient inputs to the database task-, domain- and implementation-oriented operations required to construct actual search specifications than the raw questions texts. These task-specific operations are then essentially devoted to interpreting a high-level formal query against three declarative knowledge bases: information about the domain; information about the administrative structure of the database; and information about the syntax and semantics of the target low-level search query language (3).

Moreover, with the powerful general linguistic knowledge and semantic apparatus underlying the operations of the front end at our disposal, it is easy to introduce sophisticated, focused evaluative feedback to the user at successive checkpoints in the input question processing: thus in order to confirm thre system's 'understanding', or at any rate interpretation, of the input, a natural language generator offers paraphrases derived by converting the meaning representation embodying the results of lexical and structural disambiguation of the input back into English; in addition, at a much later stage in the processing, the specific characteristics of the data which will be sought from the database as an answer to the user's question can be described in natural language by a powerful and general query reformulator which is not applied to, and does not require, a user-supplied schedule of equivalences between data language expressions and terms and English phrases and words.

Thus the front end processing is essentially in two stages: analysis of the English question, followed by translation of the resulting representation into target query language for searching. The analysis component is further broken down into analyser and extractor modules; these use linguistic and logico-linguistic knowledge respectively to construct a meaning represesentation of the input question and to extract from it a formal query in logical form, the question's logic representation. Most of the question interpretation work in this first stage of processing is done by the analyser, so at present checking feedback to the user is only provided for after analysis, and not after extraction. Thus the language generator works from the initial unambiguous meaning representation and offers paraphrases of the input back to the user.

In the second stage of processing, translation, the translator module interprets the semantic content of the logic representation with reference to the segment or variant of the real world modelled by the database: it essentially substitutes high-level data language expressions within the logic representation framework. Its output query representation is then passed over to the convertor to obtain first a generalised algebra expression, and then to derive from this the target search representation, which may be regarded as a low-level data (or query) language expression, and which is appropriate to the implementation DBMS. This last can be re-interpreted in English for final validation by the search query reformulator, before being presented to the DBMS for execution.

The motivation for the overall front end design, and justification for the design choices made for each component, are discussed elsewhere (3). Sections 3 and 4 below therefore simply describe the system, illustrating its various operations through the processing of the input question "Green parts are supplied by which status 30 suppliers?", and in particular through the sequence of question representations output by the successive interpretation steps. The illustrative question and other examples are treated as relating to Date's Suppliers and Parts relational database which has three relations with the following structure: Supplier(Sno, Sname, Status, Scity), Part(Pno, Pname, Colour, Weight, Pcity), and Shipments(Sno, Pno, Qty) (cf. (6), p.79).

## 3. THE ANALYSIS COMPONENT

### 3.1 The analyser
The analyser has been very fully described elsewhere (1), (2), with particular emphasis on its characteristics and capacities as a general-purpose natural language processor. The account which follows therefore simply summarises its main features, and focuses on the properties of the text meaning representation output by the processor, which are critical for the design and performance of the Cambridge database front end.

The analyser combines conventional syntactic analysis for question constituents with Wilks'-derived semantics (17) for the evaluation of intermediate results and their incorporation into larger semantic constructs. Thus the semantic procedures make use of lexical entries defining word senses by semantic primitive formulae, and of a range of text patterns referring to preferred combinations of primitive descriptions. The meaning representation output by the analyser is a dependency tree with case-labelled components grouped round verb elements. Lexically-derived items are characterised by semantic category primitives, and the case labels which define semantic relation primitives express constituents' functions in the overall textual unit. The form of representation achieves considerable expressive power while maintaining structural simplicity. The function of the analyser is to select the appropriate sense of input words, given that natural language words have many meanings, and to determine the semantic structure of the input sentence, given that word strings in natural language may typically be syntactically structured in many alternative ways: for example, the analyser has to decide, on semantic grounds, what word in the sentence a prepositional phrase is attached to, given that syntax may allow alternative points of attachment.

The underlying philosophy of the analyser - a passive parsing strategy based on semantic pattern matching - together with its powerful and flexible semantic apparatus for representing linguistic and linguistically-conventionalised real-world knowledge offer distinct advantages in the context of accessing databases. The semantic apparatus of category and case primitives is a rich one, providing a large amount of information about the meanings of words and texts (though it is not claimed that this apparatus explicitly captures, in its full refinement, all the specific meaning of the input: for this traces of source lexical items are needed as well). The apparatus thus offers a large number of leads, or 'hooks', for the subsequent interpretation processes. 'Traps for the unexpected' in the input are easy to implement, because the later translation procedures operate not on unrestricted and variegated natural language inputs, where unexpected trees are difficult to distinguish from expected woods, but on well-defined and rigidly structured formal objects. Furthermore, as will be discussed more fully later, the semantic apparatus can be used to characterise both the terms and expressions of the front end's input natural language and the terms and expressions of its output data language, thus making it possible to reconcile the user's view of the world with the databases's domain model and its associated administrative structure. Finally, because the analyser is independent of the database, no changes should be required in the lexicon as the application moves from one domain or database to another, only expansion to allow for the semantic definitions of new words (or word-senses) relevant to the new application.

```
(clause (type dcl) (tns present) (aspect (passive))
   (v (supply1
      ((*org subj)
       ((*inan obje)
        ((*org recipient)
         (((((@recipient subj) have) cause) goal) give))))
   (@@agent
      ((trace (clause v agent))
       (clause
          (v (be2 ((*ent subj) (((own state) obje) be))
             (@@agent
                (n (supplier1 (((*inan obje) give) (subj man))
                   (@@number many)
                   (@@defn (query (dummy)))) ))
             (@@state
                (st (n (status1 ((man poss) sign)))
                   (val (!30 (count sign)))) ))) )))
   (@@object
      ((trace (clause v agent))
       (clause
          (v (be2 ((ent subj) (((own state) obje) be))
             (@@agent
                (n (part1
                   ((*inan poss) ((work goal) (subj thing)))
                   (@@number many))))
             (@@state
                (st (n (colour NIL))
                   (val
                      (green1
                         ((*inan poss)
                          (((man subj) (see sense))
                           (obje kind)))) ))) ))) )) ))
```

The meaning representation for the example question "Green parts are supplied by which status 30 suppliers?" is illustrated above. In the figure, case labels are marked by @@, and word senses appear as numbered words, e.g. 'part1', with their characterising semantic formulae following (these have a complex syntax, with their governing primitive at the right). Thus, for example, 'supplier1', characterisied by the head primitive **man**, is an agent who is in state 'status1' (characterised by **sign**, and with value 30), and is also the agent of the higher-level propositional structure focussed on 'supply1', with object 'part1' (itself further characterised).

### 3.2 The extractor

The extractor begins the work of task-oriented abstraction of the user's input by manipulating the analyser's meaning representation to emphasise the input's function as a question. Thus the extractor processes the meaning representation to obtain a logic representation from which the high-level query representation can in turn be derived. Since this query representation is constructed from simple propositions (atomic formulae), the extractor seeks to identify these in the dependency structure. It turns out that this can be done in a straightforward way. The extractor simply pulls out verbs and their case role fillers, to form 'triples'. These are of two types, [$Obj $Link $Obj] and [$Obj $Poss $Prop], appropriate to such inputs as "suppliers supply parts" and "parts are red" respectively. The extracted triples form a tree which is subsequently reorganised and amplified to take account of quantifier information conveyed by items like determiners, and to raise the queried element to top propositional level. The result is a tree of predicate expressions with appropriately scoped quantifiers and quantified variables. The general form of this logic representation is that of Woods' LUNAR system (18), with variables ranging over classes and possibly restricted by further predications. However this representation, unlike Woods', is still only a skeleton as far as the database application is concerned: the detailed semantic information associated with the constituents of the predicate expression remains uninterpreted and is passed on for the next component to translate into domain concepts.

After the first domain- and database-independent analysis phase of question processing therefore, the example question "Green parts are supplied by which status 30 suppliers?" will be transformed into the logic representation skeleton

```
(For Every $Var1 / supplier1
   : (AND (status1 $Var1 30)
              (For Some $Var2 / part1 : (colour1 $Var2 green1)
                  - (supply1 $Var1 $Var2))
   - (Display $Var1)),
```

where the lexically derived items indicating the ranges of the quantified variables ('supplier1', 'part1'), the relationships between the variables ('supply1') and the predicates and predicate values ('colour1', 'green1') in fact carry along with them their complete semantic formulae and case labels. These are omitted here, and in the rest of the paper, to save space, but their presence in the intermediate representations must be emphasised since it is this information which provides the essential leverage in the translation to the data language forms of the input.

## 4. THE TRANSLATION COMPONENT

### 4.1 The translator
In the process of transforming the semantic content of the user's question into a low-level search representation geared to the administrative structure of the target database, it is necessary to reconcile the user's view of the world with the domain model. Before even attempting to construct, say, a relational algebra expression to be interpreted by the back-end DBMS, we must try to interpret the semantic content of the logic representation with reference to the segment or variant of the real world modelled by the database.

An obvious possibility here is to proceed directly from the variables and predications of the logic representation to their database counterparts. For example,

(supply1 (**give**) $Var1/supplier1 (**man**) $Var2/part1 (**thing**))

can be mapped directly onto a relation <u>Shipments</u> in the Suppliers and Parts database. The mapping could be established by reference to the lexicon and to a schedule of equivalences between logical and database structures.

This approach suffers, however, from severe problems: the most important is that end users do not necessarily constrain their natural language to a highly limited vocabulary or give categorial or relational concepts a particular form of expression. Even in the simple context of the Suppliers and Parts database, it is possible to refer to "firms", "goods", "buyers", "sellers", "provisions", "customers", etc., and it is possible to use, for example, both the noun "supplier" and the verb "supply" for the same underlying concept. In fact, it was precisely in order to bring variants under a common denominator that semantic grammars of the kind illustrated in (16) were employed, but these in turn are likely to lack extensibility, and hence flexibility. We, in contrast, have a more powerful, because more flexible, semantic apparatus at our disposal, capable of drawing out the similarities between "firms", "sellers", and "suppliers", as opposed to taking them as read. Thus a general semantic pattern which will match the dictionary definitions of all of these words is (((•ent obje) give) (subj •org)). Furthermore, if instead of attempting to define any sort of direct mapping between the natural language terms and expressions of the user and corresponding domain terms and expressions, we concentrate on finding the common links between them, we can see that even though the domain and, in turn, database terms and expressions may not mean exactly the same as their natural language relatives or sources, we should be able to detect overlaps in their semantic characterisations. It is unlikely that the same or similar words will be used in both natural and data languages if their meanings have nothing in common, even if they are not identical, so characterising each using the same repertoire of semantic primitives should serve to establish the links between the two. Thus, for example, one sense of the natural language word "location" will have the formula (this (where spread)) and the data language word "&city" referring to the domain object &city will have the formula (((man folk) wrap) (where spread)), which can be connected by the common constituent (where spread). (As noted in section 2, the data language we are using here is a high-level one distinct from any lower-level data (or query) language pertaining to the DBMS and explicitly referring to the database administrative structure.)

One distinctive feature of our front end design, the use of general semantics for initial question interpretation, is thus connected with another: the more stringent requirements imposed on natural language to data language translation by the initial unconstrained question interpretation can be met by exploiting the resources for language meaning representation initially utilised for the natural language question interpretation. We define the domain world modelled by the database using the same semantic apparatus as the one used by the natural language front end processor, and invoke a flexible and sophisticated semantic pattern matcher to establish the connection between the semantic content of the user question (which is carried over in the logic representation) and related concepts in the domain world. Taking the next step from a domain world concept or relationship between domain world objects to their direct model in the administrative structure of the database is then relatively easy.

Since the domain world is essentially a closed world restricted in sets if not in their members, it is possible to describe it in the data language in terms of a limited set of concepts and relationships: we have possible properties of objects and potential relationships between them. We can talk about &suppliers and &parts and the important relationship between them, namely that &suppliers &supply &parts. We can also specify that &suppliers &live in &cities, &parts can be

&numbered, and so on.

We can thus utilise, either explicitly or implicitly, a description of the domain world which could be represented by dependency structures like those used for natural language. The important point about these structures is the way they express the semantic content of whole statements about the domain, rather than the way they label individual domain-referring terms as, e.g. "&supplier" or "&part". It is then easy to see how the logic representation for the question "What are the numbers of the status 30 suppliers?", namely

> (For Every $Var1/supplier1 : (status1 $Var1 30)
>  - (Display (number1 $Var1))),

can be unpacked by semantic pattern matching routines to establish the connection between "supplier1" and "&supplier", "number1" and "&number", and so on. In the same way the logic representations for "From where does Blake operate?" and "Where are screws found?" can be analysed for semantic content which will establish that "Blake" is a &supplier, "operate" in the context of the database domain means &supply, and "where" is a query marker acting for &city from which the &supplier Blake &supplies (as opposed to street corner, bucket shop, or crafts market); similarly, "screw" is an instance of &part and the only locational information associated with &parts in the database in question is the &city where they are stored. All this becomes clear simply by matching the underlying semantic primitive definitions of the natural language and domain world words, in their propositional contexts.

The translator is also the module where domain reference is brought in to complete the interpretation of the input question where this cannot be fully interpreted by the analyser alone. The semantic pattern-matching potential of the translation module can be exploited to determine the nature of the unresolved domain-specific predications (both 'dummy' relationships and those implicit in compound nominals), and vacuously defined objects ('query' variables). Thus the fragment of logical form for "... London suppliers of parts ...", namely

> (For <quant> $Var1/supplier1
>  : (AND
>         (For <quant> $Var2/part1 - (dummy $Var1 $Var2))
>         (For <quant> $Var3/London  - (dummy $Var1 $Var3)))
>  - ........ ),

is broken down into the corresponding domain predications

> (&supply $Var1(&supplier) $Var2(&part))

and

> (&live $Var1(&supplier) $Var3(&city)),

while translating the logic representation for the example

question "Green parts are supplied by which status 30 suppliers?" gives the query representation

(For Every $Var1 / &supplier
  : (AND (&status $Var1 30)
       (For Some $Var2 / &part : (&colour $Var2 green)
          - (&supply $Var1 $Var2))
     - (Display $Var1)),

Apart from the fact that semantic pattern matching seems to cope quite successfully with unexpected inputs ('unexpected' in the sense that in the alternative approach no mapping function would have been defined for them, thus implying a failure to parse and/or interpret the input question), having a general natural language analyser at our disposal offers an additional bonus: the description of the domain world in terms of semantic primitives and primitive patterns can be generated largely automatically, since the domain world can be described in natural language (assuming, of course, an appropriate lexicon of domain world words and definitions) and the descriptions simply analysed as utterances, producing a set of semantic structures which can subsequently be processed to obtain a repertoire of domain-relevant forms to be exploited for the matching procedures.

### 4.2 The convertor

Having identified the domain terms and expressions, we have a high-level data language equivalent of the original English question. A substantial amount of processing has pinpointed the question focus, has eliminated potential ambiguities, has resolved domain-dependent language constructions, and has provided fillers for 'dummy' or 'query' items. Further, the system has established that "London" is a &city, for example, or that "Clark" is a specific instance of &supplier. The processing now has to make the final transition to the specific form in which questions are addressed to the actual DBMS. The semantic patterns on which the translator relies, for example defining a domain word "&supplier" as (((*ent obje) give) (subj *org)), while adequate enough to deduce that Clark is a &supplier", are not informative enough to suggest how "&suppliers" are modelled in the actual database.

Again, the obvious approach to adopt here is the mapping one, so that, for instance, we have:

&supplier ==> relation Supplier
Clark    ==> tuple of relation Supplier where Sname="Clark"
. . . . . . . .

But this approach suffers from the same limitations as direct mapping from logic representation to search representation; and a more flexible approach using the way the database models the domain world has been adopted.

In the previous section we discussed how the translator uses an inventory of semantic patterns to establish the connection between natural language and domain world words. This inventory is not, however, a flat structure with no internal organisation. On the contrary, the semantic information about the domain world is organised in such a way that it can naturally be associated with the administrative structure of the target database. For example in a relational database, a relation with tuples over domains represents properties of, or relationships between, the objects in the domain world. The objects, properties and relationships are described by the semantic apparatus used for the translator, and as they also underlie, at not too great remove, the database structure, the domain world concepts or predications of the query representation act as pointers into the data structures of the database administrative organisation.

For example, given the relation Supplier as defined in section 2, the semantic patterns which describe the facts that in the domain world **&suppliers &have &status, &numbers, &names** and **&live** in **&cities** are crosslinked, in the sense that they have the superstructure of the database relation Supplier imposed over them. The figure below shows (in a somewhat simplified form) an example declaration to the translator procedures which links the representative semantic patterns describing some aspects of the domain world associated with **&suppliers** with the structure of the associated relation in the database.

```
(Models-relation
    Supplier  (&exist &supplier)
        Sno         (&number &supplier ?num-val)
        Sname       (&name &supplier ?nam-val)
        Status      (&status &supplier ?s-val)
        Scity       (&live &supplier &city))
```

We can then use such declarations to avoid explicit, direct mapping from query data references to template relational structures for the database. From the initial meaning representation for the question fragment "... Clark, who has status 30 ...", namely

```
(be2 ... be
    (@@agent (Clark ... man))
    (@@state
        (st (status1 ... sign) (val (30 ... sign)))))),
```

through to the query representation

```
(For The $Var1/Clark : (&status $Var1 30) ...),
```

the semantic pattern matching has established that Clark is an instance of **&supplier**, that the relationship between the generic **&supplier** and the specific instance of **&supplier** (i.e. Clark) is that of **&name**, and that the query is focussed on his **&status** (whose value is supplied explicitly). Now from the position of the query predication '**&status &supplier** 30' in the characterisation of the relation <u>Supplier</u> given above, the system will be able to deduce that the way the target database administrative structure models the question's semantic content is as a relation derived from <u>Supplier</u> with "Clark" and "30" as values in the columns Sname and Status respectively.

The convertor thus employs declarative knowledge about the database organisation and the correspondence between this and the domain world structure to derive a generalised relational algebra expression which is an interpretation of the formal query in the context of the relational database model of the domain. We have chosen to gear the convertor towards a generalised relational algebra expression, because both its simple underlying definition and the generality of its data structures within the relational model allow easy generation of final low-level search representations for different specific database access systems.

To derive the generalised relational algebra form of the question from the query representation, the convertor uses its knowledge of the way domain objects and predications are modelled in the database to establish a primary or derivable relation for each of the quantified variables of the query representation. These constituents of the algebra expression are then combined, with an appropriate sequence of relational operators, to obtain the complete expression.

The basic premise of the convertor is that every quantified variable in the formal query representation can be associated with some primary or computable relation in the target database; restrictions on the quantified variables specify how, with that relation as a starting point, further relational algebra computations can be performed to model the restricted variable; the process is recursive, and as the query representation is scanned by the convertor, variables and their associated relational algebra expressions are bound by an 'environment-type' mechanism which provides all the necessary information to 'evaluate' (in the Lisp sense) the propositions of the query. Thus conversion is evaluating a predicate expression in the context of its semantic interpretation in the domain world and in the environment of the database models for its variables.

For example, given the query representation fragment for the phrase "... all status 30 London suppliers who supply red parts ...", namely

```
(For Every $Var1/&supplier
  : (AND
      (&status $Var1 30)
      (For The $Var3/London - (&live $Var1 $Var3))
      (For Every $Var2/&part : (&colour $Var2 red)
        - (&supply $Var1 $Var2))) ... ,
```

early in the processing $Var1 will get its database equivalent
computed as (relation Supplier). Integrating the first restriction
on the variable, the program establishes that the **&status** of the
**&suppliers** is modelled by the column Status in relation Supplier,
so the database reference for $Var1 now becomes

(select Supplier where Status equals 30).

Computing the reference for $Var1 is now pended, as an
embedded logical form is encountered. Out of context $Var3,
which is an instance of **&city**, is associated with two different
database equivalents, Scity and Pcity. However, the semantic
content of the underlying domain predicate which is evaluated
next, i.e. **(&live &supplier &city)**, together with the structure of
the relation which models this domain world relationship,
eliminates Pcity, and we therefore obtain the partial relational
expression

(select
    (select relation Supplier where Status equals 30)
    where Scity equals "London").

Similar processing will (eventually) associate $Var2 with

(select relation Part where Colour equals "red").

This is the environment of partially-computed equivalents for
$Var1 and $Var3 when the proposition (**&supply** $Var1 $Var3) is
evaluated. The domain relationship for this is modelled by the
relation Shipments in the database, and the evaluation of the
complete predication therefore yields

(join
    (select
        (select relation Supplier where Status equals 30)
        where Scity equals "London")
    (join Shipments
        (select relation Part where Colour equals "red"))).

At this point, the information that the user wants has been
described in terms of the target relational database: names of
files, fields and columns. The search description has, however,
still to be given the specific form required by the back end
DBMS. This is achieved by a fairly straightforward application of
standard compiling techniques, and does not deserve detailed
discussion here. We can currently generate search specifications
in several relational search languages including SALT (a simple
relational algebra query language (9)) and QUEL (14).

The process of generating a QUEL query, for example, is
controlled by a recursive scan of the generalised relational
algebra expression, during which information is extracted and
classified to fill in predefined slots in a template: the relations
used define ranges of QUEL variables; select expressions define
qualifications of the target QUEL query; project expressions are
used to establish the shape of the tuples of the resulting

relation being constructed by the QUEL query; joins are
performed over the common columns of the two (or more)
relations to be joined; and so on. Thus the expression generated
for the example question "Green parts are supplied by which
status 30 suppliers?" is:

```
Range of (Ql-var1,Ql-var2,Ql-var3) is (Shipments,Supplier,Part)
Retrieve  into Terminal (Ql-var2.Sname)
          where  (Ql-var1.Pno    = Ql-var3.Pno)
          and    (Ql-var1.Sno    = Ql-var2.Sno)
          and    (Ql-var2.Status = 30)
          and    (Ql-var3.Colour = "green")
```

(Note that query optimisation for search purposes is assumed to
be a matter for the DBMS, and not for the front end.)

## 5. INTRODUCING EVALUATIVE FEEDBACK

As indicated in the introduction, means of generating natural
language are needed for a variety of purposes to enable the
user to check the operation of a database search system. Thus
the system may need to produce natural language in the course
of clarifying inadequate inputs, explaining and justifying its own
actions, and, possibly, presenting its search output. The
processes underlying these system responses, e.g. selecting
explanations, are extremely difficult to design, and little
progress has been made with them. However natural language is
also required as the system's means of communicating with the
user for a more limited, but still most useful, purpose, namely to
exhibit, for the user's evaluative inspection, the interpretation
the system is giving to the user's question. We have labelled this
'evaluative feedback'.

This feedback could in principle be supplied after each of the
four major processing steps, though the utility of the individual
outputs would naturally vary with the user's knowledge (or lack
of knowledge) of e.g. the domain definition or database
organisational structure. However two points of particular
importance for natural language feedback are after the initial
analysis step, when any linguistic ambiguities in the input
question have been either resolved or laid bare, and after the
final conversion step, when the question has been explicitly
interpreted as a set of database search operations.

The rest of this section describes the provision for these
forms of system response currently made in the Cambridge
system. It might be argued that natural language generation
from later representations in the question processing should in
principle be the product of a full reversal of the input
processing, that is, an inversion of the forms and direction of
processing through all the steps involved (though this cannot be
guaranteed to recover the exact form of the input question, as
opposed to some equivalent: see (13)). However, whether this is

desirable or not, production of natural language output should not be done autonomously, and possibly ad hoc, from each form of representation: a preferable approach is to push the source representation through a common, general-purpose, and hence more powerful, natural language generator. This is the approach adopted in Cambridge, where natural language reflections of both the first meaning representation and the last search representation of a question are obtained through a common generator.

### 5.1 The English language generator

The immediate need for this module, generating text from meaning representations, follows from the fact that the meaning representation for the source question is the input to all subsequent processing; checking the correctness of its semantic content is therefore a very valuable, and perhaps essential, adjunct to the whole front end operation. Fortunately, the character of the analyser and its output allow this to be done in a very natural and convenient way: since the dependency structures produced by the analyser are substantially removed from the given surface text, generating natural language from the representation of the input text meaning is an adequate test for the precision and depth of the initial interpretation, i.e. it allows a reasonable check on the analyser's success in selecting the correct senses of the words, and correct structural relations between the words, of the input. The generator is thus a general-purpose program, independent of the domain of discourse or database structure. Its function is to take a meaning representation of an input question and express its semantic content in English.

Clearly, control over the coherency and validity of the results of natural language analysis must be an essential part of the evaluative feedback. Moreover, within the transportable system framework we are assuming, the possibilities for effective control are very limited indeed in any system which does not carry out in-depth semantic processing of the input before applying any domain-dependent information in its interpretive operations. Understanding the question as an English utterance is a prerequisite to its interpretation in the context of the database and failures here should be trapped at once - there is no point in invoking all the sophisticated machinery of the front end to attempt translation of misunderstood input. This point can indeed be generalised: the necessary checkpoints in the processing cycle of a natural language database interface can only be easily established in a modular system architecture; further, the particular modular design of the front end described here means that the database application can take advantage, effectively for free, of the benefit of a powerful general natural language generation program, capable of expressing the content of any well-formed meaning representation in a fluent and coherent way.

The generator achieves this by applying knowledge about the content and format of semantic structures, as well as linguistic knowledge pertinent to the related problems of what to say, when to say it, and how. In addition, the generator can be driven not only in single but in multiple paraphrase mode, which further enhances the clarity of feedback offered to the user, given that individual natural language expressions generated can themselves, for the good reason that they are just natural language expression, be ambiguous. Indeed this module has been designed (see (15)) to meet the fundamental requirements of a generator in a user-friendly and cooperative interface: it speaks the user's language and, because it is both domain-independent and analyser-compatible, is adaptable to the specific vocabulary of the user; it can paraphrase and hence clarify on demand; and it can produce output which is fluent and natural, in principle, though it has not been significantly tested for this purpose, over larger structures of discourse than a single sentence.

At this checkpoint after the analyser's initial processing of a question, the user can be offered, for example as a paraphrase of the illustrative question: "Green parts are supplied by which status 30 suppliers?", the form "Which suppliers with status 30 supply green parts?". In order to be able to generate this paraphrase, the system had (among other things) to select, in analysis, the appropriate word senses of "supply" and "green", and to understand that the property of 'having status equal to 30' is a qualifying phrase for "suppliers", i.e. that the structure of the question is not the same as, for example, that of the the question "Green parts are supplied by which London parts suppliers?", where the qualification "London" in the complex noun phrase applies to "parts suppliers", and not to "suppliers" alone. The generated paraphrase makes the structure of the question message more explicit than it was in the original.

## 5.2 The query reformulator

Another checkpoint in the evaluative feedback establishes the correctness of the system-generated low-level search specification before it is sent for execution against the database. Conceptually similar to the generator, this module takes as input a query in, for example QUEL, and reformulates it as a natural language expression. However this final English expression conveys the semantics of the technical search specification in terms understandable to the natural language user, i.e. using domain-referring words, as opposed to elaborating the contents of the query using concepts relevant to the detailed administrative structure of the particular database (such as names of files and records for example) which are typically of no interest to the end user. (The same program can, however, be driven by an informed user in a mode where the semantics of the query are explicitly expressed in terms of the administrative structure of the database - which also makes it possible to use essentially the same apparatus for a different task, namely that of user-tutoring).

The two most distinctive features of our query formulator are its ability to operate without having to recourse to an explicitly supplied mapping between data language terms and expressions and natural language words and phrases, and the fact that it is data-driven, as opposed to based on fixed inventory of "canned" phrases.

Little work has been done, in the context of responsive dialogue with the user, on natural language generation to allow precise query reformulation. First, in most cases where feedback is supplied, the problem is that the process operates without any linguistic knowledge and thus has to be driven by a set of explicitly supplied "canned" phrases, or rather, phrasal templates: these represent the semantics of basic data language formulae and have slots which are filled by the natural language counterparts of, for example, relation and column names (these counterparts also have to be explicitly supplied as a necessary part of the environment for natural language generation: see, for example, (10)). Apart from the inconvenience of providing different generation environments for each different database application, the lack of general linguistic knowledge, and specifically the shortcutting of natural language grammar, makes for fairly turgid, and even unnatural, linguistic phrasing; indeed it can be argued that the generated query reformulation is a mere 'syntactically sugared' variant of the original formal expression. A more significant point is that complex queries, when syntactically sugared, in a supposedly helpful way with natural language words, in fact become virtually unreadable. The approach usually adopted in reformulation, namely that of expressing queries as crude sequences of simple natural language propositions, only emphasises their formal nature; the generation process does not have the flexibility needed to produce the apposite and expressive outputs, for instance involving clause embedding, which are required for effective interaction with the user.

Additional problems with query reformulation based on an inventory of canned phrases are posed by the fact that in this case it is impossible to design a system capable of producing linguistically-motivated paraphrases, which violates one of the fundamental requirements of a generator in a friendly user interface as set out in 5.1; it is also impossible to maintain fluent discourse if this requires higher-level linguistic knowledge related to constraints about, for example, elision, pronominalisation, etc. A recent, more motivated approach, has been that of (11), where the generation process goes through a surface English grammatical structure, thus making it possible to apply grammatical constraints to the output sentence. Even so, the fact that the search query is manipulated by a set of query language-based formal translation rules (in the form of attribute grammars), where the attributes (i.e. lexical translations) for specific column and relation names, SQL key words etc., have to be explicitly supplied for different database applications, makes it difficult, if not impossible, to incorporate paraphrase capabilities into the query reformulation procedure.

In striking contrast, the natural language system discussed here has access to the precisely the kind of knowledge (both general linguistic and domain- and database-dependent) and apparatus necessary for the smooth operation of general query reformulation procedure. The English generator used for producing question paraphrases from meaning representations discussed in 5.1 has the machinery for expressing semantic networks (which are the obvious convenient abstraction of the analyser's dependency structures and so can be used for data language-derived expressions as much as for natural language ones) in English; accesses a fairly comprehensive natural language grammar; possesses the power and flexibility to generate coherent and readable descriptions of complex objects by applying linguistic procedures like relativisation, subordination, pronominalisation, etc.; and is capable of maintaining continuous discourse. Since this knowledge is represented in modular form, and the procedures are independent of the applications domain, it is natural to design the query reformulator in such a way that it utilises this apparatus.

This is straightforward, because all the modules of the front end use and maintain, in a uniform manner, the essential semantic content of the original input question. Identical processes to those employed by the translation component (semantic pattern matching which links the semantic definitions of the natural language words and phrases with their domain world object and relationship counterparts, and subsequently relates them to the way they are modelled in the database), can be essentially applied in reverse, so that during a systematic and exhaustive scan of the low-level query, its well-formed subcomponents can be related to the domain-world concepts or predications which they model. These can be linked, in their own turn, through the semantic patterns of the translator, to the appropriate entries in the natural language lexicon, which are then passed over to the generator procedures as data for the general linguistic manipulation.

Thus the QUEL query for the example question "Green parts are supplied by which status 30 suppliers?" is processed 'backwards' to retrieve the underlying predications (&supplier &supply &part), (&status &supplier 30), (&colour &part green), etc.; from here the translator semantic patterns in turn eventually recover natural language words suited for expressing those same patterns, and by extension the initial QUEL fragments, in English. The process effectively constructs a semantic representation of the content of the search query 'on the fly', which is then processed by the general-purpose generator procedures, delegating the otherwise tedious chores of what to pronominalise, when to relativise, etc. to the generator's internal low-level book-keeping specialists, and getting all the benefit of a powerful program capable of utilising extensive linguistic knowledge.

This approach clearly does not require any extensions to the environment of the front end: the semantic patterns (used by the translator) and the generator dictionary, which is part of the generator environment, are sufficient. In addition, since no "canned" phrases are needed, similar database (and hence query) constructs - for example (Ql-var3.Pcity = "London") and (Ql-var3.Colour = "green") - are expressed naturally as "parts stored in London" and "green parts", and not, unnaturally, as "parts with location = 'London'" and "parts with colour = 'green'" (10). Note, also, that the decision as to how to express a fragment naturally is made by the generator coherence specialists, is totally divorced from any constraints related to what to say, and is based entirely on considerations about how best to express a given semantic structure.

For the QUEL query derived from the example question we therefore obtain, by our 'reverse' reformulation operations, "Show me those suppliers whose status is 30 and who make shipments of green parts".

Clearly, given the way the reformulation process described works for the final search specification, we can envisage, though this is not yet implemented, producing natural language expressions for the intermediate front end processor outputs, namely the logic and high-level query representations of the input question. These would be particularly useful, for instance, in exhibiting the system's interpretation of the quantifier structures underlying input questions. Indeed work on the feedback capabilities of the system began only comparatively recently, and further testing is required. Thus, as noted earlier, the current implementation of feedback from the search representation does not go through all the question processing steps in reverse, but proceeds directly from the search representation to a meaning representation, though it uses the resources of the translator in making the step. It is possible that the absence of an explicit reverse query or logic representation could lead to inappropriate production of natural language quantifiers, but we have not been able to investigate this because the quantifier concepts allowed in the search representations we have been working with are mostly so crude.

## 6. CURRENT STATUS AND FUTURE WORK

All of the modules described have been implemented (in Lisp) and are currently operational. The system has so far been tested on the Suppliers and Parts database, which, though it is a toy from a practical point of view, is capable of offering considerable challenges to a natural language interface processor, and especially one not relying on domain-specific semantic processing. Work is currently in progress to apply the front end to a different database containing urban planning information in a test designed to compare front end performance with that of IBM's TQA system (4).

As anticipated, the bulk of the work in moving the front end to a new application seems to be in extending the linguistic capabilities of the natural language analyser and expanding the lexicon, which is hardly surprising, given our approach to schema acquisition: namely that the compilation of the set of representative semantic patterns which describe the relevant (from the point of view of the system's application) aspects of the domain world, is largely automated and employs the same natural language analyser as the one used by the front end, working on natural language description of the domain world. This is one advantage of our utilisation of general, as opposed to domain-specific, semantics. However, though this method of schema acquisition appears a convenient one, it has not been tried out sufficiently to establish that its informal style is adequate in all cases for both domain and database schemas.

The nearest to automatic schema acquisition that other related projects come to is the approach taken by TEAM (7): the process there relies on a fairly fixed format dialogue between the system and a database expert, where the system asks questions and uses the answers to provide parameters to the semantic operators which interpret the result(s) of syntactic analysis of the user's input, as well as to the basic pragmatic functions and the schema translator. However, neither this, nor (to our knowledge) any other approach to building transportable natural language front ends to database systems, takes advantage of the fact that a strong connection can be established between the real and domain worlds by examining their semantic descriptions within the same semantic representation language. When coupled with flexible semantic pattern matching, this provides a framework for question interpretation and translation quite suited to the task of applying the same set of question interpretation procedures to different database domains and applications (which early front end projects like LUNAR (18) and TQA (4) did not).

The project explicitly assumes interfacing to standard DBMS, but we have so far considered only relational databases and the convertor is currently restricted to relational database search languages. Thus our system, in its present state, does not compare directly with, say Kaplan's (8), which operates with a typical CODASYL DBMS (on the other hand it is not clear how much work would be involved in applying Kaplan's system to, say, a relational database). It should also be noted that as long as our test databases have significant complexity, we are not concerned with large databases, which pose problems more for the DBMS than for the front end, though ultimately problems arise for the front end too, for example in connection with the implications for the lexicon of large sets of attribute value terms.

So far we have not addressed the question of providing the front end with inference capabilities, which are required for fully effective natural language question interpretation; we are, however, about to begin work on this. We expect to be aided both by the modularity of the system and by the separate, comprehensive treatment of the input question as a natural language utterance: a good deal of mileage can be got out of applying common-sense inference procedures to general semantic representations of text input. On the other hand, experience suggests that it will be hard (and impractical) to merge common-sense inference with the domain-specific, i.e. pragmatic, inference which is also needed. Major issues for future research, therefore, will be the distribution of reasoning capabilities across the system architecture; and the study of the properties of a data model required to support the inference capabilities of the domain-dependent (translator) component of the front end.

## 7. CONCLUSION

The results so far suggest that developing a natural language front end to databases employing a rich and powerful semantic apparatus both for question analysis and for query translation offers distinct advantages in at least two respects: portability is promoted by the fact that domain-specific knowledge is restricted in application and declaratively expressed; and utility is promoted by the fact that user feedback is varied in form and easily achieved. Both of these advantages follow from the uniformity of the underlying representation of the semantic content of the input which is maintained throughout the complete system processing cycle.

## 8. ACKNOWLEDGEMENTS

This research is supported by the U.K. Science and Engineering Research Council.

## 9. REFERENCES

1.  Boguraev, B.K. (1979). "Automatic Resolution of Linguistic Ambiguities". Technical Report No.11, Computer Laboratory, University of Cambridge.
2.  Boguraev, B.K. and Sparck Jones, K. (1982). A natural language analyser for database access, *Information Technology: Research and Development*, vol.1, pp.23-39.
3.  Boguraev, B.K. and Sparck Jones, K. (1983). How to drive a database front end using general semantic information, *Proceedings of Conference on Applied Natural Language Processing*, Santa Monica, CA, pp.81-88.
4.  Damerau, F.J. (1980). "The Transformation Question Answering (TQA) System: Description, Operating Experience, and Implications". Report RC8287, IBM Thomas J. Watson Research center, Yorktown Heights, NY.
5.  Crout, J.N. (1981). Evaluation of natural language interfaces to database systems: a panel discussion, *Proceedings of the 19th Annual Meeting of the Association for Computational Linguistics*, Stanford, CA, pp.29-42.
6.  Date, C.J. (1977) "An Introduction to Database Systems". Addison-Wesley, Reading, Mass.
7.  Grosz, B. (1983). TEAM: a transportable natural-language interface system, *Proceedings of Conference on Applied Natural Language Processing*, Santa Monica, CA, pp.39-45.
8.  Kaplan, S.J. (1983). Cooperative responses from a portable natural language database query system, *In* "Computational Models of Discourse", (Eds. M.Brady and R.Berwick). pp.167-208. The MIT Press, Cambridge, Mass.
9.  King, T.J. and Moody, J.K.M. (1983). The design and implementation of CODD, *Software: Practice and Experience*, vol.13, No.1, pp.67-79.
10. Longstaff, J. (1982). ERQ: controlled inference and instruction techniques for DBMS query languages", *Proceedings of International Conference on Management of Data*, Orlando, FL, pp.111-117.
11. Mueckstein, E.M. (1983). Q-TRANS: query translation into English", *Proceedings of the Eighth International Joint Conference on Artificial Intelligence*, Karlsruhe, pp.660-662.
12. Shneiderman, B. (1978). Improving the human factors aspect of database interactions, *ACM Transactions on Database Systems*, vol.3, No.4, pp.417-439.
13. Sparck Jones, K. (1983). Shifting meaning representations,

*Proceedings of the Eighth International Joint Conference on Artificial Intelligence*, Karlsruhe, pp.621-623.

14. Stonebraker, M. et al. (1976). The design and implementation of INGRES, *ACM Transactions on Database Systems*, vol.1, No.3, pp.189-223.

15. Tait, J.I. and Sparck Jones, K. (1983). "Automatic Search Term Variant Generation for Document Retrieval". Technical Report (forthcoming), Computer Laboratory, University of Cambridge.

16. Waltz, D. (1978). An English language question answering system for a large relational database", *Communications of the ACM*, vol.21, pp.526-539.

17. Wilks, Y. (1975). An intelligent analyser and understander of English, *Communications of the ACM*, vol.18, pp.264-274.

18. Woods, W. (1972) "The Lunar Sciences Natural Language Information System". Final Report, Bolt, Beranek and Newman, Cambridge, Mass.

Expert Systems and Data Bases

# DATABASES AND EXPERT SYSTEMS:
## OPPORTUNITIES AND ARCHITECTURES FOR INTEGRATION

Matthias Jarke and Yannis Vassiliou

*Graduate School of Business Administration,*
*New York University, New York, USA*

## ABSTRACT

Using a combination of technologies for database management systems (DBMS) and artificial intelligence-based expert systems (ES) may prove beneficial to future management information systems. A DBMS can be used more intelligently and efficiently if enhanced with ES features, while an ES can effectively access very large databases through existing DBMS technology.

Isolated efforts to combine these two technologies started several years ago, however, the implementation of the ES-DBMS cooperative use has proven difficult. The benefits derived from cooperation between ES and DBMS, important approaches, and the research challenges presented are reviewed in this paper, together with a research effort underway at New York University.

## 1. INTRODUCTION

Expert systems are programs working in complex knowledge-intensive domains with a performance matching that of human experts (40). With the rapid technological advent of expert systems, and all the sensation they have recently created in the business community, a question of substance is often raised: "What are expert systems good for in a management information systems environment?"

NEW APPLICATIONS OF DATA BASES
ISBN 0-12-275550-2

This paper presents a partial answer, possibly quite different from the ones commonly found in AI literature or business journals.

Conventional management information systems used for transaction processing or decision support have relied on large databases, mathematical formulas and models, business rules and forms (documents), and the experience and expertise of various human specialists. Where expert systems are introduced, there is yet another type of subsystem which interacts with the human decision-makers to complement their expertise. It is not hard to see that much effort is duplicated if all these systems operate independently of each other.

Some progress has been made towards integrating the subsystems. Decision support systems have to base their mathematical modelling capabilities on solid database management technology to become cost-effective. By analogy, it can be argued that many expert systems which use a large population of specific facts need a communication channel to the corporate databases. Going a step further, we expect that future decision support systems will have to integrate all three components: database system, mathematical subsystem, and knowledge-based or expert system.

In this paper, we shall focus on the interaction of two of the subsystems, namely, knowledge-based expert systems and databases. Researchers who have addressed these problems typically looked at certain aspects of one of the two directions of ES-DBMS cooperation. In our research (see also (20, 37)), we try to view them together. First, expert system features can be used to improve interfaces to databases. Furthermore, they can support essential database features such as query optimization and transaction management.

Second, we address the other direction in the ES-DBMS cooperation: how the capability of ES to access and use existing very large databases as extensions of their own knowledge base can be improved. Elegant, long range overall system architectures are discussed, but particular emphasis is given to more practically oriented approaches, which take advantage of existing software systems.

As an illustration, consider an ongoing project at New York University in which a logic-based business expert system is developed and interfaced with an existing relational database system. The system will support underwriters in evaluating applications for life insurance policies. Such a system needs:

(a) information about customers and actuarial table data from an existing very large database;

(b) a mathematical subsystem to execute actuarial computations efficiently;

(c) knowledge-based expert subsystems for classifying applications and checking time-varying legal and corporate constraints (the underwriting expert), for identifying the appropriate actuarial models for customized premium computations (the actuarial expert), and for explaining problems and alternatives in these domains.

We are implementing the system using the logic language Prolog, a relational database system, and a mathematical subroutine library. The project is meant to serve as a demonstration of a typical architecture we expect for upcoming knowledge-based business decision support systems.


## 2. APPLICATIONS OF ES - DBMS INTEGRATION


### 2.1 Database Enhancement by Expert Systems Methods

When the requirements for advanced business applications such as decision support for managerial users are considered, current database management systems display a number of weaknesses. In this section, we highlight these problems and identify some strategies for overcoming the limitations by the use of rule-based techniques. Other artificial intelligence approaches such as natural language interfaces (39, 40) or conceptual modelling techniques (1) also contribute to better database design and usage but will not be examined here in detail.

## 2.1.1 Intelligent Database Interfaces

With the advent of decision support systems and the
proliferation of computers and databases in general, the
target user population for database query languages has
changed: there are more (potential) users, such as managers
and application specialists who have a high degree of
application knowledge but little patience to acquire much
familiarity with programming concepts.

For such users, higher-level query languages are
required which allow powerful operations without demanding
technical skills for the interaction. Besides the more
ergonomic approach taken by the so-called second generation
query languages (38), reasoning capabilities embedded in the
system could allow for a wider range and more concise
formulation of queries.

A second problem arises if users want fairly complex
operations to be performed on the data, operations which are
not provided directly by the query language. Currently,
users are forced to use a database programming language (35)
instead of an ad-hoc query language, and program the
operations on the data explicitly. This is not easy for
non-computer specialists. In addition, it often prevents
the use of standard DBMS report generation facilities
burdening the user with even more programming tasks.

In the past few years, much research has been directed
towards making database interfaces more intelligent. The
main thrust is towards more deductive capabilities. One of
the most important applications in this context is the
generalization of <u>view</u> concepts.

Early DBMS allowed access only to the stored files,
records, and fields. More recent systems provide view
mechanisms that allow the user to name windows through which
only a subset of the database is visible. For example, a
view "whole life insurance bearers" can be defined that
contains customers who have a whole life insurance policy.

Traditional view mechanisms are somewhat limited since
they are 'static': a separate view of customers would have
to be defined for each type of insurance benefit. Recently,
researchers in database programming and in logic programming
have devised more flexible mechanisms. The most recent
example are the 'dynamic' views in Morgenstern (27) which
are based on semantic templates for associatively accessing

and manipulating data objects. Similarly, the <u>selector</u> concept introduced in Mall et al. (26) allows the definition of views with parameters. In a database of customers and policies, a selector

with_benefit (T) for customer_relation

can be defined where T can assume values such as "whole life insurance" or "term annuity". The user can now request or alter the value of selected variables such as

customer[with_benefit("whole life")]

which defines a moving window whose focus depends on the parameter chosen. For querying purposes, logic programming offers similar facilities through the use of variables in rules and queries; in Prolog (23), a similar view as above could be queried by

:- covered_by(Who_has, whole_life).

which would return as the value of the variable, Who_has, the customers with whole life insurance.

   Queries to views are automatically interpreted by the built-in inference mechanisms. However, in case the view definitions (or rules in logic programming terminology) are evaluated frequently, it may be better to pre-compile queries to views into queries to base relations (stored predicates). This can be done quite easily unless recursion appears in the view definitions (9, 33). Otherwise, an iteration construct may sometimes be required in the target language of the precompilation (15).


2.1.2 Intelligent Database Operation

Besides not being as user-supportive as desired, database systems could be improved towards more safety of the data and more efficiency of the execution of read and write transactions. The addition of general rules and inference mechanisms to a database system presents a challenge to the database implementation researcher. The objective is to execute efficiently deductive queries as well as more traditional database operations. We investigate two areas: deduction-based query optimization methods, and deduction-based integrity checking for update transactions.

Query Optimization. A query evaluation subsystem within the DBMS tries to identify efficient ways to execute any submitted query. For this purpose, a query is usually standardized, simplified, and transformed in an attempt to enable the application of fast special-purpose algorithms.

A deductive component may use meta rules that guide the choice among the many applicable query transformation rules. Grishman (11) and Reiter (33) describe applications of deduction to the simplification step. Warren (41) implements the well-known query transformation heuristics of testing sharp restrictions first, and separating detachable subqueries in logic.

Jarke and Koch (17) develop a generalized heuristic called range nesting that combines both ideas. The deduction mechanism, however, is deterministic and contained in the query language compiler. An extension to this mechanism will use meta rules to generate alternative strategies and compare their evaluation costs based on knowledge about storage structures and database statistics.

Another deduction-based transformation strategy makes more direct use of the general rules that define the database intension (33). Semantic query processing (13, 22) applies the integrity constraints of the database to simplify the execution of queries. Since typically many constraints can be used to transform a given query, this strategy again needs meta rules for selecting among them.

Finally, the simultaneous optimization of multiple queries (18) can be supported by an ES. One strategy tries to remember selected query results to be used later (4), another to recognize common subexpressions in a batch of queries, in order to create suitable temporary or permanent access paths. The execution of deductive queries also may require a sequence of related queries to be submitted to the database. The relationship between these queries can be exploited for optimization (9).

Consistency Maintenance. The expression of semantics and the maintenance of data consistency (7) have been ongoing goals in database research from early DBTG network procedures on. Semantic data models (12), procedural attachments to data definitions as in TAXIS (28), and rule-based extensions to INGRES (36) all try to provide better abilities for consistency maintenance.

Recent approaches propose rule-based (8) or logic-based (23) AI techniques for semantic integrity checking. The DBMS has to determine which of the many general laws apply to a specific operation on specific data. A pattern-matching oriented deduction process can be used for this purpose (14, 29).

A second question affects the user interface of the system: how to react to violations? Nicolas and Yazdanian (29) see three alternatives: reject the operation; accept the operation but do not change the database until further operations are submitted so that the transaction as a whole leaves the database in a consistent state (10); or trigger automatic changes to other data items to bring the database back to a consistent state.

The appropriate choice depends on many factors which can be partially controlled by meta rules and partially by the user. A knowledge-based database architecture proposed in Jarke and Shalev (19) contains an input management system to avoid unnecessary resubmission of transactions.


## 2.2 Expert Systems Access to Databases

In a rule-based expert system, the "inference engine" uses a set of rules (the knowledge base) and a collection of specific facts (database) to simulate the behaviour of a human expert in a specialized problem domain.

For instance, the life insurance consulting expert system uses rules like:

```
IF   C is a customer of a certain age and
     when C dies a certain amount becomes payable
THEN C has a whole life insurance benefit.
```

and a database containing data about actual customers, insurance and annuity benefits, mortality values, etc.

A database is represented in terms of two basic dimensions: variety and population. For example, in a logic-based representation the different logic predicates ("customer", "covered by", etc.) reflect the variety, and the instances of these predicates ("Smith is a customer", "Smith is covered by term annuity", etc.) refer to the population.

Most expert system databases exhibit a large variety of facts. In contrast, the population of facts in such databases is more variable, ranging from a small "laboratory" set to a very large collection of facts. Thus, expert system databases differ from traditional commercial databases in that they tend to be more "wide" and less "deep".

In the simplest case, all data is kept in main memory and stored in mostly ad-hoc data structures. Application-specific routines for data retrieval and modification are implemented.

When the expert system database is too _large_ to fit in core, such elementary data management is not sufficient. Techniques are needed for external file management. They should preferably be application independent, since otherwise a small change in application descriptions may require an altogether different mechanism.

Furthermore, depending on the multiplicity of database use and the extent of fact variety required for the ES, general purpose database management facilities may be needed. Such facilities include views, and an integrated data dictionary that allows for queries about the database structure. In a nutshell, a generalized DBMS integrated in the expert system may be necessary to deal effectively with large databases.

Often, the need for consulting _existing_ very large databases arises. Such databases will normally be managed by a commercial DBMS. In a typical example, Olson and Ellis (30) report experience with PROBWELL, an expert system used to determine problems with oil wells. A very important source of information for such determination is a large database stored under the IMS database system. Unfortunately, this database cannot be made available to the ES in a timely manner.

Existing external databases are often very large, highly volatile, and used by several applications. Costs of storing data and maintaining consistency may prohibit the duplication of such a database for the sake of the expert system alone. During the same ES session, many different portions of the external database may be required at different times; the requirements may be _dynamic_ and unpredictable. In addition, if the external database is continuously updated, for instance in databases for commodity trading or ticket reservation, the snapshots become rapidly obsolete. Tight coupling of an ES with an external DBMS refers to the use of the communication channel between the two systems in such a way that the external database appears to the ES as an extension of its own.


## 3. TECHNOLOGY OF ES - DBMS INTEGRATION

To summarize the overview given in the previous section, it can be said that the techniques used in both application areas of integration are very similar. A system that incorporates most of the proposed strategies should be clearly feasible. In this section of the paper, we pose some architectural questions looking at the interaction between ES and DBMS from a more technical perspective.


### 3.1 Basic Architectural Decisions

The interaction between DBMS and ES can be organized along a spectrum of architectures ranging from expert systems with integrated data management facilities, to the coupling of independent expert and database systems, finally to DBMS with integrated deductive capabilities.

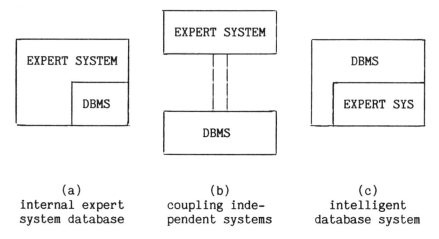

|          (a)          |      (b)       |       (c)        |
| internal expert       | coupling inde- |   intelligent    |
| system database       | pendent systems | database system |

Fig. 1: Basic Architectures for ES-DBMS Cooperation

Database access can be provided to expert systems by one of the first two basic solutions using one of four strategies detailed in (37). Starting from elementary facilities for data retrieval, these strategies progress to a generalized database management system within the expert system, to a 'loose' and, finally, to a 'tight' coupling of the expert system with an external DBMS. Examples of expert systems with internal DBMS include the systems presented in Pereira and Porto (32) and Lafue (25). Dahl (3) describes an implementation of a DBMS in Prolog.

Expert systems designers may opt for one configuration over another depending on data volume, multiplicity of data usage, data volatility, or data protection and security requirements. Regardless, in a careful design these strategies are incremental allowing for a smooth transition from a less to a more sophisticated environment.

Database enhancements by expert systems technology can be effected using architecture (b) or (c) in Fig. 1. Strategies described in the literature can be classified as: integrated systems containing both the ES and the DBMS (41); loosely coupled systems where the ES does all its work before the DBMS is called (2, 5, 11, 32); and finally the tightly coupled system DADM (21) that interleaves deduction in the ES with partial search in the DBMS.

Besides offering the user a deductive formal query language, such systems can also support other high-level user interfaces such as natural language (3, 34).

One might think that the natural architecture would be a uniform integrated system written in and usable through one language: either an extended database programming language with deductive capabilities, or an ES language with general programming capabilities, such as Prolog (31). Indeed, as seen above, many attempts to integrate DBMS and ES capabilities follow this approach.

Unfortunately, each of these languages has its own idiosyncrasies making it awkward to use in certain subsystems (e.g., complex computations in Prolog). This architecture also defeats the purpose of exploiting existing DBMS while introducing new domain-dependent expert systems. Therefore, the following two subsections focus on system architectures and communication strategies between an expert system and a database existing independently of each other.

## 3.2 Coupling Independent ES and DBMS

Three candidate architectures for the coupling of independent systems can be distinguished by the main location of processing and type of interaction control.

A first strategy calls for a total distribution of processing and control. The two systems interact by exchanging messages, as in an "actor" approach (16). Each interaction assumes a master to slave relationship between the originator and the receiver of the message, but both systems are self-contained and can be operated independently. An advantage of this architecture is a large degree of application and system independence, allowing for transportability to other ES and DBMS. How much each system has to know about the other's capabilities is an important consideration. The duplication of knowledge representations may introduce the usual dangers of redundancy: inconsistency and incompatibility.

At the other extreme, concentration of processing and control, a system integration can be envisioned. One of the two subsystems (ES or DBMS) may assume a more dominant role. This approach has naturally been followed by most researchers who focus on one direction of the interaction between ES and DBMS, for example (2, 21). The architecture suggests a more variable distribution of labor (e.g. where query optimization is done) than the typically predetermined separation of labor under fully distributed control. There is much flexibility and potential in such an architecture, at the expense of transportability. Another difficulty with this solution is the integration of additional external subsystems.

Finally, in a third architecture, processing is distributed but control is now the responsibility of a separate subsystem, a supervisor program. In essence, the supervisor performs all the necessary steps for interfacing the ES with the DBMS (e.g., translations), and manages the interaction between them. This appears as a compromise architecture with the main advantage of allowing for a smoother interaction with other subsystems. The challenging research question would be how to implement a supervisor that makes full use of the capabilities of the various subsystems without duplicating their features.

## 3.3 Optimizing ES - DBMS Communication

Within each architecture, means must be provided to translate knowledge representations and transaction requests between subsystems. In Vassiliou et al. (37), we distinguish between loose and tight coupling approaches.

Loose coupling of an ES with an existing DBMS refers to the presence of a communication channel between the two systems which allows for data extraction from the existing database, and subsequent storage of this "snapshot" as an expert system database. Data are extracted statically before the actual operation of the ES. We note that the availability of generalized database management facilities within the expert system may greatly facilitate this process.

The main disadvantage of loose coupling is the non-applicability in cases where automated dynamic decisions, as to which database portion is required, are necessary. Tight coupling supports dynamic decisions and keeps the communication channel open during expert system execution. Our suggested strategy for implementing tight coupling assumes the existence of a high-level, sophisticated mechanism within the ES - an expert system itself. The implementation of such an expert raises interesting questions of efficiency: the element-by-element reasoning of the expert system must be connected with a set-oriented DBMS access language.

The optimization of database references is designed as a three-step process. First, a precompilation mechanism implemented by an amalgamation of the ES language with its metalanguage collects ES requests for data while simulating the ES deduction process. Then, the collected database calls are simultaneously optimized by simplification and recognition of common subexpressions. Finally, the optimized query is translated to the DBMS query language and executed by the DBMS. The answer is loaded into the internal expert system database; garbage collection may be required for preserving the internal database as a rapidly accessible buffer in the presence of multiple unrelated database calls.

In (24, 37), a solution for the collection step in coupling logic-based expert systems with relational databases has been devised. Solutions for the other two steps will be reported in a forthcoming paper.

## 4. CONCLUSION

The integration of expert systems into existing data-based management information systems can avoid frictions and duplication of effort. While long-range projects such as the Japanese Fifth Generation Computer (6) stress uniform integrated solutions, our research tries to improve the interaction of existing subsystems, supporting in particular the coupling of expert subsystems with existing large databases. A number of architectures and optimization methods are currently being designed, implemented, and compared.

## ACKNOWLEDGMENTS

Parts of this paper are based on earlier work presented in more detail in Jarke and Vassiliou (20). The work was supported in part by a joint study with the International Business Machines Corporation. Jim Clifford co-developed the four-stage approach to database access by expert systems. Taracad Sivasankaran did a major part of the initial design and preliminary implementation of the actuarial expert system.

## REFERENCES

1.  Brodie, M. Mylopoulos, J., Schmidt, J.W. (eds.) (1983). On Conceptual Modelling: Perspectives from Artificial Intelligence, Databases, and Programming Languages, Springer, Berlin-Heidelberg-New York.

2.  Chang, C.L. (1978). Deduce 2: Further investigations of deduction in relational databases. In Logic and Databases (Eds H. Gallaire, J. Minker), pp. 201-236. Plenum, New York.

3.  Dahl, V. (1979). Logical design of deductive natural language consultable data bases. Proceedings 5th VLDB Conference, pp. 24-31. Rio de Janeiro.

4.  Finkelstein, S. (1982). Common expression analysis in database applications. In Proceedings ACM-SIGMOD Conference, pp. 235-245. Orlando, Florida.

5. Fishman, D., Naqvi, S. (1982). An intelligent database system - AIDS. In Proceedings Workshop on Logical Bases for Data Bases. Toulouse.

6. Furukawa, K., Fuchi, K. (1983). Knowledge engineering and fifth generation computers. Database Engineering 6, 4.

7. Gardarin, G., Melkanoff, M. (1979). Proving consistency of database transactions. In Proceedings 5th VLDB Conference, pp. 291-298. Rio de Janeiro.

8. Goldstein, I.P., Bobrow, D.G. (1980). Descriptions for a programming environment. In Proceedings AAAI-80. Stanford, Ca.

9. Grant, J., Minker, J. (1981). Optimization in deductive and conventional relational database systems. In Advances in Database Theory (Eds H. Gallaire, J. Minker, J.M. Nicolas), pp. 195-234. Plenum, New York.

10. Gray, J. (1981). The transaction concept: virtues and limitations. In Proceedings 7th VLDB Conference, pp. 144-154. Cannes.

11. Grishman, R. (1978). The simplification of retrieval requests generated by question answering systems. In Proceedings 4th VLDB Conference, pp. 400-406. Berlin.

12. Hammer, M., McLeod, D. (1981). Database description with SDM: A Semantic Database Model. ACM Transactions on Database Systems 6, 4, pp. 351-386.

13. Hammer, M., Zdonik, S. (1980). Knowledge-based query processing. In Proceedings 6th VLDB Conference, pp. 137-147. Montreal.

14. Henschen, L., McCune, W., Naqvi, S. (1982). Compiling constraint-checking programs from first-order formulas. In Proceedings Workshop on Logical Bases for Data Bases. Toulouse.

15. Henschen, L., Naqvi, S. (1982). On compiling queries in recursive first-order databases. In Proceedings Workshop on Logical Bases for Data Bases. Toulouse.

16. Hewitt, C. (1976). Viewing control structures as patterns of passing messages. AI Memo 410. MIT, Cambridge, Mass.

17. Jarke, M., Koch, J. (1983). Range nesting - A fast method to evaluate quantified queries. In Proceedings ACM-SIGMOD Conference, pp. 196-206. San Jose, Ca.

18. Jarke, M., Koch, J., Mall, M., Schmidt, J.W. (1982). Query optimization research in the database programming languages (DBPL) project. Database Engineering 5, 3, pp. 11-14.

19. Jarke, M., Shalev, J. (1984). A database architecture for supporting business transactions. Journal of Management Information Systems.

20. Jarke, M., Vassiliou, Y. (1984). Coupling expert systems with database management systems. In Artificial Intelligence Applications for Business (Eds W. Reitman). Ablex, Norwood, N.J.

21. Kellogg, C. (1982). Knowledge management: A practical amalgam of knowledge and data base technology. In Proceedings AAAI-82. Pittsburgh, Pa.

22. King, J.J. (1981). Quist: A system for semantic query optimization in relational data bases. In Proceedings 7th VLDB Conference, pp. 510-517. Cannes.

23. Kowalski, R. (1981). Logic as a database language. Unpublished manuscript. Imperial College, London.

24. Kunifuji, S., Yokota, H. (1982). Prolog and relational databases for fifth generation computer systems. In Proceedings Workshop on Logical Bases for Data Bases. Toulouse.

25. Lafue, G.M.E. (1983). Basic decisions about linking an expert system with a DBMS: A case study. Database Engineering 6, 4.

26. Mall, M., Reimer, M., Schmidt, J.W. (1983). Data selection, sharing, and access control in a relational scenario. In On Conceptual Modelling: Perspectives from Artificial Intelligence, Databases, and Programming Languages (Eds M. Brodie, J. Mylopoulos, J.W. Schmidt). Springer, Berlin-Heidelberg-New York.

27. Morgenstern, M. (1983). Active databases or a paradigm for enhanced computing environments. In Proceedings 9th VLDB Conference, pp. 34-42. Florence.

28. Mylopoulos, J., Bernstein, P.A., Wong, H.K.T. (1980). A language facility for designing database-intensive applications. ACM Transactions on Database Systems 5, 2, pp. 185-207.

29. Nicolas, J.M., Yazdanian, N. (1978). Integrity checking in deductive databases. In Logic and Databases (Eds H. Gallaire, J. Minker). Plenum, New York.

30. Olson, J.P., Ellis, S.P. (1982). Probwell, An expert advisor for determining problems with producing wells. In Proceedings IBM Scientific/Engineering Conference, pp. 95-101. Poughkeepsie, New York.

31. Parsaye, K. (1983). Database management, knowledge base management, and expert systems development in PROLOG. In Proceedings Database Week. Business Applications, pp. 159-178. San Jose, Ca.

32. Pereira, L.M., Porto, A. (1982). A implementation of a large system on a small machine. Departmento de Informatica, Universidade Nova de Lisboa. Lisbon.

33. Reiter, R. (1978). Deductive question-answering on relational data bases. Logic and Databases (Eds H.Gallaire, J. Minker), pp. 149-178. Plenum, New York.

34. Sagalowicz, D. (1977). IDA: An intelligent data access system. In Proceedings 3rd VLDB Conference, pp. 293-302. Tokyo.

35. Schmidt, J.W., Mall, M., Koch, J., Jarke, M. (1982). Database programming languages. In Proceedings Philadelphia Database Interface Workshop (Eds P. Buneman). Philadelphia, Pa.

36. Stonebraker, M., Woodfill, J., Andersen, E. (1983). Implementation of rules in relational database management systems. Memo UCB/ERL 83/10. Berkeley, Ca.

37.  Vassiliou, Y., Clifford, J., Jarke, M.  (1983).  How
     does  an expert system get its data?  NYU Working Paper
     CRIS  #50,  GBA  83-26  (CR),  extended  abstract  in
     Proceedings 9th VLDB Conference, pp.  70-72, Florence.

38.  Vassiliou, Y., Jarke, M.  (1984).  Query languages:  A
     taxonomy.  In  Human  Factors and Interactive Computer
     Systems (Eds Y.  Vassiliou).  Ablex, Norwood, N.J.

39.  Wahlster, W.  (1981).  Natural  language  AI  systems:
     state  of  the  art  and  research  perspective.  (in
     German).  In  Proceedings  GWAI  81.  Springer,
     Berlin-Heidelberg-New York.

40.  Waltz, D.  (1983).  Artificial  intelligence:  An
     assessment  of the state-of-the-art and recommendations
     for future directions.  AI Magazine 4, 3, pp.  55-67.

41.  Warren,  D.H.D.  (1981).  Efficient  processing  of
     interactive  relational  data base queries expressed in
     logic.  In  Proceedings  7th  VLDB  Conference,  pp.
     272-282.  Cannes.

# THE DESIGN OF AN EXPERT SYSTEM FOR DATABASE DESIGN

Mokrane Bouzeghoub and Georges Gardarin

*Projet SABRE, INRIA, BP 105*
*78153 Le Chesnay Cédex, France*
*Université de Paris VI, Tour 55-65, 4 place Jussieu*
*75230 Paris Cédex 05, France*

*ABSTRACT*

In this paper, we propose a new approach to database design based on an expert system. We then describe the design of a specific expert system, called SECSI, which produces a relational schema with additional integrity constraints from a description of the real world given in a subset of French. The knowledge base of the expert system is composed of a semantic network portraying the application, and a set of production rules allowing the system to transform the semantic network into a relational schema. The inference engine generates the meta-base of our relational system, called SABRE. An expert system such as the one proposed here seems to be a very attractive tool for solving the difficult problem of database design.

## 1. INTRODUCTION

Database design and modelling issues have held the attention of designers for many years. Several methods and tools have been developed under the name of logical database design. Generally, these methods fall into one of three categories :
- the first category is based upon algorithmic methods built around the relational model ; such methods provide programs deriving a normalized relational schema from a

set of attributes and constraints [CODD71, BERN76, ZAME81].
- the second category consists of manual methods that are
  generally based upon models which represent user's
  perception, like the Entity-Relationship Model [CHEN76]
  or the semantic hierarchy model [SMSM77]. All the design
  choices are left to the Database Administrator (DBA) ;
  only a few guidelines for validating the design are offered to him [HAML81, TARD79, BROD80].
- the third category is based upon interactive methods.
  Designed to aid manual methods, they often call for CAD
  techniques. Interactions between the users and the system
  are question-answering oriented [TARD79, ATZE81] or graphics language oriented [CHLO80]. These interactions are
  always guided by the system.

In this paper, we propose a new approach which consists
in developing an expert system for database design. This
system is designed to facilitate the interaction with the
designers through a subset of French. From facts described
in a quasi-natural language, our system, SECSI, produces a
conceptual relational schema in third normal form or an
internal relational schema optimized for query processing.
A set of additional integrity constraints is also generated
and is associated with the schema.

In the second section of this paper, we give a general
overview of the design tool proposed. The third section
discusses the various types of application description languages which can be offered to the data base administrator.
In a first approach, we select a subset of the French natural language which is introduced. Then, in section four, we
develop the semantic network adopted to support the representation of facts. The functional language utilized to manipulate this semantic network is also presented. Section
five is devoted to the deduction rules which define the
transformations applied for obtaining the relational schema
with the associated integrity constraints from the semantic
network. Finally, in section six, we focus on the process
of schema elaboration.

## 2.  AN OVERVIEW OF SECSI

Like most expert systems [LAUR82], SECSI is based on an
expert knowledge base. This knowledge base is composed of
facts and rules. Thus, we distinguish the base of rules and
the base of facts. These two bases are loaded by the database administrator using the dialogue modules. Then, the
inference engine carries out the deduction process. This
process generates the relational schema and the integrity

constraints which are stored in the meta-base of our relational database management system called SABRE [GARD83a].
The overall architecture of SECSI is presented in Figure 1.

The base of rules is defined at system generation time
using a dialogue module. The rules describe the algorithms
which are applied to the base of facts in order to generate
the relational schema. They are composed of general rules
such as normalization rules, but also specific rules
which can be system dependent or even application dependent.

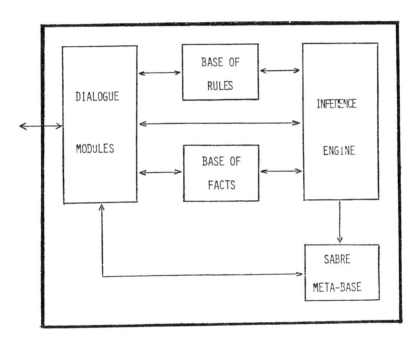

*Fig. 1  An overview of SECSI architecture*

The database administrator can always modify the base of
rules by adding new rules or deleting old rules. Rules are
expressed in an ad-hoc language based on IF-THEN statements
as we shall see in section five.

Other dialogue modules allow SECSI to fill up the base of
facts describing the application. The DBA supplies the description of his application to be modelled in a quasi-natural language. The interactive parser processes the given
description and generates partially predefined data structures which are organized as frames [MINS75] upon which the
interpreter is activated. Depending on the elements filled
in, it chooses one of the three following actions :

(1) The sentence is rejected if a minimum number of interpretable elements are not filled up.
(2) A complementary dialogue is started if a semantic interpretation of the sentence appears to be possible with some complementary information.
(3) The semantic analysis is completed and the resulting facts are stored in the base of facts if the sentence can be understood.

The inference engine performs the deduction process and generates the relational schema with the associated integrity constraints. For this purpose, it utilizes the base of rules as input. This base is a set of production rules conducting the deduction process. This process is organized into four steps corresponding to four sets of rules :

(1) The first step generates a set of first normal form relations with attribute names and domain constraints which model the application.
(2) The second step isolates functional dependencies and key constraints.
(3) The third step generates a third normal form conceptual schema.
(4) The fourth step, which is optional, produces an optimized internal schema giving the relations to be implemented and the indexes to be created.

Let us point out that during any step, the inference engine may ask the DBA for more information if necessary. Further, it only suggests results which then have to be validated by the DBA. If these results are not correct from the DBA's point of view, a new attempt is performed with new rules or updated set of old rules. Finally, SECSI produces two relational schemas with their integrity constraints which are stored in the SABRE meta-base. The conceptual schema, produced at the end of step 3, is stored as an external view for the DBA. The internal schema which is composed of the relations to be implemented is used by the SABRE system for creating the physical database.

The dialogue modules are in charge of all the dialogues with the end-user. The definition of the inference rules (base of rules) is performed in a specific language which allows the user to express the type of a rule, the condition and the action composing a rule. We intend to define several types of sentences for describing the real world application. For the time being, we have choosen a very restricted subset of French which is introduced in the next section.

## 3. THE DESCRIPTION OF THE APPLICATION

Describing the application in a comprehensive manner is one of the most important problems in database design. A first approach could be an interactive tool allowing the database administrator to define the real world attributes, to give examples of values and to introduce comments. The DBA could then define the aggregation of attributes to form entities. Also, associations between entities could be specified and finally, the generalization hierarchies and other constraints could be expressed. Such an approach would not be very flexible, but would be simple and practical.

To be more flexible, we allow the database administrator to describe his application in a subset of French. Sentences are facts describing the application to be modelled. We accept only simple declarative sentences of the type :

<SUBJECT GROUP> <VERB GROUP> <COMPLEMENT GROUP>

This language is sufficient for the descriptive aspect we are interested in and has the advantage of being simple. The <SUBJECT GROUP> and <COMPLEMENT GROUP> may include a noun or a noun group as well as an appositive or a prepositional phrase. We will not consider sentences with relative clauses or with pronouns. The verbs are classified in two types : known verbs and unknown verbs. In the very simple interface we have specified for the first version of SECSI, the known verbs are TO BE, TO HAVE, TO BELONG, TO CHARACTERIZE, MUST and MAY. All other verbs are considered as unknown ; they are accepted by the system which gives them a special meaning as we shall see later. Examples of possible sentences are given in Figure 2.

*étudiants et employés sont des personnes*
students and employees are persons
*enseignants et administratifs sont des employés*
teachers and staff members are employees
*professeurs et assistants sont des enseignants*
professors and instructors are teachers
*un étudiant est inscrit dans un ou plusieurs cours*
a student is enrolled in one or more courses
*un TD est assuré par un assistant*
a class is given by an instructor
*Bob est étudiant*
Bob is a student
*une personne a un nom, un âge et une ou plusieurs adresses*
a person has a name, an age and one or several addresses

*un cours possède un ou plusieurs TD*
one or more classes are associated with a course
*un cours est donné par un professeur*
a course is given by a professor
*un TD est donné par un assistant*
a class is given by an instructor
*un cours est caractérisé par un numéro, un nom, un jour et*
  *une heure*
a course has a number, a name, a day and an hour
*un TD est caractérisé par un numéro, un jour et une heure*
a class has a number, a day and an hour
*un étudiant a un numéro d'étudiant*
a student has a student number
*un employé a un numéro de Sécurité Sociale et un téléphone*
an employee has a social security number and a phone number
*un administratif a une adresse de travail*
a staff member has a work address
*un département est caractérisé par son nom et son adresse*
a department has a name and an address
*un employé travaille dans un département*
an employee works in a department

*Fig. 2   An example of description in natural language*

## 4. THE BASE OF FACTS

We call facts all the assertions which result from the interpretation of the natural language description of the application.
The base of facts contains these assertions which are organized as a semantic network. The following sections summarize the
concepts of the semantic network adopted and the appropriate
language needed to manipulate them. More details about this knowledge representation model and its language can be found in
[BOUZ83].

### 4.1. *The semantic network*

No precise definition exists for semantic networks other
than that of being a set of labelled nodes and labelled arcs
connecting these nodes. The precise identification of nodes
and arcs categories depends on the domain in which semantic
networks are used. More precisely, a semantic network is a
triple $(NC, AC, IC)$ where NC stands for the category of nodes,
AC the category of arcs and IC the category of constraints,
such that for each element f of AC, there exists an application :

$$f : NC \ X \ NC \longrightarrow \{True, False\}$$

such that f(ni,nj) is true if there exists an arc of class f between ni and nj, and false otherwise. Depending on the domain from which the classes are taken, the arcs have specific meanings.

In the Data Base area, several semantic networks have been introduced, among others by [ROMY76], [SMSM77], [HAML78], [BROD81]. We have kept the main concepts of these proposals and, for convenience, added some additional constraints. We distinguish four types of connections, that is, AC is composed of {g,a,c,others} defined as follows :

- A generalization arc $g$ connects a node representing a class to a node representing a super-class. For example, the fact that an instructor is a teacher is represented by a generalization arc going from INSTRUCTOR to TEACHER. Such an arc represents the verb group *is a* connecting two objects. The inverse of a generalization arc is a specialization arc denoted by $s$.

- An aggregation arc $a$ connects a node representing a part of an object to the node representing the entire object. For example, the fact that a name is a component of an entity person is represented by an aggregation are going from NAME to PERSON. The inverse of an aggregation arc is a particularization arc denoted by $p$. It represents the verb group *has a* connecting two objects.

- A classification are $c$ connects a node representing an occurrence of an object type to the node corresponding to the object type. For example, the fact that Bob is a student is represented by a classification arc $c$ going from BOB to STUDENT. Such an arc corresponds to the verb group *belongs to* connecting an element to its class. The inverse of a classification arc is an instantiation arc denoted by $i$.

- An association arc connects two nodes associated by any other king of predicate. The verb representing the association is the label of the arc. For example, the fact that a class is given by an instructor is represented by an association arc labelled "IS-GIVEN-BY" going from CLASS to INSTRUCTOR. Each association may have an inverse which is the passive form or the active form of the corresponding verb. For example, the inverse of "IS-GIVEN-BY" is "GIVES".

Some constraints have to be met by the semantic network if a normalized relational schema is to be derived. These constraints, such as functional dependencies between attributes and intersection constraints between entities, may be represented by special arcs called constraint arcs. Figure 3 portrays the semantic network corresponding to the example given in Figure 2.

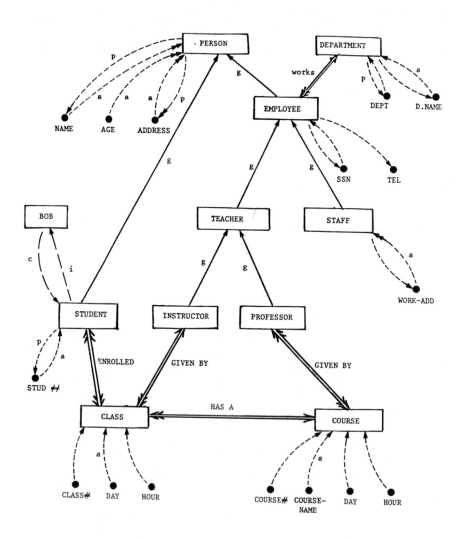

*Fig. 3   An example of a semantic network*

This semantic network may be internally represented by Prolog clauses or by a relational database of four relations:

INFO(INF-NAME,INF-CATEG)
CONNECT(ARC-NAME,INF-NAME-1,INF-NAME-2)
INTEG-CONST(CONST-NUM,INFO-NAME,CONST-CATEG,TEXTE)
COMMENT(COM-NUM,INFØ-NAME,TEXTE)

If we study a semantic network as defined so far, there appear four types of nodes : attributes, values, entities and instances of entities. Attributes and values are connected by $c/i$ arcs. Attributes and entities are connected by $a/p$ arcs. Entities may each other be connected by $g/s$ arcs or any association arc. Like attributes and values, entities and their instances are connected by $c/i$ arcs.

4.2. *The manipulation of the semantic network*

To manipulate the Semantic Network defined above, we use functional programming [BACK78]. In this section, we will summarize the functional language MORSE, that we have developed to manipulate the previous semantic network [BOUZ83]. This language is composed of a set of objects, a set of primitives, some functional forms and some derived forms.

The set of objects is composed of all categories of nodes of the semantic network defined before, including the empty set $\phi$, the undefined object, $\bot$, and the logical values $T$ and $F$.

The set of primitives is composed of the set of consulting primitives and the set of updating primitives.

(1) Consulting primitives : with each type of arc, $a,p,g,s,$ $c,i$ ...,is associated a primitive function scanning its occurrences. For example, if Y1, Y2 and Y3 are nodes connected to X by $p$ arcs, the primitive $P$ applied to X scans the $p$ arcs and gives Y1, Y2 and Y3 as a result.

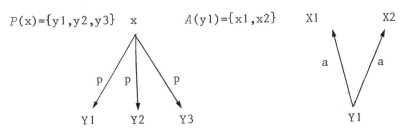

$P(x)=\{y1,y2,y3\}$      $A(y1)=\{x1,x2\}$

*Fig. 4  An example of primitives*

The symmetric primitive of $P$ is $A$. For example, if Yl is connected to X1 and X2 with $\alpha$ arcs, then $A(Yl)=\{X1,X2\}$. In the same way, $G(X)$ gives all the nodes Zi connected to X with $g$ arcs and $S(X)$ gives all the nodes Zj connected to X with $s$ arcs, etc...

(2) <u>Updating primitives</u> : nodes are simultaneously created with arcs. To create an arc $p$ between two nodes, X and Y, we use the statement $p(X,Y)$. To suppress an arc $p$, we use the statement $delete(p(X,Y))$. To suppress a node X, we use the same type of statement : $delete(i(ENTITY, X))$. ENTITY is a meta-concept to which all entity nodes are connected as its instances. Note that the basic predicates are in lower case and the corresponding primitives in upper case.

Essentially, the functional forms coincide with the set operations sum, difference, intersection and product applied to the primitives. We will likewise consider several constructions with Boolean functions as functional forms even if they are more writing conventions than compositions.

(1) *Sum of functions* : for example,
$$(G+S)(EMPLOYEE) = G(EMPLOYEE) + S(EMPLOYEE)$$
$$= \{PERSON,TEACHER,STAFF\}$$

(2) *Intersection of functions* : for example,
$$(G{\times}S)(EMPLOYEE) = G(EMPLOYEE) \times S(EMPLOYEE)$$
$$= \{PERSON\} \cap \{TEACHER,STAFF\}$$
$$= \emptyset$$

(3) *Product of functions* : for example,
$$(S*G)(EMPLOYEE) = S(G(EMPLOYEE)) = S(PERSON)$$
$$= \{EMPLOYEE,STUDENT\}$$

(4) Some particular cases :
$$G^*(PROF) = G(G(...G(PROF)...)) = \{PERSON\}.$$

This primitive is a transitive closure, it searches a tree of g arcs and returns its leaves.

$$G^+(PROF) = G^{(0)}(PROF) + G^{(1)}(PROF) + ... + G^*(PROF)$$
$$= \{PROF\} + \{TEACHER\} + \{EMPLOYEE\} + \{PERSON\}$$

This primitive searches a tree of $g$ arcs and returns all its nodes.

(5) Construction on the arcs : $p(X,Y)$ specifies that X and Y are connected by the arc $p$ going from X to Y.

$$p(\{X1,\ldots,Xn\},\{Y1,\ldots,Ym\}) \quad \leftrightarrow \quad \left\{ \begin{array}{l} p(X1,Y1) \\ p(X2,Y1) \\ \ldots\ldots \\ p(X1,Y2) \\ p(X2,Y2) \\ \ldots\ldots \\ p(Xn,Ym) \end{array} \right.$$

Derived forms : functional forms are obtained by composition (sum, product...) of primitive functions while derived forms seem more like primitives than like functional forms since they are defined with the basic predicates (arcs). But instead of using one predicate as was done for primitives, we use a combination of several predicates. The primitive function $S$(PERSON) returns all possible specializations of any person. The derived form $S'$(WATSON;PERSON) returns the actual specializations of the person Watson.

The operations defined between these functions satisfy the commutative, associative and distributive properties. $\phi$ and $|$ play the roles of either neutral element or absorbing element.

All these primitives, functional forms and derived forms allow us to specify the condition part and the action part of the production rules. If the semantic network is represented by a relational database, then it will be necessary to translate the MORSE expressions into statements in a relational language.

## 5. THE BASE OF RULES

The base of rules contains the set of rules allowing SECSI to produce a third normal form relational schema and then an optimized internal schema. The rules have the structure of production rules :

IF <CONDITION> THEN <ACTION>

The condition is expressed in terms of MORSE functions [BOUZ83], the functional language defined on our semantic network and summarized in section four. Also, the condition can include predicates on the answers given by the database administrator. The actions are either updates of the copy of the semantic network used for producing the relational schema, or messages sent to the database administrator, or

updates performed in the SABRE meta-base, or particular procedures managing specific data structures. The rules are
stored in a relational database of four relations :

- the SIMPLIFICATION relation contains all rules which allow
  SECSI to generate a first normal form schema by simplifying the semantic network
- the DEPENDENCY relation contains all rules necessary for
  finding functional dependencies
- the NORMALIZATION relation contains all rules for performing the normalization process
- the OPTIMIZATION relation contains all rules which allow
  SECSI to generate an optimized schema.

All these four relations have similar schema composed of
three attributes : RULE-NUMBER, CONDITION, ACTION. In the
following sub-sections, we give an overview of the various
categories of rules.

## 5.1. *Simplification rules*

This set of rules is used to produce a first normal form
schema. This schema is portrayed by a particular semantic
network with only two types of nodes : root nodes which represent the relations and terminal nodes which represent the
attributes. An attribute node must be connected to a set of
relation nodes by aggregation arcs. Figure 5 presents a
semantic network associated with a possible first normal
form schema representing the application described in
Figure 2. The first normal form schema corresponding to this
semantic network is presented in Figure 6. As we can see,
it is fully redundant. In addition to that first normal
form schema, the domains of the attributes are determined
and some referential integrity constraints are specified
(for example, a staff-member is an employee).
   The rules to produce a first normal form schema work on a
copy of the initial semantic network that they simplify.
That is why they are called simplification rules. More precisely, the simplifications performed are the selection of
an entity to represent a relation in a generalization hierarchy, the suppression of useless generalizations which are
replaced by attributes or virtual relations, the suppression
of association arcs which are replaced either by a redundant
attribute or by an entity node connected with the attributes
of the participating entities. In the resulting simplified
semantic network, instantiations are not considered. However,
they are kept for the next step. As an example, a basic rule

for eliminating generalizations in the inheritance of attributes. This rule is illustrated by Figure 7 and has the meaning :

> *"If X is a super-class without generalization and has several sub-classes with specific attributes then all sub-classes inherit the attributes and the associations of the super-class x".*

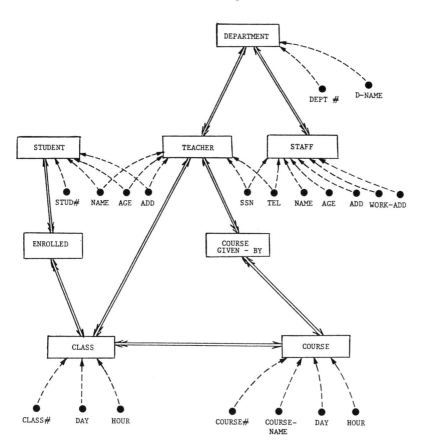

*Fig. 5   A simplified semantic network*

```
DEPT(DEPT-NUM,DEPT-NAME)
STAFF(NAME,AGE,ADDRESS,SSN,TEL,WORK-ADD)
TEACHER(NAME,AGE,ADDRESS,SSN,TEL)
STUDENT(STUD-NUM,NAME,AGE,ADDRESS)
CLASS(CLASS-NUM,COURSE-NUM,DAY,HOUR)
COURSE(COURSE-NUM,COURSE-NAME,DAY,HOUR)
ENROLLED(STUD-NUM,CLASS-NUM,COURSE-NUM)
COURSE-GIVEN-BY(COURSE-NUM,NAME)
```

*Fig. 6    The first normal form schema*

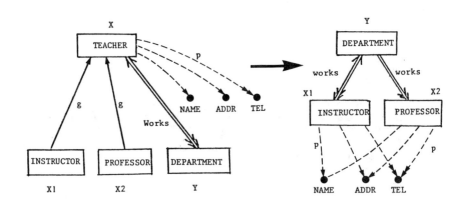

*Fig. 7    An inheritance rule*

Later, this super-class will be eliminated from the semantic network and a virtual relation will replace it in the relational meta-base of SABRE, specifying that all sub-classes Xi are included in X. In the knowledge base, this rule is converted into a condition part based on cardinalities and an action part creating and deleting sets of arcs. Such a rule is coded as shown in Figure 8.

This statement is only shown to give a flavour of how rules are represented. For more details about these functions, see [BOUZ83].

```
if      Card(G(X)) = [0,0]
    and Card(S(X)) = [0,0]
    and Card(P(X)) ≠ [0,0]
then    p(S(X),P(X))
    and r(S(X),R(X))
    and delete(p(X,P(X))
    and delete(r(X,R(X))
    and delete(i(ENTITY,X)).
```

*Fig. 8   An example of rule expressed in MORSE language*

## 5.2. *Dependency rules*

This set of rules is necessary to get the functional dependencies from the known instances of attributes and from a dialogue with the database administrator. The dialogue is directed by the structure of the semantic network obtained at the end of the simplification step. The process guesses functional dependencies between attributes connected by an aggregation arc to a given entity node. For that purpose, the system searches the instances for an example of the relation showing that there does not exist a dependency. If it does not find such an example, it asks the DBA for plausibility. If such an example is validated by the DBA, then the system assumes the non existence of the functional dependency.

After isolating functional dependencies, the transitive closure is composed and first normal form relations are proposed to the DBA. Finally, at the end of the step, a set of relation keys are proposed to the DBA who validates them. If they are not correct, the process is repeated.

## 5.3. *Normalization rules*

A normalization algorithm is applied to each entity obtained after the simplification process. The normalization algorithm is written as a set of production rules. Actions are of three types :

(1) Splitting entities which are not in third normal form. This corresponds to the normalization process.
(2) Duplicating attributes which are keys of entities, connecting them to the corresponding entities and suppressing association arcs connecting these entities.
(3) Generating additional integrity constraints such as keys , virtual relations and referencial integrity constraints.

For example, the normalized schema corresponding to the example application is portrayed as a simple semantic network in Figure 9 and as a relational schema with its integrity constraints in Figure 10.

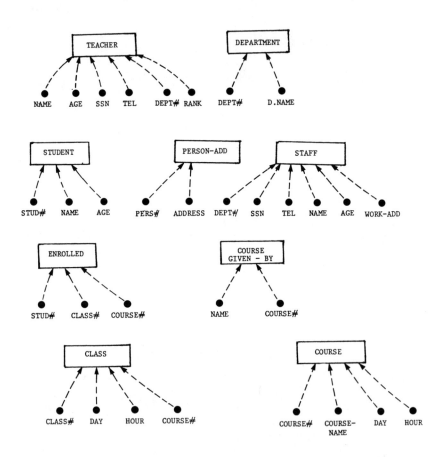

*Fig. 9  A reduced semantic network*

```
DEPT(DEPT-NUM,DEPT-NAME), KEY=DEPT=NUM
STAFF(NAME,AGE,SSN,TEL,WORK-ADD), KEY=DEPT=NUM
TEACHER(NAME,AGE,SSN,TEL,RANK), KEY=SSN
STUDENT(STUD-NUM,NAME,AGE), KEY=STUD=NUM
CLASS(CLASS-NUM,COURSE-NUM,DAY,HOUR), KEY=CLASS=NUM,
                                      COURSE-NUM
COURSE(COURSE-NUM,COURSE-NAME,DAY,HOUR), KEY=COURSE=NUM
ENROLLED(STUDENT-NUM,CLASS-NUM,COURSE-NUM), KEY=ALL
COURSE-GIVEN-BY(COURSE-NUM,NAME), KEY=ALL
PERSON-ADD(ADDRESS,NAME), KEY=ALL

PERSON(STUDENT,TEACHER,STAFF) : VIRTUAL RELATION
EMPLOYEE(TEACHER,STAFF) : VIRTUAL RELATION
DOMAIN(RANK) = {PROF,INSTRUCTOR}
```

*Fig. 10   The normalized relational schema*

## 5.4. *Optimization rules*

The optimization rules allow the system to produce the
internal relational schema. At first, a set of typical
queries with associated frequencies is given by the database administrator. These queries are stored in a relation
QUERY containing the selection attributes, the join attributes, the projection attributes and the query frequency.
Also, for each third normal form relation, an update frequency is given and stored in a relation UPDATE. Using cost
functions, computed from these relations as conditions, a
set of production rules defines conditional transformations
of the normalized semantic network in order to replace relations by their joins. The transformations are applied
only if the gain in query processing is greater than the
loss in updating. When applied, they also generate integrity constraints to keep redundancy (join dependencies). In
addition, other production rules define conditional generation of indexes. All decisions may be controlled by the
DBA.

## 6. INFERENCE ENGINE

The inference engine is based on a stepwise transformation
of the semantic network to compose the base of facts. The
transformation aiming for the normalized relational schema
is composed of the following steps which are applied recursively :
- select a fact in the base of facts
- find a rule to apply to this fact

- store the deduced or the modified fact in the base of
facts.
Actually, this schema is used for various purposes :
- simplification of the semantic network and generation of
first normal form relations
- search for functional dependencies
- normalization of each 1 NF relation
- generation of the optimized internal schema.
The most important point is how to determine the production
rule to be applied. The base of facts has the structure of
a semantic network. Each node of this network may be involved in a transformation determined by the environment which
characterizes this node, (i.e., the arcs starting or ending
at this node). This environment dictates the conditions of
some transformations. Thus, the problem of identifying a
production is equivalent to that of finding a semantic network node and exploiting the knowledge of its environment.
Given this environment, we are able to select the appropriate rule to apply by accessing sequentially the base of rules
and comparing premises of each rule with the environment
characterizing the node. Another promising method is selec-
tivity accessing actions by means of predicate-trees, an
original method developed in the SABRE project [GARD83b].

The general principle of the inference engine is based
on the forward chaining. This choice is inherent to the
nature of our problem. The inference engine starts with a
base of facts corresponding to the application description
and tries all the appropriate rules over and over, adding
new facts (constraints, nodes, arcs) or modifying old facts
until no rule applies.

Pattern matching depends on the internal organization of
rules. Rules are organized into named packets, each one
contains the rules whose premises reference the same type
of environment. For example, a packet looks as follows :

```
packet-name-1(Pred1,Pred2,Pred3) → Act1,Act2
packet-name-1(Pred1',Pred2',Pred3) → Act1,Act3
packet-name-1(Pred1,Pred2',Pred3) → Act3,Act4
```

In each packet, rules are sorted from the most particular
case to the more general case. Then the pattern matching
operates at two levels : search for the packet name and
search for appropriate premises. Each action "Acti" may be
a call for another rule whose packet name is "Acti".

7. CONCLUDING REMARKS

In this paper, we have described an expert system approach for data base design. We have summarized the methods of knowledge representation and the deduction process of the conceptual and internal relational schema. A quasi-natural language improves the communication between the end-users and the system.

With regard to the relational schema design, the synthesis algorithm [BERN76] produces a schema whose consistency is higher than that produced by a decomposition algorithm because it integrates all the functional dependencies. Unfortunately, the acquisition of all functional dependencies of the universal relation may lead to a combinatory explosion. The decomposition algorithm [CODD71] is more attractive because it reduces to a very limited set of attributes and functional dependencies. However, the 1 NF relations are subjectively declared by the DBA and the relational concepts are not sufficient to express the entire semantics of the application. SECSI adopts the latter approach ; starting from facts described in a natural language, it tries to produce more relevant a priori relations which are normalized by a decomposition algorithm. With regard to the implementation of this schema, it is known that the normalization process is often opposed to the desired level of performance. Indeed, a normalized schema contains a large number of relations which implies, if implemented just as it is, a large number of relational operations for each query. For this reason, we have made SECSI able to choose the relations to be implemented with their access paths according to the performance needs of the user's transactions.

The originality of our approach is inherent to that of expert systems. A good tool for database design should be an intelligent aid for the database administrator. Therefore, it is important that SECSI be able to explain why a choice is made ; it could also explain to the DBA in what condition it is possible to modify a schema if needed ; finally, it should be a very helpful tool to teach the DBA how to build a good schema.

This system could be extended to perform more work. We can envision database restructuring and also translation of queries expressed in a subset of natural language using the semantic network, into relational queries expressed on the relational schema. This could be a good approach for translating queries expressed in natural language.

ACKNOWLEDGEMENTS

*We wish to thank Prof. Joachim SCHMIDT of Hamburg University and Patrick VALDURIEZ from INRIA for their helpfull comments and all other members of the SABRE Project for the fruitful discussions we had together.*

REFERENCES

[ATZE81] ATZENI C., LENZERINI M., VILANELLI F. : "INCOD : a system for conceptual design of data and transactions in the E-R model", Int. Conf. on ERA, P.P. Chen Ed., ER Institute, 1981.

[BADA81] BARR A., DAVIDSON J. : "Representation of knowledge in handbook of AI", Barr & Feigenbaum Ed., Comp. Sce Dept., Stanford University.

[BERN76] BERNSTEIN P.A. : "Synthesising third normal form relations from functional dependencies", ACM-TODS, V1, N4, Dec. 1976.

[BOUZ83] BOUZEGHOUB M. : "MORSE : a functional query language built on a semantic network", to be published.

[BROD81] BRODIE M.L. : "On modelling behavioural semantics of data bases", Proc. of 7th VLDB, Conf. IEEE, 1981.

[BUNE79] BUNEMAN O.P. & FRANKEL R.E. : "FQL : a functional query language", Proc. ACM-SIGMOD, May 1979.

[CHLO80] CHAN E.P.F., LOCKOVSKY F.H. : "A graphical database design aid using the E-R model", Int. Conf. on ERA, P.P. Chen Ed., North-Holland, 1980.

[CHEN76] CHEN P.P. : "The entity relationship model - Toward a unified view of data", ACM-TODS, V1, N1, March 1976.

[CODD71] CODD E.F. : "Further normalization of the database relational model", in Courant Comp. Sce Symposia 6 : DB System, Prentice-Hall, 1971.

[GARD83a] GARDARIN G., BERNADAT P., TEMMERMAN N., VALDURIEZ P., VIEMONT Y. : "Design of a multiprocessor relational database system", IFIP Conf. Proc., Paris, 1983.

[GARD83b] GARDARIN G., VALDURIEZ P., VIEMONT Y. : "Predicate trees", Report n°4, June 1983, INRIA.

[HAML81] HAMMER & McLEOD : "Data base description with SDM : a semantic data model", ACM-TODS, V6, N3, Sept. 1981.

[LAUR82] LAURIERE J.L. : "Les systèmes experts", AFCET-TSI, n°1 et 2, 1982.

[MINS75] MINSKYM. : "A framework for representing knowledge", in Winston Ed., The psycho of Comp. Vision, NY, 1975.

[ROMY76] ROUSSOPOULOS N., MYLOPOULOS J. : "Using semantic networks for data base management", Proc. of VLDB Conf., Sept. 1976

[SHIP81] SHIPMAN D.W. : "The functional data model and the data language DAPLEX", ACM-TODS, V6, N1, March 1981.

[SMIT77] SMITH J.M., SMITH D.C.P. : "Data bases abstractions aggregation and generalization", ACM-TODS, June 1977.

[TARD79] TARDIEU H., NANCY D., PASCOT D. : "Conception de systèmes d'information, construction de la base de données", Edition d'Organisation, Paris, 1979.

[WOOD75] WOODS W.A. : "What's in a link : foundation for semantic networks" in Representation and Understanding Studies in Cognitive Science, Bobrow and Collins Ed., Academic-Press, NY, 1975

[ZAME76] ZANIOLO C., MELKANOFF M.M. : "On the design of relational data base schemata", ACM-TODS, V6, N1, 1981.

# INTERFACING PROLOG AND RELATIONAL DATA BASE MANAGEMENT SYSTEMS

G. Marque-Pucheu*, J. Martin-Gallausiaux,
and G. Jomier

*ISEM, Bât 508, Univeristé Paris-Sud, Orsay, France*
*\*Ecole Normale Supérieure, 45 rue d'Ulm, 75005 Paris, France*

ABSTRACT

In this paper we are interested in interfacing PROLOG and the
relational data base management system PEPIN.
In the first part we present the theoretical basis of this
work and in the second the implementation aspects.

## 1. INTRODUCTION

The close relationship between relational data base and predicate logic have been emphasized by several authors (GALL 78,
GALL 81, NICO 82). So, the use of PROLOG as a host language
for RDBMS is a natural choice since it is a way to "program
in Logic". This choice and the way to implement it have been
investigated in (CHAK 82, KUNI 82, MIYA 82, CHOM 83).

Three main reasons may justify this choice. First, a logic
programming language permits the definition of "virtual relations", i.e, relations defined by rules upon facts. A good
example is the relation GRANDFATHER in a data base containing
the relation FATHER. The explicit storage of the relation
GRANDFATHER leads to the waste of large amount of space and
to problems in the updates in order to maintain the consistency of the whole data base. All these problems can be
avoided by the use of the rule :

$$\forall x, \forall y, \forall z \; FATHER \, (x,y) \land FATHER \, (y,z) \Rightarrow GRANDFATHER \, (x,z)$$

In this case, no space is wasted, but the evaluation of a query
to the GRANDFATHER relation must use the rule deductively to
access the physical data.

Second, the logic programming language can be used as a host language for the processing of the data.

Third, the growing use of logic programming in the processing of natural language makes it the right language to program user-friendly interfaces.

Interfacing PROLOG and RDBMS sets a problem of efficiency. The design of PROLOG deduction strategy assumes that the cost of accessing a fact is uniform. So, resolution can be simply done by accessing facts one by one. This assumption is true when the facts are stored in main memory, but it is no longer true when the facts are stored on secondary memory. For example, the computation of the intersection of two relations A and B defining the relation C by

$$\forall x, \ A(x) \wedge B(x) \Rightarrow C(x)$$

is very inefficient with the PROLOG strategy which instanciates x upon all the individuals in the relation A and then searches these individuals in the relation B. On the other hand a RDBMS can execute operation in a very efficient way using algorithms adapted to the data access paths. Local optimizations like those proposed in (STAB 83, WARR 81) cannot give solutions in the general case, when the size of relations cannot be evaluated.

IMPLEMENTING THE INTERFACE : THE INTERPRETATIVE AND THE COMPILED APPROACH

Several propositions have been made to interface PROLOG with RDBMS in order to combine their different advantages. All of these approaches separate the knowledge base into a data base of facts managed by a conventional RDBMS and a set of rules processed by a PROLOG interpreter. In these approaches, PROLOG is considered both as a language and as a processing language.

In the compiled approach (CHAK 82, KUNI 82) deduction and evaluation are completely separated. If a query contains no virtual relation, it is sent for evaluation to the RDBMS, otherwise the rules are applied until the query contains no more virtual relations. The implementation of the version proposed by (CHAK 82) is very simple. Two methods can be used. In the first one, no modification is done in the PROLOG interpreter which operates on a metalanguage program. In the second method, the PROLOG interpreter is slightly modified to delay the evaluation of relations in the data base.

The main drawback in this approach is that the full expressive power of Horn clauses is not used. Recursive virtual relations cannot be evaluated and no further processing of the result of the query can be done.

In the interpretative approach, the deduction and the evaluation process are intermixed, and the deduction mechanism of the PROLOG interpreter is deeply modified to deal with sets of values instead of individual values. The main problem in this approach is the problem of storage of the tables and of table sharing. The two main drawbacks of this approach are the severe limitation in the size of the relations and the impossibility of query optimization.

The main reasons of the drawbacks of these solutions are in a mismatch between the structure of control and the information. PROLOG usually controls the recursivity in the rules but only the RDBMS is able to know when the recursion must stop.

A simple way to avoid these drawbacks is to define a high level interface between PROLOG and the RDBMS which does not describe the individual queries, but all the queries generated by recursive rules. This interface enables also some kind of global optimization since the RDBMS has a global information about all the processing to be done. This approach is described in this paper.

This high level interface is not limited to the interface of PROLOG with RDBMS. The proposed description of queries generalize the transitive closure (which is not sufficient to implement the full power of logic data base) while keeping the essential features of this operator : iteration of relational operators until saturation. But, the main difference is that our description is sufficient to implement the full expressive power of logic data base.

## 2. ALGEBRAIC STRUCTURE OF THE ANSWERS TO A QUERY

To define an implementation of an interface between a RDBMS and PROLOG, it is first necessary to precisely define what is the answer to a query in the general case, i.e. with recursive rules. We are going to precisely state the problem and its proposed solutions.

A first distinction must be made between the evaluation of a query and the further processing in a logic programming

language. In the processing the full power of Horn clause logic (CHAN 73) is used. In the evaluation of a query which
works only on tuples of terms without functions, we can restrict ourselves to the function free Horn clause logic. We will
assume that facts and rules are separated by using different
predicate names to define the real physical relation and the
virtual relations. We will also assume that the facts are
fully intanciated.

## DEFINITION 1

A *term* is either a constant or a variable.
An *atomic formula*, or *unit*, is a formula $R(t_1,...,t_n)$ where
R is a n-adic predicate symbol and where $t_1,...,t_n$ are terms.
A *ground unit* is an unit without variables, i.e. fully in-
tanciated.
The *extensional data base (EDB)* is a finite set of ground
units (the facts).
A *Horn clause* is a formula $A \leftarrow B_1 \wedge B_2 \wedge ... \wedge B_k$ $k > 0$, where
$A, B_1,...,B_k$ are units.

A *ground instance of a Horn clause* H is a Horn clause obtained from H when all the variables have been substituated by
constants.
The *intensional data base (IDB)* is a finite set of Horn clauses. The set of predicate symbols occuring in the units of
the EDB and of those occuring in the left hand side of Horn
clauses in the IDB are disjoint.
A *logic data base* consists of an IDB and of an EDB.
The *Herbrand universe* $\mathcal{U}$ of a logic data base in the set of all
the ground units constructed with the predicate symbols defined in the data base.
After the definition of the syntax we need a definition of
the semantics of logic data base.

## DEFINITION 2

An *interpretation* I of a Horn theory is a set of ground
units.
A *model of a logic data base* in an interpretation M such
that :

1)    $EDB \subseteq M$

2)    for each ground instance of each Horn clause of the IDB :

$$A \leftarrow B_1 \wedge ... \wedge B_k$$

$A \in M$ or for some i, $B_i \notin M$

Logic data bases as Horn theories have the "model-intersection property".

Proposition 1 : Logic data bases have the "model-intersection property", i.e. any intersection of models is itself a model. Consequently, a logic data base has a least model which is the *intersection of all models* (in the sense of the set inclusion).

DEFINITION 3

A *query* is a finite conjunction of units $B_1 \wedge \ldots \wedge B_\ell$. An *answer* to a query is a ground substitution $\sigma$, such, that, for each i ($1 \le i \le \ell$) $B_i \sigma$ belongs to the least model of the underlying logic data base.

So, the main problem in the evaluation of the answer to a query is the computation of the least model. Usually, the definition of the least fixpoint is done by fixpoint method.

DEFINITION 4

Let S be a logic data base. We define an operator $T_S$ in the powerset of the Herbrand universe by :

$$T_S : \varphi(u) \rightarrow \varphi(u)$$

such that

$A \in T_S(I)$ if A belongs to I or A belongs to the EDB or $A \leftarrow B \wedge \ldots \wedge B_k$ is an instance of clause of the IDB and for each i ($1 \le i \le n$) $B_i$ belongs to I.

Proposition 2 :   $\underset{n \in N}{U} \quad T_S^n(\phi)$ is the least model of S.

This result is not practically useful, and a more algorithmic approach is needed.

A first step in an algorithmic definition of the least model is the "normalization" of the Horn clauses in the IDB.

DEFINITION 5

The *block decomposition* of a clause is the finest partition such that two units sharing a variable belong to the same block. A logic data base is *normalized* if all the clauses in IDB have only one block.

<u>Proposition 3</u> : Each logic data base is equivalent to a normalized logic data base.

The second step is the definition of the least model using equations.

<u>DEFINITION 6</u>

Let $P_1, \ldots, P_h$ be the predicate symbol of the logic data base and $\mu$ its least model. We define $L_1, \ldots, L_h$ as :

$$L_i = \{\vec{t} \mid P_i(\vec{t}) \in \mu \}$$

<u>DEFINITION 7</u>

Let $t = (t_1, \ldots, t_n)$ be a n-tuple of terms in variables $\vec{x} = <x, \ldots, x_p>$ if R is a p-adic relation ($R \in D^p$, where D is a set), we extend t into a mapping from $\varphi(D^p)$ into $\varphi(D^n)$ by letting :

$$t.R = \{(t_1(\vec{x}), \ldots, t_n(\vec{x})) \mid \vec{x} \in R\}$$

i.e. the set of the images of t by the substitutions of $<x_1, \ldots, x_n>$ by the p-tuples belonging to R.

We define also, for each R $D^n$, $t^{-1}.R$ by :

$$t^{-1}.R = \{\vec{x} \mid (t_1(\vec{x}), \ldots, t_n(\vec{x})) \in R\}$$

<u>DEFINITION 8</u>

The system associated with a logic data base is defined as follows :

Let $\mathcal{C}_1, \ldots, \mathcal{C}_\ell$ be the clauses in the IDB. Let $J_i$ be the set of $j \in [1, \ell]$ such that $P_i$ is the predicate symbol of $\ell_j$.

The clause $\mathcal{C}_j$ for $j \in J_i$ can be written :

$$P_i \; t_j^i \leftarrow P_{n_{j,1}} \; t_{j,1} \wedge \cdots \wedge P_{n_{j,k_j}} \; t_{j,k_j}$$

$t_j^i, t_{j,1}, \ldots, t_{j,k_j}$ being the tuples of terms involved in the clause.

Let $\mathcal{R}_i$ be the set of ground tuples $\vec{t}$ such that $P_i(\vec{t})$ belongs to the EDB.
The system of equations associated with the logic data base is written :

$$
\begin{cases}
X_i = \underset{j \in J_i}{U}\ t'_j\ [\ \overset{k_j}{\underset{k=1}{\cap}}\ t_{j,k}^{-1}\ X_{n_{jk}}\ ] & \text{for } P_i \text{ is defined in the IDB} \\[2ex]
X_i = \mathcal{R}_i & \text{for } P_i \text{ defined in the EDB}
\end{cases}
$$

<u>Proposition 4</u> : The system associated to a logic data base has a least solution for set inclusion. (MARQ 81).

The *least solution* is defined by :

$$
\begin{cases}
X_{i,o} = \mathcal{R}_i & \text{if } P_i \text{ is defined in the EDB} \\[1ex]
X_{i,o} = \emptyset & \text{if } P_i \text{ is defined in the IDB}
\end{cases}
$$

$$
\begin{cases}
X_{i,n+1} = X_{i,n} & \text{if } P_i \text{ is defined in the EDB} \\[2ex]
X_{i,n+1} = \underset{j \in J_i}{U}\ t'_j\ \overset{k_j}{\underset{k=1}{\cap}}\ t_{j,k}^{-1}\ X_{jk,n} & \text{if } P_i \text{ is defined in the IDB}
\end{cases}
$$

$$
X_i = \underset{n \in \mathbb{N}}{U}\ X_{i,n}
$$

The main purpose of this system is to give another way of computing the least model.

<u>Theorem 1</u> : If $X_i$ is the i-st component of the least solution of the associated system and     the least model of a logic data base then $P_i(\vec{t}) \in \mu$    iff $\vec{t} \in X_i$.

Let us emphasize the intuitive meaning of the construction in the right hand side of the equations. Constructions like $t'\ [\ \overset{\ell}{\underset{k=1}{\cap}}\ t_k^{-1}\ X_k\ ]$     generalize all the monotonic relational operators. For instance :

1)-    with $t' = (x_1, x_3)$, $t_1 = (x_1, x_2)$, $t_2 = (x_2, x_3)$

$t'[t_1^{-1}\ X_1 \cap t_2^{-1}\ X_2]$ is the equijoin of $X_1 \subset D^2$ and $X_2 \subset D^2$

2)-    with $t' = t_1 = t_2 = (x_1, \ldots, x_n)$

$t'[t_1^{-1} X_1 \cap t_2^{-1} X_2]$ is the intersection if $X_1$ and $X_2$.

3)-    with $t' = (x_1, \ldots, x_{n+p})$, $t_1 = (x_1, \ldots, x_n)$

$t_2 = (x_{n+1}, \ldots, x_{n+p})$

$t'[t_1^{-1} X_1 \cap t_2^{-1} X_2]$ is the cartesian product of $X \subset D^n$
and $X \subset D^p$.

4)-    with $t' = (x_1, \ldots, x_p)$, $t = (x, \ldots, x_n)$, $p < n$
$t'[t^{-1} X]$ is the projection of the relation $X \subset D^n$ on
its p first components.

5)-    with $t = t' = (x_1, \ldots, x_{p-1}, b, x_{p-1}, \ldots, x_n)$, $t' \, t^{-1} X$
selects in the relation $X \in D^n$ the tuples with the
individual b as p-st component.

To have a simple notation for reasoning about queries, we
shall use a classical trick in algebraic semantics : we
define a symbolic notation for operators and the interpretation of these symbols as relational operations. We can
then show that the interpretation of the solution of the
symbolic system is equal to the solution on the interpreted
system.

DEFINITION 9

To define an interpretation of symbolic operators over a logic data base, we associate for each nil-adic symbolic operator A, a relation $\bar{A}$ defined in the EDB and for each poly-
adic symbolic operator h, a relational operator $\bar{h}$ of the
above defined type.

We extend inductively the interpretation to trees by letting :

$$\overline{h(t, \ldots, t_n)} = \bar{h}(t, \ldots, \bar{t}_n)$$

and then to set of trees by letting

$$\bar{T} = \bigcup_{t \in T} \bar{t}$$

Example : We shall use as an example the classical "Ancestor" relation :

$$A(x_1,x_2) \leftarrow A(x_1,x_3) \wedge F(x_3,x_2)$$
$$A(x_1,x_2) \leftarrow F(x_1,x_2)$$

The interpreted version of the system may be written :

$$X_A = \{(x_1,x_2) \; [(x_1,x_2)^{-1} \; X_A \cap (x_3,x_2)^{-1} \; X_F]\}$$
$$X_F = \mathcal{R}_F$$

and the uninterpreted version may be written :

$$Y_A = h(Y_A,Y_F) \cup Y_F$$
$$Y_F = R_F$$

its solution is the rational set of trees

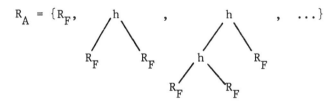

$\bar{h}$ is interpreted as a join operator and $R_F$ is interpreted as $\bar{R}_F = \mathcal{R}_F$.

Theorem 2 : The interpretation of the solution of the uninterpreted system is equal to the least solution of the interpreted system (MARQ 83).

The algebraic structure of the solution of the uninterpreted system is always simple.

DEFINITION 10

An *automaton* $\mathcal{A}$ is a quadruple $\mathcal{A} = (Q,\Sigma,Q_F,\delta)$ where $Q$ is a finite set of states, $\Sigma$ a (weighted) set of functional symbols, $Q_F \subset Q$ the subset of final states and $\delta$ is a mapping such that, for each $f \in \Sigma$ of arity $p$, $\delta(f)$ is a mapping $Q^p \to Q$. We can extend $\delta$ into a mapping $\delta : T_\Sigma \to Q$ (where $T_\Sigma$ is the set of trees constructed with the symbols of $\Sigma$) by letting :

$$\delta(f(t, \ldots, t_p)) = \delta(f) [\delta(t), \ldots, \delta(t_p)] .$$

A set of trees is called *rational* if there exists an automaton $A$ such that :

$$R = \{t \in T_\Sigma \mid \delta(t) \in Q_F\}.$$

Theorem 3 : The solution of the uninterpreted system associated with a logic data base is a rational set of trees. (MARQ 83).

The definition of rationality and of interpretation leads to an algorithm to compute a virtual relation defined by a rational set of trees recognized by an automaton $A$ and an interpretation.

*ALGORITHM* : Let $A = (Q, \Sigma, Q_F, \delta)$ be an automaton recognizing the set of trees which define the relation.

- For each $q \in Q$, let $R_{q,o} = \emptyset$
- For each "transition" $q_1, \ldots, q_p \overset{h}{\to} q'$ in    (a picturial notation for $\delta(h) [q_1, \ldots, q_p] = q'$) and each n add $\bar{h}(R_{q_1,n}, \ldots, R_{q_p,n})$ to obtain $R_{q',n+1}$ after all adjunctions.
- Stop when $R_{q,n+1} = R_q$ for each $q \in Q$
- Define the resulting relation R as :

$$R = \underset{q \in Q_F}{\cup} R_{q,n}.$$

This algorithm is close to the one developed in (NICO 81). It can be practically improved in several ways :

• All the unnecessary transitions can be first deleted from the definition of the automaton ($\delta$ is then a partial mapping)

• The increments of relations can be computed with the increments of relations of the precedent step.

This algorithm to compute a relation is in fact an algorithm to compute the answer to a given query. In this case, we only need to add a dummy rule with the query at the right-hand side and a new predicate symbol at the left-hand side.

Example : In the case of the ancestor relation, the computation proceeds as follows :

$$\begin{cases} R_{1,o} = \emptyset \\ R_{2,o} = \emptyset \end{cases}$$

$$\begin{cases} R_{1,1} = \mathcal{R}_F \\ R_{2,1} = \mathcal{R}_F \end{cases}$$

$$R_{1,n+1} = \bar{h} \ ([R_{1,n} - R_{1,n-1}], \ \mathcal{R}_F) \cup R_{1,n}$$

$$\mathcal{R}_A = R_{1,n} \quad \text{as soon as} \quad R_{1,n+1} = R_{1,n}.$$

$\bar{h}$ is in this case, an equijoin.

This computation in rather efficient if all the relations
are sorted with the appropriate keys, since no redundant
computation is done in this case.

4 - OPTIMIZATION OF QUERIES

The previously defined algorithm is rather efficient in some
cases. It can be very inefficient in the case of late selection. Let us show it on an example :

Example : We define the ancestor relation as above, and a
query :

$$?x \quad A(x,a)$$

asking about the ancestor of the individual a. In
this case, the rational set of trees defining the
answer is :

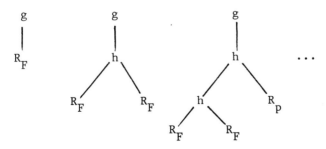

let $\bar{g}$ be an unary operator (selection-projection) defined
by :

$$\bar{g}(X) = (x_1) \ [(x ,a)^{-1} \ X \ ]$$

This definition of the answer to a query leads to a very
inefficient computation since we compute all the ancestor
relation before the selection. To optimize this query, we
can use a reordering of the relational operators similar to
the one described in (CHU 82). A simple computation shows
that for any relations X and Y, the following equality holds :

$$g[h(X,Y)] = h'[X,g(Y)]$$

h' being a new symbol interpreted as :

$$\bar{h}'(X,Y) = (x_1) \ \{[(x_1,x_2)^{-1} \ X] \cap [(x_2)^{-1} \ Y]\}$$

By successive applications of this equality, we obtain a
different but equivalent rational set of trees

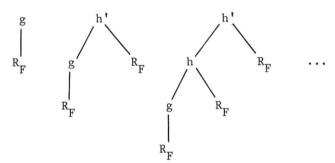

which is much more efficient.

So, the problem of optimization comes down to a transformation of a set of trees into another set of trees giving the
same answer. This is rather different from the optimization
of non-recursive queries. With recursive queries, the finite
description of all the optimized trees is the main problem.
*The RDBMS cannot optimize the individual trees since they do
not appear in any moment of the query evolution. Only their
global (finite) description can be used, and so, a different
approach is necessary to optimize the queries.* In fact it is
not obvious that the set of optimized trees obtained by
optimization of a rational set of trees is also rational. It
is possible to show with a counterexample that this property
is not true. But, for the most important optimizations, this

property is hopefully true thus enabling a simple and efficient interface between the RDBMS and PROLOG.

### DEFINITION 11

A dyadic operator $\bar{h}$ defined by

$$\bar{h}(X,Y) = t \ [(t_1^{-1} \ X) \cap (t_2^{-1} \ Y)]$$

is called *normal* if the tuples of terms t, $t_1$, $t_2$ do not contain constants and if all the variables involved in each of these terms are distinct. A monadic operator $\bar{g}$ defined by $g(X) : t'[t^{-1} \ X]$ is called a *selection* (resp. an *extension*) iff t' (resp. t) does not contain constants and if all the variables involved are distinct.

A first optimization can be done by putting the "selections" down to the leaves and the "extensions" up to the root of the trees.

### DEFINITION 12

A rational set of trees defining the answer to a query is in *first normal form**, if all its trees contain only normal dyadic operators, selections and extensions and if the extensions appear only at the root and the selections are applied only on the leaves.

Theorem 4 : For each rational set of trees defining the answer to a query, there exists a rational set of trees in first normal form defining the same answer (MARQ 83).

The queries can be further optimized.

### DEFINITION 13

A normal dyadic operator $\bar{h}$ defined by

$$\bar{h}(X,Y) = t\{ \ [\ t_1^{-1} \ X]\cap [t_2^{-1} \ Y \ \}]$$

is a cartesian product f $t_1$ and $t_2$ have no variable in common. It is called a semijoin operator if all the variables in $t_1$ appear in $t_2$ or if all the variables in $t_2$ appear in $t_1$. It is called a join operator otherwise.

---

\*
   *N.B. no connection with Codd's normal forms.*

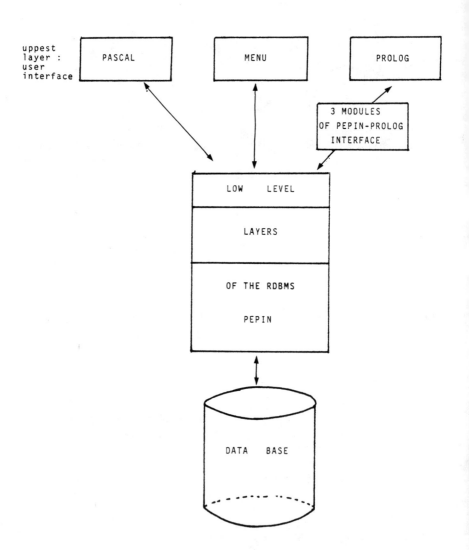

*Fig. 1   The RDBMS PEPIN*

DEFINITION 14

A rational set of trees defining the answer to a query is in *second normal form* if the cartesian product appears only at the top of the trees and the semijoin and intersection operators only at the bottom.

Theorem 5 : For each rational set of trees defining the answer to a query, there exists a rational set of trees in second normal form defining the same answer.

We can also note that the property is also true for some optimizations using the associativity of the join operator (MARQ 83).

5 - IMPLEMENTATION ON THE RDBMS PEPIN

1)- Some elements about PEPIN

PEPIN is a rational data base management system which has been developped first at INRIA then at PARIS-SUD University (I.S.E.M. Laboratory). (BOUC 81).

This system, which is operational, offers a relational interface. More precisely the operations are

- at the level of the tuples :

  • insertion
  • retrieve, modification and deletion of the tuples of a relation which verify a condition. The conditions are conjunctions and disjunctions of elementary conditions. The elementary conditions are

        (ATTRIBUT, OPERATOR, CONSTANT)

    or   (ATTRIBUT 1, OPERATOR, ATTRIBUT 2)

    where operator is = , < , ≤ , > , ≥ , < >   ;

- at the level of the relations :

  • unary operations : projection, selection, sort, aggregates
  • binary operations : join, intersection, union, difference, cartesian product.

PEPIN is written in PASCAL and has a structure with layers (BOUC 83). The uppermost layer is the user interface which

transforms the requests of the user in operations on the data
or in operations of "management" of transactions (initialisa-
tion, locks, commitment , abort, end of session), which are
executed by the low level layers of the RDBMS.

Until now the users access to PEPIN via a menu or using interfaces (conversational or not) written in PASCAL and specially
adapted to an application (cf. Fig. 1). The goal of this
work was to offer to the users a third possibility of interface via PROLOG, for the reasons explained in the introduction.

## 2)- The implementation of the interface PROLOG-PEPIN

To implement this interface we had at our disposal a PROLOG
interpreter written in PASCAL.
So the realization of the above explained method leads to
three different modules, two written in PROLOG and the last
one in PASCAL.

### a) Module 1 : the "clauses compiler"

As shown on Fig. 2 the first module is a "clauses compiler"
- its inputs are the user interactively defined virtual relations
- its output is the automaton (definition 10).

It provides the normalization of the clauses of the logic
data base (definition 5).
In our example (Fig. 2) defining the virtual relation Ancestor
the two first clauses correspond to the IDB (definiton 1) and
the third one indicates that Father is a real relation which
belongs to the relational data base (EDB). In the automaton
appear the transitions and the relational operations (here
a join) to be done.
The purpose of the "clauses compiler" for the virtual relations may be compared to the purpose of the definition module
in a data base management system for the real relations.
Now the virtual relations are defined : it is possible to
use them in PROLOG queries which will use the second and the
third modules of the PROLOG-PEPIN interface.

### b)- Module 2 : transmission of parameters and optimization

The module 2 is activated when the user formulates a query
to the data base through the built-in PROLOG predicate "eval".
In our example we ask for Jim's ancestors.
The information contained in the query, particularly the value of some parameters (here Y = Jim, i.e. we are going to

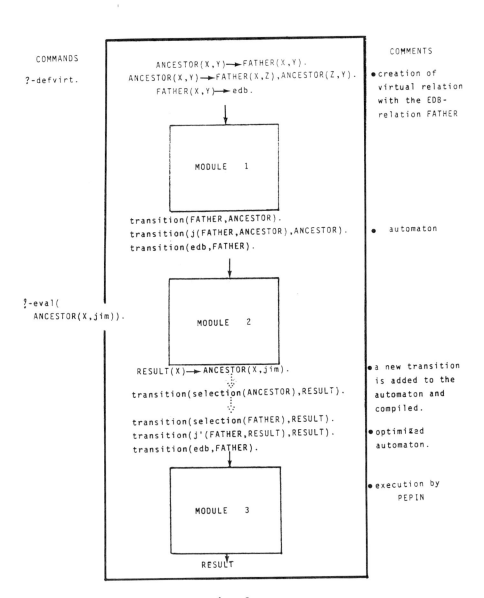

COMMANDS

?-defvirt.

ANCESTOR(X,Y)⟶FATHER(X,Y).
ANCESTOR(X,Y)⟶FATHER(X,Z),ANCESTOR(Z,Y).
FATHER(X,Y)⟶edb.

COMMENTS

● creation of
virtual relation
with the EDB-
relation FATHER

MODULE    1

transition(FATHER,ANCESTOR).
transition(j(FATHER,ANCESTOR),ANCESTOR).
transition(edb,FATHER).

● automaton

?-eval(
ANCESTOR(X,jim)).

MODULE    2

RESULT(X)⟶ANCESTOR(X,jim).

transition(selection(ANCESTOR),RESULT).

transition(selection(FATHER),RESULT).
transition(j'(FATHER,RESULT),RESULT).
transition(edb,FATHER).

● a new transition
is added to the
automaton and
compiled.

● optimized
automaton.

● execution by
PEPIN

MODULE    3

RESULT

*Fig. 2*

perform a selection on the Ancestor relation), must be transmitted to the automaton. This is done by adding a clause to
the automaton.

Here the query generates a clause

$$Result(X) \rightarrow Ancestor\ (X, Jim)$$

which is compiled in :

$$transition\ (Sélection(Ancestor),\ Result)$$
$$Y = Jim$$

and added to the automaton.
After this modification the automaton must be transformed,
taking into account the optimization rules of relational
queries. For instance the selection $Y = Jim$ on the relation
Ancestor must be changed in the same selection on the relation Father in order to diminish the size and eventually the
number of intermediate results (temporary relations) generated by the RDBMS.

The optimization is divided in two parts. The first one is
based on some classical criteria (cf. definition 12 "first
and second normal forms") : the selections, projections, semi-
joins and intersections are to be executed as soon as possible and the cartesian products as late as possible.
After this first step of the optimization another one would
be necessary to determine the order of execution of the other
operations, such as the joins. But the results available to-
day in the area of relational query evaluation and query optimization do not yet allow the realization of the tool we
would like to have here.

   c)- Module 3 : execution of the optimized automaton

The optimized automaton is sent to the third module of the
interface which executes it using the saturation algorithm
detailed at the end of section 3 of this paper in order to
control the end of recursions. As this module follows step
by step the execution of the relational operations it is
written in PASCAL, like PEPIN.
At the end of the execution the values corresponding to the
answer to the relational query are returned, through a buffer
to PROLOG, using the backtrack mechanism on the predicate
"eval".
In case of necessity for the continuation of the PROLOG program it is easy to transfer the results of a query to facts
of PROLOG. In order to do that a predicate "assert-in" can
be defined using "eval".

Some parts of those modules have already been implemented but the work is still in progress. Nevertheless the performances of the resulting system will depend for a part on future results on relational queries optimization.

CONCLUSION

In the introduction we pointed out the two main problems appearing in the works on the Interface PROLOG-RDBMS : the control of the recursion and the optimization.
The algorithm presented in this paper, which uses a technique of saturation, ensures that the recursion will end in any case, so the answer to the relational query will always be obtained. This technique had been used before for generative data bases (NICO 81): in this case the deductive rules are applied each time an update is performed. As a result the answers to all the possible queries are generated, but at the same time much information, which will never be used is created and stored. However we only use the technique of saturation to build the answer to the query. In this way we deal with one aspect of the optimization problem, which is to avoid the generation of useless relational data. Nevertheless, as we saw before, different aspects of the general problem of optimization remain opened.

REFERENCES

(BOUC 81) : P. BOUCHET, A. CHESNAIS, J-M. FEUVRE, G. JOMIER, A. KURINCKX : "Data bases for microcomputers : the PEPIN approach". ACM SIGMOD workshop on small data base systems, Orlando (Florida). Oct. 1981, SIGSMALL NEWSLETTER, vol. 7, n° 2.

(BOUC 83) : P. BOUCHET, A. CHESNAIS, J-M. FEUVRE, G. JOMIER "PEPIN : Un SGBD relationnel pour microordinateurs". Workshop on Relational DBMS Design/Implementation/Use on microcomputer, 14-15 Feb. 1983, Toulouse (France).

(CHAK 82) : U.S. CHAKRAVARTHY, J. MINKER, D. TRAN "Interfacing predicate logic languages and relational data bases". Proc. of the 1st Int. Logic Programming Conf., Marseille (France), Sept. 82.

(CHAN 73) : C.L. CHANG, R.T.C. LEE : "Symbolic logic and mechanical theorem proving". Academic Press, 1973.

(CHOM 83) : J. CHOMICKI, W. GRUDZINSKY : "A data base system support for PROLOG". Proc. of the Logic Program. Workshop 83, Univ. Nova de Lisboa, Algarve (Portugal)

(CLOC 81) : W.F. CLOCKSIN, C.S. MELLISH : "Programming in
PROLOG". Springer Verlag 1981.

(GALL 78) : H. GALLAIRE, J. MINKER, J.M. NICOLAS (Ed.)
"Advances in data base theory", vol. 1, Plenum
Press 1981.

(KUNI 82) : S. KUNIFUJI, H. YOKOTA : "PROLOG and relational
data bases for fifth generation computer systems".
in (NICO 82).

(MARQ 81) : G. MARQUE-PUCHEU : "Quelques applications de la
logique du premier ordre à des problèmes de pro-
grammation". Thèse d'Etat, Paris-VI, 81 (France).

(MARQ 83) : G. MARQUE-PUCHEU : "Algebraic structure of the
answers to a query in a logic data base".
To appear.

(MIYA 82) : N. MIYAZAKI : "A data sublanguage approach to
interating  predicate logic languages and relational data bases". Techn. Memo. n° 1, ICOT,
Tokyo (Japan), 1982.

(NICO 81) : J-M. NICOLAS, J. MINKER : "On recursive axioms
in relational data bases". TR-1119 University
of Maryland (USA), 1981.

(NICO 82) : J-M. NICOLAS : "Logical bases for data bases".
Preprint of the workshop. Toulouse (France),
Dec. 1982.

(STAB 83) : E.P. STABLER, G.W. ELOCK : "Knowledge representation in an efficient deductive inference system". Proc. of the Logic Programming Workshop 83.
Univer. Nova, Lisboa Algarve (Portugal).

(ULLM 80) : J. ULLMAN : "Principles of data bases systems".
Pitman 1980.

(WARR 81) : D.W.D. WARREN : "Efficient processing of interactive relational data base queries expressed in
logic". Proc. of the VLDB Conf. Cannes (Frances)
1981.

# Engineering Data Bases

# DATABASES FOR COMPUTER-AIDED DESIGN

## Mike Gray

*Shape Data Ltd, Cambridge, England*
*Present address: IBM UK Science Centre,*
*St Clement's Street, Winchester, England*

## INTRODUCTION

A computer-aided design system will contain many tools. For example, in the field of machined-metal component design, there might be tools for solid modelling, for finite-element analysis, for the production of engineering drawings, production of numerically-controlled machine tapes, and so on. These programs may be concerned with slightly different subsets of the design data, and may use it in different ways; hence there are integration problems.

Database systems are intended to solve this kind of problem by providing a robust store for data that can be accessed in a high-level data-independent way. A computer-aided design system will need to be integrated around such a database. However the DBMSs developed for commercial data processing are unsuitable in a number of ways for the requirements of CAD. The characteristics of design data are different:

- the data has a complex structure with entities interlinked in many ways.
- much of the information consists of the structure of these linkages.
- consistency and transactions are harder to define
- the conceptual schema may change frequently

This applies to the design of mechanical components, of electronic hardware, and of software. For definiteness, the discussion here will be in terms of mechanical components.

THE DATABASE MUST REALLY BE USED

The intention is for the database to be the authoritative version of the design. Only then can it really integrate and control the various activities. Engineering drawings and other representations should be derived from the database, rather than the other way round, so that anyone who needs to find out the current state can use the database.

This means that the database must be very flexible in allowing information to be added. Any information or annotation that someone could add to paper drawings, they must be able to record in the database. If this is not possible, a designer will end up keeping notes on the back of envelopes, and any chance of creating an integrated CAD system will vanish. The conceptual schema must be able to evolve during the design process to accommodate the necessary data. The function of the database system is to allow existing tools to continue to function despite this change or evolution in the data. This is "data independence".

DATA INDEPENDENCE

Data independence is usually achieved by the provision of "external schemas" or "views" of the database. Each tool has a view of the data containing those elements which it relies upon, and the database system maintains the availability of this view despite changes in the conceptual schema. The changes in the schema which can be catered for include the addition of new information, a change in the representation or units of some item, or a simple change in the logical structure.

This process of providing a view tailored to a particular program must be reversible, so that updates generated by that program can be applied to the database. It must be possible to propagate updates through whatever views are provided. The problem of propagating updates through views has been widely studied; see for example (1), (2). It largely concerns what to do with the information that the program does not know about, and how it is affected by the updates. In general it will be necessary to "discard" or "unset" some of this information, and so a design database requires a simple mechanism for taking care of "null values" (3).

## THE DATA MODEL

A conventional database consists of a collection of records making up a model of a given "universe of discourse" or "enterprise". This model is normally considered in terms of entities and their attributes, and relationships between them. A typical update transaction on such a database consists of creating or deleting entities, altering their attributes or altering relationships between them.

When we consider a design database, containing the descriptions of metal components, the situation looks similar. There are many of these entities, with attributes, and some relationships between them. There will be details of different versions of a component, of which versions are compatible with which other versions, which drawings relate to which versions, and all the usual apparatus for controlling the design process. A designer, when he is working on a given component, will retrieve its description from the database, make some changes to it, and put it back.

However, when we look at a given metal component, the shape information upon which the designer works is not a simple attribute. It will be a 3-d model of the component. This can consist of a number of bodies of certain fixed primitive types (such as boxes, cylinders, cones etc.) to be combined together to give the component shape. Alternatively it can consist of a number of edges, faces and vertices, and their positions in space and topological connections. This latter way of describing the shape is more likely to be useful for attaching other information in the database, and so the discussion here will be in terms of it.

A solid body owns a set of faces, each of which lies in some geometric locus in space such as a plane. Each face surrounded by a ring of edge and vertices, which are linked together so as to travel round the face in a particular direction. The edges and vertices also have locations in space.

We can regard this 3-d description as one of the attributes of the component, along with other attributes such as component name, date designed, version number or material. If we treat the 3-d description simply as an atomic attribute of the component, there is no difficulty in handling it. The DBMS stores the 3-d description, and hands it over to any program that asks for it. The problem with

this is that the designer will often wish to record other
information not just about the component as a whole but
about some part of the 3-d model.  For example, he may want
to record in the database that a particular face of the body
is to have a given surface finish.  This information is not
part of the 3-d shape information, yet needs to point into
it.  If the 3-d description is a single atomic value to the
database, this will not be possible.  Thus if the database
is ignorant of the details of how 3-d shapes are described,
the designer will be severely restricted in recording
information.

The database should therefore be aware of the 3-d
description of the component.  The conceptual schema should
mention such things as edges, vertices and faces.  These
belong to a given component, but they cannot simply be
attributes of it because they have attributes of their
own and there are relationships amongst them.  They must
therefore be stored in the database as entities.

These entities which make up the 3-d model of a component
clearly belong to that component in some sense.  Although
"vertex" and "face" are entities in the database, they
cannot exist other than as part of a component.  This
dependency can be handled using the mechanism of referential constraints in the relational model, but this is not
entirely satisfactory.  The referential constraint mechanism
was set up to handle cases such as an employee belonging to
a department.  This does not imply that an employee is only
able to exist in the context of a department; employees can
be moved from department to department, for example, but one
cannot simply move a vertex from one body to another.

It seems more natural to have a two-level system of
entities, where the vertices, edges and so on are sub-
entities of the component.  Their names will then be local
to this component, so that rather than each vertex in the
database having a globally unique database identifier, it
has an identifier unique within the component, and the
component has a unique identifier.  This is equivalent in
the relational model to having a compound key for vertices,
one part being the component key, and a referential
constraint to the component relation ensuring that the
appropriate component exists.

A related problem is that of fetching "all the information" about a given component (for example to archive it
to tape, or copy it to another database).  This involves

fetching its attributes, and some of the entities related
to it both directly and indirectly. It is necessary to
output the edges and vertices connected with it, and any
information connected with them. It is thus a problem of
traversing the data-structure by following pointers, rather
like marking garbage collection. However, not all pointers
are followed; if the object belongs to a set, it is not
necessary to output all the information about that set
(which would include all the other members). In this way,
the pointer from the component to the set in which it
belongs is different from the pointers to the sub-entities
defining the shape. We wish to treat the shape information
as a whole as if it were a single attribute.

The meaning of the sub-entities in a 3-d model differs
from those in more conventional applications of databases
in that much of the information carried by them is in
their connections to one another. Vertices edges and faces
will have a position in space recorded with them, but they
also form a complex network with one another, and this
information is crucial to the model. It is this greater
emphasis on information recorded in relationships rather
than attributes that makes the CAD problem different from
conventional database use. The significance of an entity
is as much in its position in the network as in the values
recorded in it. This makes it very hard to express
constraints non-procedurally, for example, or to transform
the information into another representation.

Given that the 3-d description of a component is held
in the database system, how can the solid modeller make
alterations to it? The operation of the solid modeller is
typically expensive, and involves very intensive access to
the model. It is therefore essential that the 3-d model
should be resident in store, and should be uncluttered by
other information not relevant to the operation of solid
modelling. Thus we must have a "scratchpad" mode of
working. (This can also deal with the problem of rolling
back the current update). The question is where to draw the
line between DBMS and solid modeller. One method is to have
the solid modeller request the 3-d model from the database,
act upon it at will during the session, and present the
altered model to the database for storage at the end. The
other possibility is for the modeller to make the changes to
the model by calling the DBMS, which will keep the model in
store and write it back to disk at the end of the session.
It will be up to the database administrator to see that if
the database contains information which has been computed

from the shape, it is discarded when the shape is altered.

## THE PROBLEM OF RETAINING CONTINUITY OF NAMES

The problem comes from information which refers not to the
component itself, but to the sub-entities making up the 3-d
model. If there is a "surface finish" attached to a face in
the model, when the designer works on the model, that
information should not be lost. Whenever the designer uses
a tool, he does not expect it to throw away all the
information he has recorded about his design that it does
not understand. This information must be retained across
the operation of that tool. If no changes have been made
anywhere near a face, then the designer will certainly
expect the system to retain information about it such as
surface finish. What happens if the shape or position of
the face is altered? What if it is cut into two parts by
the designer? Do both parts that have that surface finish,
or only one of them? The problem amounts to knowing what
is the "same face" after changes have been made to the 3-d
model of the component.

The same applies to other features such as vertices or
edges. Many of these may be created or deleted during a
design session. It will not always be clear how they
correspond. For example, if a designer shortens a rod or
bar, is the new end face the "same face" as the old end
face? (See Figure 1).

If the operation is accomplished by sectioning the body
with a plane, and then discarding the small body cut off,
then this will not be so. If it is done by a more local
operation, reducing the length of the bar or moving the
defined position of the end face, then it will stay the same
face. This is rather unsatisfactory. We could ask the
designer, as he performed each operation on the component,
which parts now correspond to which, but this is tiresome:
on the other hand any default assumptions might well go
wrong.

The problem is for the DBMS to know what is the "same
face". There must be some way for information about sub-
entities such as faces to be preserved across modelling
operations.

If we adopt the method of working where the modeller
makes changes to the model by calling the DBMS, then the
DBMS must keep track of these entities as the modeller

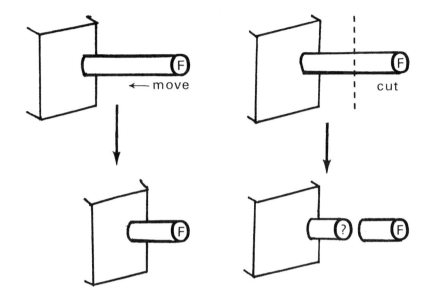

Fig. 1   Shortening a bar by two different methods.

alters the shape.  If the operations on the shape are of the
forms "create edge", "delete face" and so on, then the DBMS
will have little chance of doing anything intelligent with a
problem such as that in Figure 1.  An improvement is for the
DBMS to understand more of the semantics of the data.  This
is usually regarded as being a good thing in commercial
applications, but here it means that the database will end
up having to know as much about solid models as the solid
modeller.  The operations available will be some set of
transactions embodying the semantics of solid models, for
example the "Euler Operations".  (4) These are simple
combinations of creating and deleting faces, edges and so
on, which model rather better the operations performed on
solids.  These transactions will have to cope with all the
information in the schema.  Having the interface to the DBMS
at the Euler Operation level so that the solid modeller
can be built on top of that is an attractive solution, but
does not seem practical at the moment.  It would still not
entirely solve the problem of understanding the operations
done on the shape; even if the operation of removing the end
of the bar in Figure 1 is described in Euler operations, it
is still ambiguous as to which face the designer wants to
inherit the name F.

If we adopt the other level of interface, where the modeller fetches the solid model from the database and works on it directly, then the modeller will need to keep with each entity some kind of database identifier so that when the model is replaced the database can know which faces correspond. In areas of the model where no change is made, the identifiers will remain fixed so that the faces etc. will keep their other attributes in the database. In areas where the designer has made changes during the session, the modeller will have to find out which faces should now have those identifiers. This can be done by a combination of careful algorithms and asking the user. Thus in the case of shortening the bar, the modeller will have to deduce or ask the user which face was required.

EXTERNALLY NAMED FEATURES OF BODIES

One improvement is to have a list of those features of the model requiring this continuity. The modeller then only need ask the designer about cases where one of the features has been affected. This amounts to having a "spec" of the object, containing statements such as "there is a face F having surface-finish 35". Then if the model is changed in the region of F, the designer can in some way be offered the chance to specify which face of his new model now fills the role of F. This effectively provides high-level names for features such as faces, which can be bound to different actual faces after a design change.

This process of separating out those features of the component which can be referred to from outside is similar to the usual methods of separating the interface definition from the implementation of a hardware or software module. For example, in a database for VLSI design, there could be two levels of description. There might be a description at one level of a component in terms of logic naming certain inputs and outputs and describing the required behaviour in terms of these. The designer who was implementing this would be working with a model describing areas of silicon and their coordinates; at the end of a session he would have to re-establish the correspondence between this and the higher-level names, where it had been affected by his work. It would then be possible, for example, to perform a simulation to ensure that the given silicon design would match the logic-level description.

We can regard the running of such a program as a consistency constraint on the database, but it is unreasonable to expect the DBMS itself to enforce such a constraint automatically. However, the fact that the program can be run to verify consistency can be recorded in the conceptual schema. In many ways the information in the higher-level (logic level as opposed to silicon layout level) description of the circuit corresponds to the kind of information which would be in the conceptual schema in a conventional application. It gives a higher level, more slowly changing description which the values in the lower level model must satisfy. In this kind of application there might not be just two levels of description, but many: there might be silicon layout, transistor-level description, logic gate level description, register-level description and so on. Each of these constrains the one below it. The relationships between the levels can be recorded in the conceptual schema, and this information combines with each level to give a schema for the level below.

WHAT ARE CONSTRAINTS?

Constraints are statements about the values in a database which are explicitly stored with the database, and checked (enforced). Not every statement about the values will be stored; we cannot completely describe the semantics of an application. The description and enforcement of constraints on a design database is a problem.

There are several reasons for storing constraints about a database explicitly and enforcing them. Firstly, there are those constraints that are necessary in order to organise the database. For example, limiting the range of values of some attribute so that space can be allocated for it, or specifying the uniqueness of certain fields so that they can be used as keys. These fundamental constraints create little problem.

Secondly, constraints are stored explicitly that would otherwise be coded as tests in application programs. These constraints ensure that the data is at least such that the programs should not crash. The advantage of storing them explicitly in the database rather than in programs is just that they are easier to find and maintain there, and uniformity is ensured. A programmer wishing to see which characteristics of the data he can rely on can look at the list of constraints.

Finally, constraints are stored so that there is some chance of detecting errors in the data; if an update is applied which does not reflect the truth about the world it might also violate one of the constraints, and so be caught and rejected. This last reason is less meaningful in the design environment, as there is no one "correct" state of the database; it is not a model of a well-defined universe of discourse.

CONSTRAINTS ON DESIGN DATA

The problem with design data is that it does not exactly model a real world, and there can be different levels of consistency. Consider a data structure describing a three-dimensional shape. The simplest level of consistency of this structure is that the pointers involved are valid, so that following the "next edge" pointer from an edge leads to another edge. A higher level of consistency is "Euler consistency", meaning that the topological arrangement of faces, edges and vertices is consistent with a closed solid. Above this is geometrical consistency, meaning that the body is not self-intersecting according to the positions defined for the parts of the shape. Finally there might be constraints on the object concerned with its use; in other words design constraints that it must satisfy.

The first level of these constraints must always hold in the database, although it can be violated by a program while re-arranging part of the data structure. Such a re-arrangement will therefore be a "transaction" at this level, in order to conceal the invalid state from any other program, or to prevent it from ending up in the database in the event of a crash. The Euler consistency level is also required for almost any purpose, and is maintained by having as transactions the Euler operations. The above operations are very small, and transactions on so fine a grain must be entirely in-store operations to allow adequate performance. Any model stored by the designer into the database will satisfy these constraints. The higher-level constraints are the ones that cause problems. They can only be checked by running quite long programs.

The main purpose of consistency constraints in a CAD application is the second one mentioned above: defining the properties that a given program can rely on, and must preserve; but different levels of consistency may be necessary in the input to different processes. A design to be released to other people might have to satisfy the

full design constraints, so that it could be input to a
simulation. On the other hand, the simple tools used by the
individual designer might rely only on the lower level of
consistency. Hence other people would see the designer as
locking a design for a considerable time while he performed
some long transaction on it, whereas the tools used by
the designer would work in smaller transactions taking
the design from one state to the next. Thus the smaller
transactions are nested inside the longer one. Different
methods of handling nested transactions have been suggested
by several authors. (5), (6).

What is required here is that the system will be aware of
several different definitions of consistency, and will know
which definitions apply to which programs. This will induce
a structure of nested transactions whereby at a certain
point it will be possible to use some program on a design,
but others will be locked out because the design is invalid
to them. This can be compared with the technique developed
in System R, where there is one definition of consistency,
but programs differ in the extent to which they need to see
consistent data. (7).

CONCLUSIONS

Applications such as CAD involve data where a high propor-
tion of the information is carried by the structure of
linkages between the entities. This makes it more difficult
to handle the data by conventional techniques: constraints
are harder to express non-procedurally, and it can be harder
to retain meaningful names for entities. For example, an
item of information in the database may refer to face F of
a model, where F is "the end face", but operations carried
out on the model can change which face is "the end face"
in an unpredictable way. We therefore need to have a set
of external names, such as "the end face", which can be
associated with the actual entities in a flexible way. This
set of names and the statements made about them constitute a
higher-level description of the object. There may be
many levels of description. There may also be different
levels of consistency for the data-structure appropriate
for different purposes, and this will require a more
intelligent way of handling transactions.

REFERENCES

1. Chamberlin D., Gray J. and Traiger I. (1975)
   Views, authorisation and locking in a relational database
   system. In: "Proc of ACM National Conference 1975" p. 425

2. Furtado, Sevcik and Dos Santos. Permitting updates
   through views of databases. In: "Information Systems"
   Vol 4 Page 269

3. Gray M. A. (1983) "Views and Imprecise Information in
   Databases". Technical Report 38; University of Cambridge
   Computer Lab, Cambridge, England.

4. Braid I. C., Hillyard R. C., Stroud I. A. (1980)
   Stepwise construction of polyhedra in geometric modelling
   In: "Mathematical Models in Computer Graphics and Design"
   Academic Press, New York

5. Gray J. (1981) The transaction concept : virtues and
   limitations. In: "Proceedings Eighth VLDB Conference"

6. Moss J. (1982) Nested transactions and reliable
   distributed computing. In: "Proceedings Second Symposium
   on Reliability of Distributed Software and Database
   Systems" IEEE

7. Gray J., Lorie R., Putzolu G. and Traiger I. (1976)
   Granularity of locks and degrees of consistency in a
   shared database. In: "Modelling in DBMSs" North Holland

# TRANSACTION MANAGEMENT IN THE DESIGN ENVIRONMENT

## Randy H. Katz

*Computer Science Division, Electrical Engineering
and Computer Sciences Department, University of California,
Berkeley, California 94720, USA*

*ABSTRACT:* We define a *design transaction* as a sequence of operations that map a consistent version of an engineered artifact into a new consistent version. Because design transactions are unconventional, we argue that traditional notions of consistency, atomicity, and durability are irrelevant when defining them. We describe a design transaction management mechanism, based on version checkout and change files, that supports controlled sharing and is resilient to system crashes. The mechanism is well suited for a computing environment of engineering workstations and database servers.

## 1. Introduction

Sophisticated techniques have been developed to support transaction processing in a database system. These systems are characterized by high volume, short duration, simple units of work. Database systems are now being employed in application environments with very different characteristic workloads. An active area of research involves extending the existing techniques for the new environments (see [HASK82a, HASK82b, LORI83]).

We are interested in applying database techniques to support VLSI design activities [KATZ82a]. A *design management system* manages the information about the design of complicated "engineered" artifacts, such as VLSI circuits. Database facilities are an important service of such a system.

---

[1]Research supported by NSF Grant MCS-8201860

NEW APPLICATIONS OF DATA BASES
ISBN 0-12-275550-2

Engineered objects are built by teams, simultaneously working on different portions of an overall design. A design system supports controlled sharing of data through mechanisms that avoid designer interference. Further, design data must survive across even catastrophic system crashes. A *shared* repository for design data that is *resilient* to system crashes is perhaps the most important facility provided by a database component. The collection of mechanisms that provide these are called *transaction management* [GRAY78, GRAY81].

A database transaction is an *atomic* unit of work that keeps the database *consistent* and whose effects are *durable* across system crashes. [HASK82a, HASK82b, LORI83] describe approaches for supporting "design transactions" on top of existing database transaction management services, generalizing conventional consistency, atomicity, and durability notions as little as possible. We believe that new approaches can be effective in the design environment, and can significantly reduce the complexity of supporting design transactions.

Our purpose is to examine how design transactions differ from conventional database transactions. In the next section, we describe our model for the design environment and indicate how its requirements are different from those of conventional transaction processing. In section 3, we define design transactions and discuss the concurrency control and recovery issues in the design environment. An overview of the transaction processing mechanism is given in section 4. A more detailed presentation can be found in [KATZ83]. Our conclusions are given in section 5.

## 2. Design Environment

The environment for design activity is substantially different from the con-

ventional environment. These differences, and their effect on system requirements, are discussed in this section.

The debit/credit transaction of [GRAY78] is representative of conventional
transactions. The database consists of bank accounts, teller cash drawer, bank
branch balance, and account history records. Requests must be handled quickly,
and many simultaneous transactions can be in progress. A typical request
accesses a single account records, checks the balance to insure that there are
sufficient funds if a withdrawal, modifies the balance, and makes the modified
account record available to other transactions. The teller cash drawer and
branch balance are also modified. A history record is created to provide an audit
trail. Updates may be lost and the database may be left in an inconsistent state
if more than one transaction is allowed to modify these records simultaneously.

On the other hand, a typical "design transaction" is much more like an
editing session. It begins when a designer extracts a logical portion of the design
from the shared repository into his private workspace. During the lifetime of the
transaction, he interacts with his data through an ensemble of sophisticated
design tools, such as editors, design generators, and analysis programs. When his
design activities are complete, the data must pass a battery of tests for self-
consistency. This validation process is specific to the object being designed. For
example, a VLSI circuit is validated by (1) checking that its layout does not
violate any geometrical rules, (2) checking that the circuit is electrically well
formed, and (3) simulating the circuit to insure that its behavior is as expected.
The design system is responsible for insuring that all checks are performed in the
desired sequence. When the data is once again consistent, it is returned to the
shared repository to "release" it to other designers. However, older versions of a

design file are rarely discarded once a new version has been created. The new version is added to those that are available on-line in the repository.

Several observations are possible:

(1)    Design Transactions Are Long Duration.

Designers interact with their data for long periods, while conventional transactions are short. Thus, concurrent transactions cannot be controlled by forcing them to wait. On the other hand, the rapid response needed in conventional transaction processing is not as important in the design environment.

(2)    Design Transactions Touch Large Volumes of Data.

While conventional transactions touch few records, large collections of data are accessed by design transactions. Given the volume of data, entering the database system to update records one-at-a-time remains prohibitively expensive. Conventional database systems appear suited for managing shared repositories from which data is extracted for more intensive access. Conventional transactions can be used to implement the atomic merge of in-progress changes back into the repository.

(3)    Design Transactions Need More Than Serial Consistency.

Serializability is an insufficient correctness criterion. Special validation programs determine the consistency of design data. Serializability refers to interleaved access to shared data, which is both undesirable and unlikely in the design environment.

(4)    Design Transactions Are Not All Or Nothing.

Conventional transactions are atomic: either all updates may by a transaction become visible (it commits) or none are visible (it aborts). Exposure of intermediate states is forbidden. In the design environment, intermediate states are acceptable as long as they are file system consistent.

(5)    Design Transactions Are Not Ad Hoc.

Actual designer interference is rare because of the strict partitioning of responsibility among members of the design team. Situations may arise where designers are mutually waiting for data held by each other. Because design transactions are interactive, these can be resolved through designer negotiations. "Deadlocks" should not be resolved by system induced abort, since valuable design work will be lost.

Design transactions do not fit the traditional notions of consistency, atomicity, and durability. Serial consistency is insufficient for determining the self-consistency of design data. The data itself, rather than the order in which it is accessed, determines the correctness of a transaction. Further, simultaneous update access to the same design data is not correct, and need not be supported by the system.

Design transactions are not atomic. Visibility of intermediate states of design data is acceptable, and may even be desirable. While only one designer is allowed to update the data, many may be simultaneously browsing it to check on an in progress portion of a design. Browsers can tolerate a lower level of consistency.

Designers demand that as much of their work as possible be saved if the system fails. Savepoints guarantee that changes are saved, but it should be possible to restore the database to its *latest* possible state.

The durability of design transactions is also unusual. Old versions of design data persist even after newer consistent versions have been created. Support for versions is already a requirement of the design environment. They simplify many aspects of concurrency access and recovery. Since transaction management components of existing systems do not support versions, they are somewhat unsuitable as a basis for supporting design transactions.

## 3. Design Transactions

### 3.1. Introduction

A transaction is a unit of work that maintains the consistency of a database. A set of consistency constraints are in force at transaction begin and end, but can be violated during the transaction. In the design transaction, the definition of data self-consistency is complex. A VLSI design is consistent only if the circuit is well formed and implements its intended function with the desired performance. These constraints can only be verified by complicated checking programs.

We define a *design transaction* as a sequence of database operations that map an application consistent version of a design into a new consistent version. Design transactions are non-atomic units of design consistency. If the system crashes, then the designer can continue from the last safe state determined by transaction management, which may be *beyond* the last saved state. Old design versions are durable across transactions: an old version is not removed unless it is explicitly moved off-line.

## 3.2. Object Model for Hierarchically Constructed Designs

Design data is arranged so that logically related parts can be accessed as a single unit. Objects can be hierarchically nested within other objects. For example, a **microprocessor** consists of a **data path** and a **control unit;** the **data path** consists of a **register file, shifter,** and **arithmetic logic unit;** etc. We have called the nested structure of design data a design hierarchy [KATZ82a] (see figure 1). A designer can request access to individual objects independently of their components or the objects that contain them. For example, a designer can create a new datapath object from an existing ALU and shifter and a new register file, without affecting the current microprocesssor object.

## 3.3. Concurrency Control Issues

Designers do not work simultaneously on very fine granules of the design at the same time, such as individual transistors or gates. They work on aggregates

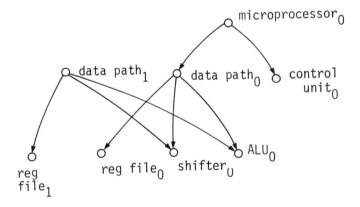

Figure 1 -- Hierarchically Constructed Design

of objects that are functional units, such as a register or register file. Consistency constraints, such as interface specifications, are associated with these units. They describe how the aggregate is to behave and with what performance. Aggregates of objects with associated interfaces form the appropriate lockable granuales.

Conventional locking cannot be used. If a design object is unavailable because it has been acquired by another designer, then the requesting designer cannot be forced to wait. Locks need to survive system crashes since design transactions are not aborted by a system crash. The solution proposed in [HASK82a] is to introduce *persistent locks* that are stored in non-volatile storage to survive crashes. A requestor need not block if the lock is unavailable.

A better paradigm for acquiring design data is to view the design database as a library [KATZ82b].[2] Design subparts are checked out to designers, who return them when done. "Concurrency control" is therefore handled by a Librarian process that traverses and manipulates the hierarchical structure of design data (see figure 2). It knows: (1) *what* parts of the design have already been checked out, (2) *who* has checked them out, and (3) *when* they are expected to be returned to the repository. This information is stored in the design database, and is thus durable across system crashes. A designer who must have access to data can determine who currently holds it, enabling him to request its early return.

When a designer is through with the data, it is checked back into the repository as a *new* version. The modified design data cannot become the current version ("released"), until it has passed the necessary self-consistency checks.

---

[2] One difference with a conventional library is that books cannot be changed. Every time design data is returned to the repository, a new version is created.

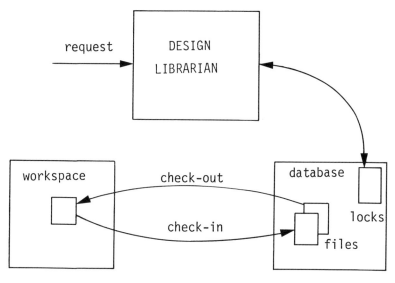

Figure 2 — Design Librarian

However, it can be read by other designers who are willing to browse inconsistent data.

## 3.4. Recovery Issues

Resiliency to system crashes is an important requirement. Conventional transactions restore the database to a transaction consistent state if a crash occurs. However, if the system crashes in the midst of a design transaction, it may be undesirable to undo *any* work done by the transaction. Savepoints within a design transaction guarantee that the database can be restored up to that point, but if possible, it should be restored beyond the savepoint. *Continuous recovery* is needed.

The computing environment for design introduces additional problems. The design environment will consist of individual workstations networked to a file server. These are inherently less resilient to crashes than the file servers, because they are located in a more hostile environment (an office instead of a machine room), and because it is more difficult to use redundancy to obtain resiliency (worrkstations rarely have more than one disk, and almost never have tape drives). Redundancy for data on the workstation must be provided by the file server.

Four kinds of failures are possible: (1) workstation soft crash (memory buffers lost), (2) workstation hard crash (local disk data lost), (3) server soft crash, and (4) server hard crash (see [BROW81, KARS82] for descriptions of conventional transaction processing in this environment). Recovery management must be able to deal with each of these. While conventional techniques can be used to make the server files resistant to crashes, e.g., duplexed logs, new approaches are needed to extend recovery to data at the workstation.

Fortunately, a transaction management approach based on versions simplifies the other aspects of recovery. While design versions are checked out to workstations, the last consistent version resides safely on the file server. Use of versions avoids updating in place, with its associated undo complexities. Incremental *change files* have a simple structure. These are associated with files rather than transactions, since only one transaction updates a given design file at a time.

## 4. Design Transaction Management

The activities of a design transaction are shown in figure 3. A design transaction begins with a *work* phase in which design objects are acquired by the designer and manipulated with his tools. When the transaction completes, and the modified collection of design data is shown to be self-consistent, new current

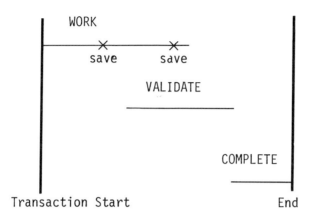

Figure 3 -- Design Transaction Activities

versions of the modified files will be created.

In a distributed design environment, the workstation's disk serves as the designer's workspace. A designer requests a design object, represented by a collection of associated files, from the file server Librarian. If it is still available, the request is granted and the files are transferred to the workstation's disk. Additional "mirrored" copies are also made in the file server. Mirrored files always contain a savepoint consistent snapshot of the data in the workstation.

If the object has already been acquired by another designer, he is identified, as is the expected time of his return of the object. The designer continues with other work, and must try to acquire the object later. A designer can negotiate the quick return of the object if he needs it immediately. "Deadlock" is a rare possibility, but can be resolved through such negotiations.

R.H. Katz

Workstation

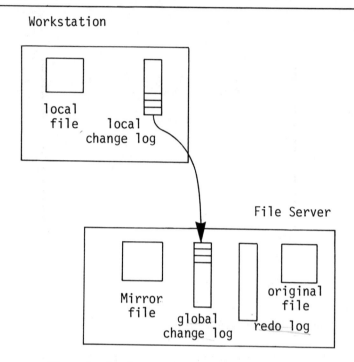

Figure 4 — Implementation of Continuous Recovery

A design transaction is punctuated with savepoints, insuring that changes will survive local failures. Activity at the workstation can continue even though the connection to the file server is broken. This is not advisable however, since it exposes the designer to serious loss of data.

The designer manipulates the design with the aid of his design tools. Changes made to files since the last savepoint are maintained in local change files. At savepoints, these are transmitted to the file server, where they are committed to the mirrored copies of the files, making the workstation and file server copies identical (see figure 4). It is possible to recover past a savepoint if the local logs have survived the crash, or are also saved on the file server. A process running on the workstation can continuously write the logs back to the server. This not only provides continuous recovery, but also reduces the latency of a save.

A beneficial side-effect of the extra redundancy in storing mirrored copies on the file server is that browsing in-progress data is simplified. A recent savepoint consistent version of the design can be viewed without accessing the workstation data.

When design work is completed, the transaction enters a *validation* phase. Validation programs are invoked to check that the modified design data is self-consistent. If the data is not valid, the transaction is not aborted! The inconsistencies are located and corrected. The transaction reenters the work phase, and validation is reattempted. Self-consistency checking may actually be distributed throughout the lifetime of the transaction, and need not only occur at the very end of design activity. However, the system must insure that the latest values of modified design data have are the ones that have passed validation.

Once shown to be valid, the transaction enters a *completion* phase. The in-progress versions of the design files are made current, the old current versions become previous, etc., and the transaction terminates successfully. The new design file versions can now be granted to other designers. If a designer decides to abort his transaction, the mirrored and local copies of files are destroyed and the original versions are made available again for checkout.

Design transactions make a heavy demand on disk resources. However, redundancy is unavoidable if resiliency is to be obtained. Since the file server is dedicated to providing file services to the network of workstations, it can be equipped with a large number of disk devices.

## 5. Conclusions

We have described a new transaction processing environment that is significantly different from that in which the standard notions of consistency, atomicity, and durability have evolved. The experience gained in building these latter systems is not necessarily appropriate for the design environment. We believe that more effective systems can be built by implementing transaction management with new techniques.

## 6. References

[BROW81] Brown, M. R., R. Cattell, N. Suzuki, "The CEDAR DBMS: A Preliminary Report," Proc. ACM SIGMOD Conference, Ann Arbor, MI, (May 1981), pp. 205 -- 211.

[GRAY78] Gray, J., "Notes on Database Operating Systems," IBM San Jose Research Report #RJ2188(30001), (February 1978).

[GRAY81] Gray, J., "The Transaction Concept: Virtues and Limitations," Proc. 7th Intl. Conf. on Very Large Databases, Cannes, France, (October 1981), pp. 144 – 154.

[HASK82a] Haskin, R. L., R. A. Lorie, "On Extending the Functions of a Relational Database System," Proc. ACM SIGMOD Conference, Orlando, Fl., (June 1982), pp. 207 -- 212.

[HASK82b] Haskin, R. L., R. A. Lorie, "Using a Relational Database System for Circuit Design," IEEE Database Engineering Newsletter, V 5, N 2, (June 1982), pp. 10 – 14.

[KARS82] Karszt, J., H. Kuss, G. Lausen, "Optimistic Concurrency Control and Recovery in a Multi-Personal Computer System," ACM SIGSMALL Newsletter, V 8, N 4, (November 1982), pp. 12 – 21.

[KATZ82a] Katz, R. H., "A Database Approach for Managing VLSI Design Data," Proc. 19th ACM/IEEE Design Automation Conference, Las Vegas, NV, (June 1982).

[KATZ82b] Katz, R. H., "DAVID: Design Aids for VLSI using Integrated Databases," IEEE Database Engineering Newsletter, V 5, N 2, (June 1982), pp. 29 – 32.

[KATZ83] Katz, R. H., S. Weiss, "Transaction Management for Design Databases," University of Wisconsin-Madison Technical Report #496, (February 1983).

[LORI83] Lorie, R. A., W. Plouffe, "Complex Objects and Their Use in Design
Transactions," Proc. ACM SIGMOD Conference on Engineering Design
Applications, San Jose, CA, (May 1983).